Lecture Notes in Computer S

T0230178

Commenced Publication in 1973
Founding and Former Series Editors:
Gerhard Goos, Juris Hartmanis, and Jan van Leeuwen

Editorial Board

Willem Jonker   Milan Petković (Eds.)

Secure
Data Management

VLDB 2004 Workshop, SDM 2004
Toronto, Canada, August 30, 2004
Proceedings

 Springer

Volume Editors

Willem Jonker
Milan Petković
Information and System Security, Philips Research Eindhoven
Prof. Holstlaan 4, 5656 AA Eindhoven, Netherlands
E-mail: {willem.jonker, milan.petkovic}@philips.com

Library of Congress Control Number: 2004110614

CR Subject Classification (1998): H.2.0, H.2, C.2.0, H.3, E.3, D.4.6, K.6.5

ISSN 0302-9743
ISBN 3-540-22983-3 Springer Berlin Heidelberg New York

Springer is a part of Springer Science+Business Media

springeronline.com

© Springer-Verlag Berlin Heidelberg 2004
Printed in Germany

Typesetting: Camera-ready by author, data conversion by Olgun Computergrafik
Printed on acid-free paper   SPIN: 11312253   06/3142   5 4 3 2 1 0

Preface

Concepts like ubiquitous computing and ambient intelligence that exploit increasingly interconnected networks and mobility put new requirements on data management. An important element in the connected world is that data will be accessible anytime anywhere. This also has its downside in that it becomes easier to get unauthorized data access. Furthermore, it will become easier to collect, store, and search personal information and endanger people's privacy. As a result security and privacy of data becomes more and more of an issue. Therefore, secure data management, which is also privacy-enhanced, turns out to be a challenging goal that will also seriously influence the acceptance of ubiquitous computing and ambient intelligence concepts by society.

With the above in mind, we organized the SDM 2004 workshop to initiate and promote secure data management as one of the important interdisciplinary research fields that brings together people from the security research community and the data management research community. The call for papers attracted 28 submissions both from universities and industry. The program committee selected 15 research papers for presentation at the workshop. The technical contributions presented at the SDM workshop are collected in this volume, which, we hope, will serve as a valuable research and reference book in your professional life.

The volume is divided into four topical parts. The first section focuses on accessing encrypted data. The first three papers of this section concentrate on the interesting problem of searching in encrypted data, while the last paper discusses the integrity of data that is shared or exchanged on the World-Wide Web. The second section addresses private data management, as well as management of private (personal) data. Research topics of this section include management of personal data with P3P for Internet services, privacy in digital rights management, as well as privacy-preserving data mining. The third section focuses on access control, which remains an important area of interest for database security researchers. Finally, two papers in the fourth section discuss specific topics within database security: release control of sensitive associations stored in databases, and a method to defend against copying a database as a whole.

July 2004   Willem Jonker and Milan Petković

Table of Contents

Encrypted Data Access

Privacy Preserving Data Management

Access Control

Database Security

Secure and Privacy Preserving Outsourcing of Tree Structured Data

Ping Lin and K. Selçuk Candan

Department of Computer Sciences and Engineering
Arizona State University
Tempe AZ. 85287, USA
phone: 480-727-3611
{ping.lin,candan}@asu.edu

Abstract. With the increasing use of web services, many new challenges concerning data security are becoming critical. Data or applications can now be outsourced to powerful remote servers, which are able to provide services on behalf of the owners. Unfortunately, such hosts may not always be trustworthy. In [1, 2], we presented a one-server computationally private tree traversal technique, which allows clients to outsource tree-structured data. In this paper, we extend this protocol to prevent a polynomial time server with large memory to use correlations in client queries and in data structures to learn private information about queries and data. We show that, when the proposed techniques are used, computational privacy is achieved even for non-uniformly distributed node accesses that are common in real databases.

Keywords: Search on Encrypted Data, Tree structured data (XML) Security, Private Information Retrieval

1 Introduction

In web and mobile computing, clients usually do not have sufficient computation power or memory and they need remote servers to do the computation or store data for them. Publishing data on remote servers helps improve service availability and system scalability, reducing clients' burden of managing data. With their computation power and large memory, such remote servers are called data stores or oracles. Typically, as the entities different than the data owners, these data stores can not be fully trusted, for they may be malicious and can be driven by their own benefits to make illegal use of information stored on them. Hence data outsourcing introduces security concerns that are different from traditional database service which always assumes that database is honest and it is the illegal users access that should protect the data from. These concerns have to be addressed effectively to convince customers that outsourcing their IT needs is a viable alternative to deploying complex infrastructures locally.

1.1 Problem Statement

Special security concerns with respect to data outsourcing can be categorized into *content privacy* and *access privacy* [12]. Clients with sensitive data (e.g.,

W. Jonker and M. Petković (Eds.): SDM 2004, LNCS 3178, pp. 1–17, 2004.

personal identifiable data) outsourced to untrusted host may require that their data be protected from such data storage oracles. This is defined as *content privacy* [12] and leads to encrypted database research [7], in which sensitive data is encrypted, so the content is hidden from the database. Sometimes not only the data outsourced to a data store, but also queries are of value and a malicious data store can make use of such information for its own benefits. This is defined as *access privacy* [12]. Access privacy leads to private information retrieval [13] research, which studies how to let users retrieve information from database without leaking (even to the server) the identity and the location of the retrieved data item.

Access privacy and content privacy are not independent. If the data has some structure, plain access may reveal this structure, hence impair content privacy. For example, if the data is in the form of an XML tree (as described in the next subsection), without proper methods to protect access privacy, the path along which to find the target data will be revealed, so will be the whole structure of the data tree, which impairs the content privacy. Hence to protect both content privacy and access privacy, we need to hide the structure of the data.

In this paper, we address secure outsourcing of tree structured data, such as XML documents. To be specific, we address hiding of tree-structured data and queries on this data. XML documents [8] have tree-like structures. XML has become a de facto standard for data exchange and representation over the Internet [9]. Some work has been done on selective and authentic untrusted third-party distribution of XML documents [3, 9–11]. The work focuses on access control and authentication of document (i.e.,query result) source and content. With more and more data stored in XML documents, techniques to hide tree structures (the content and structure of XML documents) from untrusted data stores are in great need. In an XML database, a query is often given in the form of tree paths, like XQuery. To hide XML queries and the structure of XML documents, clients need to traverse XML trees in a hidden way. Other frequently used tree-structures include indexes that are often built for convenient access to data. However, most index structures closely reflect the distribution of the data. Thus, in order to hide the data and data distribution from the database, tree structure hiding techniques must be adopted to protect index trees from oracles. Though the techniques we present in this paper can also be used for hiding index structure accesses, here we do not focus on this application. Recent work in privacy-preserving index structures includes [4].

In [1, 2], we proposed a protocol for hiding traversals of trees from oracles. Noticing that existing private information retrieval techniques require either heavy replication of the database onto multiple non-communicating servers or large communication costs or computation costs [13], we provided an one-server *tree-traversal* protocol that provides a balance between the communication/computation cost and security requirements. To protect the client from the malicious data store, some tasks (such as traversing the tree-structures) are performed interactively. Client responsibilities include encryption and decryption of the data received from the data store during the traversal of the tree. The encryption capability required at client side can be achieved by assistant hardware equipments, such as smartcards that are cheap (generally no more than several dollars) and now commonly used in mobile environments [20]. We analyzed the overhead incurred by proposed technique, including communication cost, encryption/decryption costs, and concurrency overhead. Since [13] has argued that information-theoretical private information retrieval cannot be achieved without a significant communication overhead, our proposed method minimizes those costs in a computational hiding sense.

In this paper, we build on the approaches proposed in [1, 2] to develop a computationally secure protocol for hiding correlated accesses to tree-structured outsourced data. We find that if node accesses are uniformly distributed, the original protocol achieves computational privacy [2]. To ensure computational privacy in face of non-uniformly distributed and correlated node accesses, which actually occur in real scenarios, we propose a systematic way to enhance the preliminary protocol so that from the server's view, node accesses are uniformly distributed.

2   Related Work

Besides the common data encryption methods that hide sensitive data, there are various efforts to hide other kinds of secret information from untrusted servers. Basic methods to protect content privacy include database encryption, where critical data such as credit card number can be encrypted. DBMS suppliers such as Oracle and DB2 have provided encryption functionality. Bertino and Ferrari [10] have studied how to protect sensitive XML data content from different entities by performing differentiated encryption of various portions using multiple keys. Hacigümüs, H. et al. [7] have studied how to execute SQL over encrypted data. Other recent work on querying encrypted data includes [5] and [6].

Sensitive information about data may include users queries about data. Different from traditional database security which deals with preventing, detecting, and deterring improper disclosure or modification of information in databases, private information retrieval (PIR) aims to let users query a database without leaking to the database what data is queried.

The basic idea behind any information theoretic PIR scheme is to replicate the database to several non-communicating servers and pose randomized queries to each server so that from the server's view those queries are independent of the target but the user can reconstruct the target data from query results. The privacy guarantee lies in that even computationally un-bounded server can not tell the difference between any two communications for different targets. [13] showed that if one copy of database is used, the only way to hide the query in the information theoretic sense is to send the whole database to the user. In order to reduce even one bit in communication between the server and the user, replication of the whole database is required. Hence information theoretic privacy techniques require multiple data copies and cause heavy communication overheads.

In order to achieve practical use, communication cost and the number of replicas need to be reduced. Ambainis proposed a k-server scheme that requires

$O(n^{2k-1})$ communication [14] (where n is the database size). This result is further improved to $n^{O(\frac{\log\log k}{k\log k})}$ by Beimel et al. [15]. This is the best known k-server information theoretic private information retrieval scheme so far. However, to achieve communication that is subpolynomial in the size of the database, more than a constant number of servers are needed [13]. In real world, database replication is not a preferable solution. It may not be possible to prevent servers from communicating with each other. In computationally private information retrieval (CPIR) schemes, therefore, the user's privacy requirement is relaxed so that any two communications for different targets are indistinguishable to any polynomial time server.

CPIR schemes are built on cryptographic assumptions, which enable further reduction of the communication and the number of replicas. If a one-way function exists, then there is a 2-server scheme, such that the communication is $O(n^\epsilon)$ for any $\epsilon > 0$ [16]. Under the Quadratic Residuosity Assumption, a one-server scheme can be constructed with sub-polynomial communication [17]. Under the ϕ-hiding Assumption, a one-server scheme with a poly-logarithmic communication can be achieved [18]. Based on Paillier cryptosystem which is secure under the Composite Residuosity Assumption, Chang [19] proposed a one-server scheme with logarithmic communication overhead which is the optimal for CPIR. Despite the reduced communication overhead, however, all above CPIR schemes [16–19] suffer from heavy computation cost (linear in size of the database size) at both the client and server sides. Smith et al. [12] employed the secure processor technique to achieve computational privacy by embedding a secure processor at the malicious server, let the clients encrypt their queries and let the secure processor decrypt the queries and read the database to retrieve the targets. Since the whole database should be read into the secure processor to hide the query from the server, cost linear in the database size is still incurred at the server side.

Most existing information theoretic PIR and computationally PIR schemes are built on binary data model, making it hard to be applied to real database. In the next section, we provide an overview of our previous work which enables a one-server CPIR scheme that can be easily applied to real data model and only involves moderate and adjustable computations and communications to gain content privacy and access privacy [1, 2].

3   Background: Private Tree Traversal with Access Redundancy and Node Swapping

In [1], we proposed a preliminary protocol to hide traversal paths on tree structured data. The protocol is a one server protocol. *Content privacy* is guaranteed through encryption of the tree nodes (data and pointers) before outsourcing, hence the host can not know the data content. *Access Privacy* is achieved by novel *access redundancy* and *node swapping* techniques. The data storage space is divided into units of nodes (called physical nodes) which may contain tree nodes (called data nodes) or have no content (empty nodes) and is organized

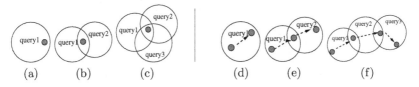

Fig. 1. (a,b,c) Leakage of the position of root node of tree structure as a result of repeated accesses and (d,e,f) node swapping eliminates leakages

into a multi-level structure with each level storing a corresponding level of the tree respectively. Whenever a client wants to retrieve a tree node, besides the target node, it asks a set of random nodes from the level. We define the set of nodes the client retrieves in order to get the target as *redundancy set*. Hence if the size of the redundancy set is m, the probability for the server to have a correct guess of the target is $\frac{1}{m}$; the probability for the server to have a correct guess of parent-child relationship is $\frac{1}{m^2}$; if the depth of the tree is l, the probability for the server to find the traversal path is $\frac{1}{m^l}$. The definition of redundancy set can be extended to contain multiple target nodes. If there are k targets in the redundancy set, the probability for the server to have correct guess of the targets is $\frac{1}{C_m^k}$; the probability for the server to have a correct guess of the parent-child relationships is $\frac{1}{(C_m^k)^2 \times k!}$; and the probability for the server to have correct guess of traversal paths is $\frac{1}{(C_m^k)^l \times (k!)^{l-1}}$.

Unfortunately, we find that repeated access for the same target (e.g. the root) may reveal the target, for the target is always in the intersection of the related redundancy sets. Figures 1(a), (b), (c) give an example showing how repeated access for the root may reveal the physical location of the root. In Figure 1, large circles represent redundancy sets and small circles represent the root. In [1, 2] we addressed this problem by requiring that each redundancy set should at least include one randomly selected empty node. After each retrieval the client should swap the target with the empty node, *re-encrypt* the redundancy set using a different key or encryption scheme (which is essential in order to hide the location of target and the empty) and then write the set back into the data storage space at the server. This is called *node swapping*. Node swapping ensures that after each retrieval, the target moves to a random position in the data store, hence making the distribution of data in the data storage space random, i.e., data keep randomly moving as queries are posed and answered. With node swapping, any correct guess of the target is transient and hence the information leaked by intersections is reduced (Figures 1(d), (e), (f)).

Since data nodes are constantly swapped, the parent-child links have to be properly maintained. The physical location of the root is maintained in a fixed encrypted special node snode [1, 2] which is the entry to the data store. In [1, 2], we developed highly concurrent techniques to maintain parent-child links as children nodes are swapped. Based on this, we have implemented a deadlock free private tree traversal algorithm [1, 2] to enable a client to query the tree by traversing the tree and locating the required data node. The total cost (includ-

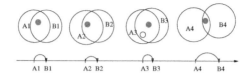

Fig. 2. Intersections may leak identical queries

ing communication cost, read/write cost and encryption/decryption cost) of the protocol is a function of the redundancy size m, the total data points num and the node size s, i.e., the maximum number of data points a data node can contain. If c, e/d, r/w denote communication cost function, encryption/decryption cost function, read/write cost function with respect to node size s, the function is $log(\frac{num}{s}) \times m \times (c(s) + e(s) + d(s) + r(s) + w(s))$. This cost is adjustable. Compared with the costs of existing one-server PIR schemes which are linear in the database size num, this cost is moderate (poly-logarithmic in num). This cost function also shows that with m and num set, there exists an optimal node size s to minimize the total cost. Experiment results [1, 2] show that the performance of the protocol is consistent with the theoretical analysis mentioned above and, compared with one-server information theoretic private information retrieval scheme, this cost is small and hence the proposed approach is more practical.

Although this algorithm hides uniformly distributed tree node accesses, when queries are correlated, the server can learn private information about queries and data. In this paper, we present techniques that guarantees computational privacy even for non-uniformly distributed accesses that are common in real databases.

4   Problem Formation: Preventing Information Leakages Caused by Intersections of Redundancy Sets

In this paper, we refer to client's retrieval of a single redundancy set as a *call*. A query then can be represented as an ordered set of calls. For instance, a path from root to a leaf would be a sequence of calls from the client to the server.

Supposing that there is a transport layer security mechanism (e.g. anonymous access protocol) that hides the identity of client, the server sees data accesses as a stream of calls from unknown origins. We define a stream of calls the server has observed during certain period of time as a *view*.

Computational privacy requires that any computationally bounded server should not be able to tell the difference between client-server communications for two different *queries*. Given the above query model, we note that the server might be able to infer information by observing the call stream, by observing the intersections of the redundancy sets of the corresponding calls in each query. For instance, if there are two queries, Query A and Query B, that are the same and consecutive, i.e., without intermediate queries' interfering, their calls for every node on the path will be intersecting, hence providing hints to the server that two identical queries have happened. Figure 2 depicts the phenomenon, with A_i and B_i denoting A and B's corresponding calls respectively.

Correct identification of identical queries not only increases the risk of leaking the traversal path (although such leakage is transient), it also leaks the information as to how frequent queries are posed. If the server happens to know the query distribution in advance, i.e., how often every query occurs, and if there are distinguished variation among query frequencies, the server can identify the queries that have been posed.

Our goal in this paper is, therefore, provide computational privacy in the presence of correlated queries:

1. **Hiding distribution of calls:** for any two different queries Q_1 and Q_2 posed in the view, the distribution of their sequences of calls are indistinguishable in polynomial-time.
2. **Hiding intersections:** for any two queries Q_1 and Q_2 in the view, it is hard to tell if they are identical or not by observing their sequences of calls.

4.1   Privacy Guarantees for Uniformly Distributed Node Accesses

In [2], we showed that if for every level at the tree, node accesses are uniformly distributed(i.e., for every level, tree nodes on this level are accessed by clients at the same probability), and if the database is randomly initialized, then the protocol has already achieved the required computational privacy.

Hiding Distribution of Calls. Our proof is based on the following proposition and corollary.

Proposition 1. *If the data storage space is randomly initialized and data nodes are uniformly accessed in each level of a tree, then data nodes are always uniformly distributed in each level of the data storage space.*

Corollary 1. *If the data store is randomly initialized and node accesses are uniformly distributed for every level of a tree, then redundancy sets posed are also uniformly distributed for any level of the data store.*

If the data storage space is randomly initialized and node accesses are uniformly distributed in every level, then data nodes will always be uniformly distributed in each level of the data storage space and calls for that level will also be uniformly distributed. So for two different queries, if their traversal path lengths are equal, the distribution of their sequences of calls are identical, hence indistinguishable in polynomial-time; if their traversal path lengths are not equal, clients can execute dummy calls at deeper levels to always make the same number of calls. Details of the proofs are omitted here due to space constraints.

Hiding Intersections. As to the second privacy requirement, the only hint server has for identifying identical queries from views are intersections between calls: if two identical queries are posed consecutively without any interfering calls, their corresponding calls will intersect. However, if node accesses are uniformly distributed, even if the server happens to know that at some time t, there is a call belonging to Q_1 such that one of its target is the data node nd, and the server observes that some time later there is a call belonging to Q_2 and the call intersects with Q_1's call at nd, it can not judge whether the later call is also targeting at nd or not, hence having no hint whether Q_2 is identical to Q_1. If, m denotes the size of the redundancy sets, n denotes the number of data nodes in tree level where nd is located and N denotes the total number of nodes in the data storage space of the level, k denotes the number of target nodes per call, then

- the call of Q_2 may intersect with the call of Q_1 at nd because it also sets target on nd. This probability $P_1 = \frac{C_{n-1}^{k-1}}{C_n^k}$
- the call of Q_2 may intersect with the call of Q_1 at nd because it selects nd as one of its random nodes. This probability $P_2 = \frac{C_{n-1}^k}{C_n^k} \times \frac{C_{N-2k-1}^{m-2k-1}}{C_{N-2k}^{m-2k}}$.

If there are enough empty nodes in the level to expand the data storage space, e.g., n empty nodes, and if m is large enough, e.g., at least $4k$, P_2 will be no less than P_1. Hence if the data storage space for the tree is expanded linearly and calls contain enough random nodes (only linear redundancy), from the intersections, the server can not tell whether two queries are identical or their corresponding redundancy sets just happen to intersect and the probability for the polynomial time server to have correct judgement whether a view contain identical queries or not cannot be non-negligibly better than random guessing.

4.2   Naive Approaches for Providing Privacy Guarantees for Non-uniformly Distributed Node Accesses

In real situations, queries and node accesses are not always uniformly distributed. If there are big variations among node access distributions, higher frequencies of intersections will be more likely a sign of repeated occurrence of high frequency queries than just random intersections. Thus intersections may leak information about occurrence of identical high frequency queries, hence enabling the server to deduce query frequencies. If the server knows in advance the tree structure and how often each tree node is accessed, such information leakage increases the risk of leaking the queries that have been posed.

These attacks by the server would rely on the intersection property mentioned above. Intuitively, such an attack by the server can be prevented by ensuring that intersections do not reveal much information. This can be achieved by modifying the client/server protocols such that the redundant sets intersect at multiple nodes as well as by inserting appropriate dummy/interfering calls.

Intuitively, dummy interfering calls add ambiguity and reduce the probability with which the server can identify the calls that correspond to identical queries. Note that in order to provide efficient and provable security, the process of introducing dummy calls have to follow a strategy which randomizes the intersections with minimal overhead. In this section, we first discuss three naive approaches

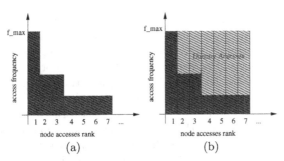

Fig. 3. Naive uniform approach: (a) original node accesses distribution and (b) adding dummy node accesses enables uniform distribution

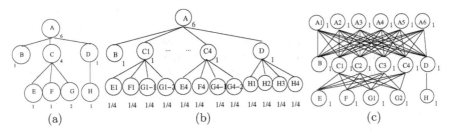

Fig. 4. Replication: (a) original tree and node access frequencies, (b) and (c) two different ways for replicating nodes

to minimize information leakage by intersections. In the next section, we present a systematic and efficient way to choose proper dummy interfering calls.

Naive Uniform Approach: A straight forward approach to make tree nodes to be uniformly accessed is to generate enough dummy accesses for low frequently accessed tree nodes so that all tree nodes are accessed at the same frequency with the most often accessed one. Figure 3 depicts the approach. In Figure 3, the X axis denotes node access rank (node ranked 1 is mostly accessed) and the Y axis denotes the number of accesses for each tree node during unit time interval. Figure 3(a) shows the original node accesses distribution and Figure 3(b) shows the uniform distribution after enough dummy accesses (depicted by grey columns) are generated. The cost of this approach is $\sum_i (f_{max} - f_i)$ (f_{max} is the maximum access frequency and f_i is the access frequency for node ranked i). In general, this naive approach leads to a large number of dummy accesses (for example, this would require exponential dummy calls for trees where the root is accessed once for each leaf), which would cause a heavy cost for the system.

Replication Approach: The idea of this naive approach is to replicate nodes that are accessed with higher frequencies into multiple copies so that each copy is accessed at the same frequency with the lowest frequency node. There are two ways to replicate nodes. The first is to make node accesses uniformly distributed at every level by applying replication repeatedly from the top to bottom, making access frequency uniform at every level. Figure 4(b) gives an example how to replicate the tree shown in Figure 4(a) in a way that at every level nodes are uniformly accessed. In this figure, the number associated with a tree node denotes its access frequency. Note that with this approach, the nodes of different levels have different access frequencies. Therefore level information is leaked. The second approach prevents leakages of level information by applying replication to all nodes of the tree, making them accessed at the same frequency with the least accessed tree node. Figure 4(c) depicts the tree structure after applying the second replication approach to the tree in Figure 4(a). Replication is simple and does not need dummy node accesses, hence is query efficient. However, since every high frequency nodes are replicated according to the lowest frequency, huge disk space is required to replicate the tree in both of these replication approaches. For the first approach, a space of size exponential in the height of the node is required to get just one extra copy of this single node. The second replication approach needs less replication (exponential in the tree depth). However, since every copy of the parent should maintain addresses of its children, when a child is swapped, all parents have to be updated to refer to the new address of the child. This will increase the access frequency of the copies of the parent, making the unified access non-uniform. Furthermore, for both approaches, if the content of a node is updated, all copies of the node should also be updated, making update a costly task and changing the uniform accesses of nodes. This problem is inherent with replication.

Clique Approach: Another naive approach to minimize information leaked by intersections is to generate calls for queries such that any two queries' corresponding calls intersect. If we use a graph to represent a view so that every vertex depicts a query and every edge depicts the intersection between two queries, with this approach, the view forms a clique. The idea behind this approach is to make the probability for non-identical queries to intersect equal the probability for identical queries to intersect (both equal 1) so that there is no way for the server to find identical queries by observing intersections. This approach is also too costly. It requires a large redundancy set, for a call should contain more than half of the data storage nodes from its level to be able to intersect with corresponding calls of all other queries. Actually this cost is comparable to sending the whole database to the client.

5   Proposed Approach: Clustering Node Accesses into Uniform Chains

From the naive approaches described above, we observe that challenges associated with hiding information that may be leaked by intersections are (a) making node accesses seem uniform, (b) without introducing many dummy node accesses, (c) without large redundancy set sizes, and (d) without requiring large storage space. In this section, we propose a *frequency clustering and chain-merging* approach to minimize information leaked by intersections.

Let D denote the total number of tree nodes. The idea behind the approach is as follows: if we can fractionally cluster D nodes into D equivalent classes

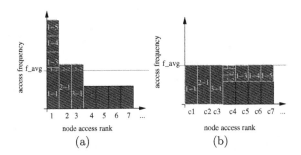

Fig. 5. Frequency clustering: (a) Splitting high frequency accesses and (b) access frequencies are uniformly distributed after merging

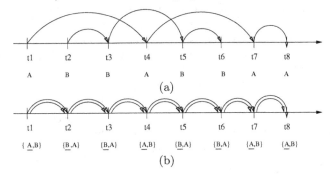

Fig. 6. Chain merging: (a) Two access chains for node A, B respectively (each edge denotes an intersection in redundancy sets as described in Section 4); (b) A's access chain and B's access chain are merged together into one single chain(each consecutive pair of calls has two intersections)

such that the total access frequency for each equivalent class is almost equal to the average access frequency, and if we can merge node accesses in each equivalent class together, the server's view of node accesses will become uniformly distributed. This is depicted in Figure 5. Accesses to high frequency nodes are split(Figure 5a). For example, the node ranked first is split into segments 1-1, 1-2, 1-3, 1-4, 1-5. Then as shown in Figure 5(b), accesses to high frequency nodes are clustered with accesses to low frequency nodes. For example, segment 1-5 is clustered with 7 to form cluster c7, segments 1-2, 2-2, 3-2 are clustered with 4 to form cluster c4. The total frequency for each cluster adds up to f_{avg}. The splitting and clustering depicted in Figures 5 exhibits the process of fractional clustering of node accesses. For example, the first cluster $c7$ in Figure 5(b) depicts that with some clustering probability (the ratio between the frequency of the segment 1-5 and the total frequency of the first ranked node access), the first ranked node access is clustered with the seventh ranked node access.

The challenge, however, is to make accesses for different nodes in each cluster look like the same. Figure 6(a) shows two different chains formed by accesses of nodes A and B that are clustered together. The shape of the individual access chains can leak information about access frequency to the server. Unless the node

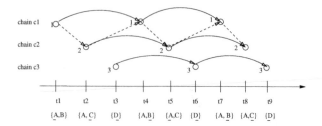

Fig. 7. Crossing among chains are denoted with dashed arrows

accesses in each cluster resembles each other, the server will observe individual accesses. To address this challenge, we propose *chain merging* (Figure 6). By merging chains, we mean that whenever a node in a given cluster is accessed by a client, then the client also accesses other nodes in the cluster together with this node in a single redundancy set. Figure 6(b) shows when accesses of A and B are merged. The access *chains* of A and B are merged together into one single chain and the resulting chain is uniform looking.

With this approach, the malicious server will observe access chains, each of which occurs with approximately f_{avg} frequency. Hence access frequency distributions will not be leaked by intersections (except the average access frequency). To achieve chain merging, however, there are three further challenges that have to be addressed:

- *Maximum cluster size:* The maximum number of node accesses per cluster should be constrained by a subpolynomial; i.e., we should avoid clusters that require redundancy sets the sizes of which are polynomial in the database size. Otherwise, merging them into one would require large redundancy, which would cause heavy communication overheads. This is discussed in Section 5.1.
- *Cluster directory size and access frequency:* We need a storage and search efficient directory structure to maintain the clustering information so that whenever a client needs to access a target node, it can quickly find the corresponding clusters and identify all nodes in those clusters. This directory will be maintained in the server in encrypted manner. Since each node access is preceded by a directory lookup, the size of the directory structure as well as its access pattern should not leak further information. This is discussed in Section 5.2
- *Chain crossings:* a node may belong to more than one cluster, making multiple chains *cross* with each other. Figure 7 gives an example. In this example, there are three clusters: $c_1 = \{A, B\}$, $c_2 = \{A, C\}$, $c_3 = \{D\}$. The axis depicts time line and the small circle that above time t_i represents the cluster that is accessed at time t_i. Since A is in clusters c_1 and c_2, we can see that besides the intersections which form a chain for each cluster (depicted by solid arrows), there are some crossing intersections (depicted by dashed arrows) between chains c_1 and c_2. However, since c_3 shares no elements with c_1 and c_3, there is no crossing associated with c_3. Such *crossings* between

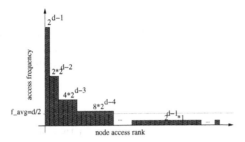

Fig. 8. Node access distribution example: a balanced tree with uniform leaf accesses

chains should have uniform pattern, otherwise a powerful server may infer extra information from their distribution. For this example, the server may deduce that cluster c_1 and cluster c_2 share some high frequency element. This is discussed in Section 5.3

In the rest of the paper, we address each of these challenges.

5.1   Minimizing the Maximum Cluster Size

In this section, we show how to restrict the maximum number of accesses per cluster to 3 (except for boundary clusters). The procedure starts from the highest and lowest frequency nodes and progressively moves towards medium frequency nodes. We first split the highest frequency node access into segments of enough volume to fill the gap between the lowest frequency and the desired average frequency. Then, we use the highest frequency node to fill as many of the lowest frequency node accesses as possible. In most cases this scheme will lead to clusters of size 2. In some cases, it may be that the segment of the highest frequency node access can not fill the gap between the low frequency and the average frequency and need to cluster with a segment from the next highest frequency, resulting in a cluster size of 3. In this way, we can continue using segments of the highest available frequencies to fill the unfilled lowest frequencies, getting clusters of size 2 or 3.

An extreme exception may happen at the final stage of the above process when the highest available frequencies are just above f_{avg}, and the unfilled lowest frequency is below f_{avg}, and the rank of highest available frequencies are immediately before the rank of unfilled lowest frequency. Let i denote the rank of the final unfilled lowest frequency node. Because the available highest frequencies $f_{i-j}, f_{i-j+1}... f_{i-1}$ are just above f_{avg}, and f_i is pretty much below f_{avg}, hence a number of node accesses (ranked $i-j$, $i-j+1$, ...$i-1$) are needed to fill the gap between f_i and f_{avg}. In the case of trees accesses (shown by Figure 8) we can show that the number of nodes in the extreme cluster is bounded by the depth, d, of the tree. Suppose there are d distinct access frequencies (one for each level) and there are 2^{i-1} different i^{th} ranked node accesses, each with access frequency 2^{d-i}. This extreme case happens if f_{i-1} is just above $\frac{d}{2}$, i.e., $f_{i-1} = \frac{d}{2}+1$ if d is even, or $f_{i-1} = \frac{d+1}{2}$ if d is odd. In both cases, the final boundary clusters have a size of $O(d)$. In conclusion, if D denotes the total number of nodes, this way of clustering generates $O(D)$ clusters of size 2, at most d boundary clusters of size 3, final boundary clusters of size $O(d)$. The advantage of this is that the number of chains that has to be merged and the required cluster size are both small.

5.2   Implementing a Storage and Search Efficient Cluster Directory

Directory information of clusters is available in two places: (a) a cluster table C maintains which nodes are in a given cluster and what their frequency shares are; and (b) for each child node in the tree, its parent keeps the list of clusters the child belongs to and the corresponding clustering probabilities (determined by the ratio of the child's frequency shares and its total access frequency) for the child. The cluster table C is encrypted and stored in a fixed address in the server space (this is called snode in [1, 2]). Entry i of the cluster table C records the identifiers of all nodes the accesses of which are clustered into cluster c_i. The tree structure is also encrypted (Section 3).

While traversing from a parent node to a child node, a client first identifies which clusters the child node belongs to and picks one of those clusters using the associated clustering probabilities. Figure 9 provides an example. In this figure, the node A is fractionally clustered into 4 different clusters: $\{A, B\}$, $\{A, C\}$ $\{A, D\}$, and $\{A, E\}$. Each time A is accessed from its parent, one of these 4 clusters will be chosen based on the clustering probabilities stored in the pointer. Therefore, the resulting cluster access pattern can be represented as a random walk graph shown in Figure 9(a), whose vertices (i.e, clusters) have equal number of visits (i.e., uniform access distribution). The weights associated with arrows are traversal probabilities for A that are calculated from A's clustering probabilities. For example, P_{12} denotes the probability with which the next access of A is clustered into c_2 if the current access of A is clustered into c_1. Once the cluster to be used is identified, the client uses the cluster table C to find other nodes in the chosen cluster and requests all the nodes in the cluster in a single redundancy set. Since the cluster table and pointers are encrypted, the only information the server observes are the *sizes* of the entries in the directory and their *access frequencies*. We can hide entry sizes from the server by extending all of them to the maximum cluster size. Since chains are uniformly accessed, entries of C are uniformly accessed, giving no extra information per access except (possibly) the random identifier of the cluster for which we do not care.

The cluster table search cost is $O(1)$: the client only needs to access one entry of C per access and each entry has a constant size (as discussed above). The storage cost of the cluster table is proportional to the size of the database. Since the cluster table maintains pure node identifiers and generally the size of a node is much greater than the size of a node identifier, the cluster table is small compared to the size of the database. However, unless properly designed, the storage cost for pointers can be prohibitively expensive: each parent stores all the clusters each child belongs to and, since (in the worst case) a node can be clustered into D (the size of the database) many clusters, the pointers could become prohibitively large.

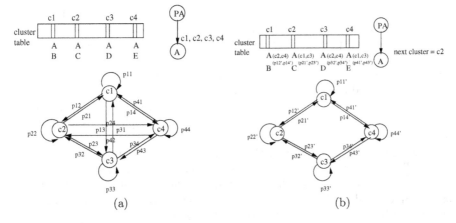

Fig. 9. Reducing pointer costs: (a) In the original structure, the pointer has to maintain all clusters of node A; (b) in the new structure, the pointer only maintains the *next cluster*

To prevent this, instead of storing all the clusters of a given child, the parent should store only a small (constant) number of clusters of the child. This would ensure that the storage requirement is small; however since not all clusters are available, the clustering probabilities for the child would be altered, destroying the uniform access distribution of the cluster chains. In order to prevent the access distribution of the chains diverging from uniform, we need to read-just traversal probabilities and modify the cluster table to let it contain more information.

Figure 9(b) shows how to reduce the storage cost for pointers from P_A to A. In this example, we first reduce the number of cluster neighbors from 3 to 2. To achieve this, we need to recompute the random walk traversal probabilities. The probabilities associated with the new random walk graph are computed so that the clustering probabilities of A remain the same and the access frequency of each cluster is kept uniform. The cluster table C is modified so that: each entry of cluster reflects the two possible *next clusters* for A and their corresponding traversal probabilities, based on the new random walk graph. Then, the parent-child pointer from P_A to A is modified such that, instead of maintaining all clusters that A belongs to, it only maintains the *next cluster* that will be used when A is accessed. Based on the pointers and traversal probabilities stored in the corresponding entry of the cluster table, the value of *next cluster* will be updated after each access.

5.3   Eliminating the Chain Crossing Problem

To address the chain crossing problem, we present two solutions. For the first solution, we borrow the idea from replication approach presented in Section 4.2: Each node is replicated according to its contribution to its clusters. For each corresponding cluster, the node has a replica. When the node needs to be accessed, one of the replicas is chosen based on how the nodes accesses are distributed among its clusters (i.e., the clustering probabilities). We call this solution *merge-replication*. Since copies of a node are independently accessed, crosses among the chains that are caused by sharing of the node is removed. Since the maximum size of the clusters is small, the amount of total replication is also small. When a child is swapped and the references to it needs to be updated, the client needs to update the physical address *only* in the corresponding entry in the cluster table. However, this solution is restricted to read only applications for update is inherently costly for replication.

If we do not use replication, the crossings will exist and be visible to the server. Therefore, in the second solution, we embed the existing chain crossings into dummy chain crossings that are uniformly distributed among the existing chains. Since, as described in the previous subsection, the number of crossings per cluster can be limited through random-walk based readjustment of the traversal probabilities, the amount of dummy crossings per cluster are small. Details of this process are omitted.

6   Conclusion

In this paper, we build on the protocol we presented in [1, 2] to develop a protocol that enable secure outsourcing of tree structured data and hides correlations in tree traversals from the untrusted server in computational privacy sense. The early protocol [2] ensured privacy when accesses were uniformly distributed. To ensure computational privacy in face of non-uniformly distributed node access which actually occur in real scenarios, in this paper, we presented a systematic way to enhance this protocol so that from the server's view, node accesses are uniformly distributed. Since a lot of data, such as XML, has tree-like structures and queries can be expressed as traversal paths on these trees, this protocol can be utilized for secure outsourcing of XML documents. Compared with existing private information retrieval techniques [13, 22], our protocol does not need replication of databases and it requires less communication, and is thus practical.

References

1. Lin P., Candan K.S.(2004) Hiding traversal of tree structured data from untrusted data stores. Proc. of the 2nd Inernational Workshop on Security In Informtion Systems, WOSIS 2004. pp. 314–323.
2. Lin P., Candan K.S. (2004) Ensuring privacy of tree structured data and queries from untrusted data stores. *Information System Security*, May/June 2004. pp. 22–38.
3. Yang X., Li C. (2004) Secure XML publishing without information leakage in the presence of data inference. VLDB 2004.
4. Hore B., Mehrotra S., Tsudik G. (2004) A privacy-preserving index for range queries. VLDB 2004.
5. Song, D. X., Wagner, D., Perrig, A. (2000) Practical Techniques for Searches on Encrypted Data. IEEE Symposium on Security and Privacy 2000. pp 44–55.

6. Damiani, E., Vimercati, S. D. C., Jajodia, S., Paraboschi, S., Samarati, P.(2003) Balancing confidentiality and efficiency in untrusted relational DBMSs. Proc. of ACM Conference on Computer and Communications Security, 2003. pp 93–102.
7. Hacigümüs, H., Iyer, B.R., Li, C., Mehrotra, S.(2002) Executing SQL over encrypted data in the database-service-provider model. Proc. of ACM SIGMOD International Conference on Management of Data. Madison, Wisconsin, USA, June 3-6, 2002. pp. 216–227.
8. Paparizos, S., Al-Khalifa, S., Chapman, A., Jagadish, H. V., Lakshmanan, L. V. S., Nierman, A., Patel, J. M., Srivastava, D., Wiwatwattana, N., Wu, Y., Yu, C.(2003) TIMBER: A Native XML Database for Querying XML. Proc. of ACM SIGMOD International Conference on Management of Data, San Diego, California, USA, June 9-12, 2003. pp. 672.
9. Bertino, E. Carminati, B., Ferrari, E., Thuraisinggam, B. M., Gupta,A.(2002) Selective and authentic third-party distribution of XML documents. MIT Sloan Working Paper No. 4343-02.
10. Bertino, E., Ferrari, E.(2002) Secure and selective dissemination of XML documents. *ACM Transactions on Information and System Security*, 5(3). pp. 290–331.
11. Damiani, E., di Vimercati, S. D. C., Paraboschi, S., Samarati, P. (2000). Securing XML documents. Proc. of the 7th International Conference on Extending Database Technology, Konstanz, Germany, March 27-31, 2000. pp. 121–135.
12. Smith, S. W., Safford, D.(2001) Practical server privacy with secure coprocessors. *IBM Systems Journal*, Vol. 40, No. 3. pp. 683–695.
13. Chor, B., Goldreich, O., Kushilevitz, E., Sudan, M.(1995) Private information retrieval. Proc. of 36th IEEE Symposium on Foundations of Computer Science. Milwaukee, Wisconsin, USA, October 23-25, 1995. pp. 41–50.
14. Ambainis, A.(1997) Upper bound on the communication complexity of private information retrieval. Proc. of ICALP 1997. Bologna, Italy, 7-11 July 1997. pp. 401–407.
15. Beimel, A., Ishai, Y., Kushilevitz, E., and Raymond, J. F.(2002) Breaking the $O(n^{1/(2k-1)})$ barrier for information-theoretic private information retrieval. Proc. of 43rd IEEE Symposium on Foundations of Computer Science. Vancouver, BC, Canada, Nov 16-19 2002. pp. 261–270.
16. Chor, B., Gilboa, N.(1997) Computationally private information retrieval. Proc. of the 29th Annual ACM Symposium on the Theory of Computing. El Paso, Texas, USA, May 4-6, 1997. pp. 304–313.
17. Kushilevitz, E., Ostrovsky, R. (1997) Relication is not needed: single database. Computationally-private information retrieval. Proc. of the 38th IEEE Symposium on Foundations of Computer Science. Miami Beach, Florida, USA, Otc 19-22, 1997. pp. 365–373.
18. Beimel, A., Ishai,Y., Kushilevitz, E., Marlkin, T.(1999) One way functions are essential for single-server private information retrieval. Proc. of the 31st Annual ACM Symposium on Theory of Computing. Atlanta, Georgia, USA. May 1-4, 1999. pp. 89–98.
19. Chang Y.C.(2004) Single database private information retrieval with logarithmic communication. eprint 2004/036.
20. Bouganim, L., Pucheral, P.(2002) Chip-secured data access: confidencial data on untrusted servers. Proc. of 28th VLDB, Hongkong, China, 2002. pp. 131–142.
21. Bayer, R., Schkolnich, M.(1977) Concurrency of operations on B-trees. *Acta Informatica*, Vol. 9. pp. 1–21.
22. Chor, B., Gilboa, N., Naor, M.(1997) Private information retrieval by keywords. Technical Report TR CS0917. Technion Israel, 1997.

Using Secret Sharing
for Searching in Encrypted Data

Richard Brinkman, Jeroen Doumen, and Willem Jonker

University of Twente, Enschede,
{brinkman,doumen,jonker}@cs.utwente.nl

Abstract. When outsourcing data to an untrusted database server, the data should be encrypted. When using thin clients or low-bandwidth networks it is best to perform most of the work at the server. In this paper we present a method, inspired by secure multi-party computation, to search efficiently in encrypted data. XML elements are translated to polynomials. A polynomial is split into two parts: a random polynomial for the client and the difference between the original polynomial and the client polynomial for the server. Since the client polynomials are generated by a random sequence generator only the seed has to be stored on the client. In a combined effort of both the server and the client a query can be evaluated without traversing the whole tree and without the server learning anything about the data or the query.

1   Introduction

Nowadays the need grows to securely outsource data to an untrusted system. Think, for instance, of a remote database server administered by somebody else. If you want your data to be secret, you have to encrypt it. The problem then arises how to query the database. The most obvious solution is to download the whole database locally and then perform the query. This of course is terribly inefficient.

We propose a method that looks like secure multi-party computation where two parties, a client and the database server, together evaluate a query. Before we will present our solution (section 4) we will say a few thinks about secure multi-party computation in general (section 3).

2   Related Work

Most modern database management systems (DBMS) include functionality to encrypt records. However, they lack native support to query these records. Bertinoro [1] have studied how to protect XML data by using a diversified key approach.

In [2] techniques are presented to support keyword-based search on an encrypted textual string. We adapted this work to exploit the tree structure in XML documents in [3].

W. Jonker and M. Petković (Eds.): SDM 2004, LNCS 3178, pp. 18–27, 2004.

Other techniques to support keyword-based search on encrypted textual strings are presented in [4]. All these keyword based search techniques can only be used to find exact matches. [5] provides an order-preserving scheme for numeric data that allows any comparison operation directly applied on the encrypted data. In [6, 7] techniques are explored which execute SQL-based queries over encrypted relational tables in a database-service provider model, where an algebraic framework is described for query rewriting over encrypted attribute representation.

In [8] a single-server solution for remote querying of encrypted relational databases on untrusted servers is presented. The approach is based on the use of B+ tree indexing information attached to the relations. The designed indexing mechanism can balance the trade-off between efficiency requirements in query execution and protection requirements due to possible inference attacks exploiting indexing information.

Traditionally, databases are protected against a malicious intruder by means of an access control mechanism. However, the database management system itself is trusted. When the data is outsourced the database system cannot be trusted any more to keep the query and the answer secret. Private Information Retrieval [9] aims at letting a user query the database without leaking to the database which data was queried. The idea behind PIR is to replicate the data among several non-communicating servers. A client can hide his query by asking all servers for a part of the data in such a way that no server will learn the whole query by itself. [9] proves that PIR with a single server can only be done by sending all data to the client for each query. In practice database replication is not preferable. Computational PIR [9–11] aims at achieving the same goal as information theoretic PIR but uses cryptographic techniques. [12] uses a single server scheme which is a compromise between total privacy and efficiency. A query is hidden by asking for more nodes than required. The server cannot tell which nodes are really needed and which ones are just dummy nodes. To avoid replay attacks and server learning, all nodes in the retrieved set are shuffled and stored at different locations after each query.

3   Secure Multi-party Computation

We speak of secure multi-party computation when several parties calculate a function result without giving the other parties access to their input. More precisely, the parties want to evaluate the function result $(y_1, \ldots, y_n) = f(x_1, \ldots, x_n)$ where each parameter x_i is the private input of party P_i and y_i its private output. It is also possible that all y's are equal. In that case it is written as $y = f(x_1, \ldots, x_n)$. In principle there exist schemes that can evaluate any function securely using secure multi-party computation [13]. However, no efficient multi-purpose schemes are known to us at the moment.

For example, let f be an anonymous voting function. Each voter P_i can vote for a decision ($x_i = 1$) or against it ($x_i = 0$). The function f can be defined as the function $f(x_1, \ldots, x_n) = \sum_{i=1}^{n} x_i$ (in case of a majority vote) or as $f(x_1, \ldots, x_n) = \prod_{i=1}^{n} x_i$ (in case of a veto system).

One characteristic of secure multi-party computation is the lack of a trusted third party. In our example there is no need for a trusted party to count the votes.

Many secure multi-party computation protocols are based on Shamir's secret sharing scheme [14]. These protocols have at least two phases. In the first phase each party P_i splits up its input x_i in such a way that at least $t \leq n$ shares are needed to reconstruct x_i. In the second phase each party P_i calculates its share of the function result given only his own input and the shares of the other parties. Now, the complete function result is shared over all parties.

We will now give the implementation of one specific secure multi-party computation protocol. In this protocol P_i shares its input variable x_i by choosing a random polynomial g_i of degree t such that $g_i(0) = x_i$. P_i sends to each other party P_j the value of $g_i(j)$. When t parties collaborate they can reconstruct the original polynomial g_i by interpolating the t points $(j, g_i(j))$. With the polynomial it is easy to recalculate $x_i = g_i(0)$.

The second phase consists of the local computations with the distributed shares $g_i(j)$ and depends on the function f. For simplicity reasons we consider only our voting case where $f(x_1, \ldots, x_n) = \sum_{i=1}^{n} x_i$. Each party P_j locally calculates the sum $h(j) = \sum_{i=1}^{n} g_i(j)$. Having at least t collaborating parties and thus t points $\langle j, h(j) \rangle$ it is possible to construct the polynomial $h = \sum_{i=1}^{n} g_i$ and also $f(x_1, \ldots, x_n) = h(0)$.

4   Searching in Encrypted Data

One way to look at the problem of searching in encrypted data [3, 15, 16] is to consider the search algorithm as a *search* function that is to be evaluated in the sense of secure multi-party computation. The function takes two arguments, *data* and *query*, as input. *data* is the private input of the client but stored on the server and *query* the private input of the client. We achieved this by splitting the original *data* into a random part $data_{client}$ and a server part $data_{server}$ such that $data = data_{client} + data_{server}$. Since $data_{client}$ is generated by a pseudo random generator it can be forgotten provided that you keep the random seed. Damiani et al [17] use the same strategy in the relational setting. Thus the search function becomes $search(data_{server}, query)$. Both the client and the server contribute to the evaluation of this function. The representation and the splitting of the data is not a trivial problem. One way to represent the data is explained in the following section. In section 4.2 we will solve the problem of sharing and in section 4.3 the querying of the data.

4.1   Data Representation

Secure multi-party computation works best with simple algebraic expressions like polynomials. It is possible to map the tree of elements from an XML file to a tree of polynomials. We will demonstrate this mapping by way of the example shown in figure 1(a).

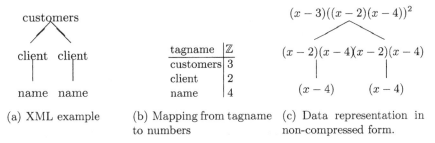

tagname	$\mathbb{Z}$
customers	3
client	2
name	4

(a) XML example

(b) Mapping from tagname to numbers

(c) Data representation in non-compressed form.

Fig. 1. XML example and its non-reduced representation as a tree of polynomials

First we introduce a mapping function from tag names to integers ($map : tagnames \rightarrow \mathbb{Z}$). The mapping function may be chosen arbitrarily. For our example we choose the mapping function displayed in figure 1(b). The mapping function should be private to avoid the server to see the query (see section 4.3).

The tree of XML elements is represented as a tree of polynomials. The tree is built from the leaves up to the root node. The leaf node *name* is translated into the polynomial $(x - map(name)) = (x - 4)$. Every non-leaf node is calculated as the product of the polynomials of all its children times itself. For instance, in figure 1 *customers* is represented as $(x - map(customers))((x - 2)(x - 4))^2$, where $(x-2)(x-4)$ represents each *client* node. Figure 1(c) shows all represented elements.

To avoid large degree polynomials we will work in a finite ring. We have investigated two different rings: $\mathbb{F}_q[x]/(x^{q-1}-1)$ (where q is a prime power $q = p^e$. For the reader's convenience, all proofs will be given for q prime) and $\mathbb{Z}[x]/(r(x))$ (where $r(x)$ is an irreducible polynomial). In the first case the coefficients of the polynomials are reduced modulo q. If p is prime then $\forall a \in \mathbb{F}_p : a^{p-1} \equiv 1$ (mod p). Since these polynomials will only be used for evaluation in points of $\mathbb{F}_p[x]$, it makes sense to store the polynomials modulo $x^{p-1} - 1$. In effect, this means we are working in $\mathbb{F}_p[x]/(x^{p-1} - 1)$. In order to avoid zero divisors, we will avoid mapping a tagname to $p - 1$. Thus we reduce every polynomial to a polynomial of degree less than $p - 1$ with coefficients in $\mathbb{F}_p$.

When working in $\mathbb{Z}[x]/(r(x))$, the polynomial is reduced modulo an irreducible polynomial $r(x)$. The resulting degree is less than the degree of $r(x)$. However, the coefficients are elements of $\mathbb{Z}$ and can get quite large for large trees.

Although we calculate in a finite ring, no information about the original tag names is lost. We will prove this in theorems 1 and 2 for the respective cases $\mathbb{F}_p[x]/(x^{p-1} - 1)$ and $\mathbb{Z}[x]/(r(x))$. But before we can prove theorem 1 we need some lemmas.

Lemma 1. *If p is prime then $\prod_{i=1}^{p-1}(x - i) \equiv x^{p-1} - 1$ (mod p).*

Proof. Let $f(x) = \prod_{i=1}^{p-1}(x - i)$ and $g(x) = x^{p-1} - 1$. Two polynomials are the same if they have exactly the same roots. All elements of $\mathbb{F}_p^* = \{1, \ldots, p - 1\}$

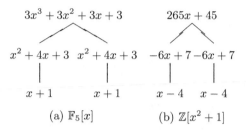

(a) $\mathbb{F}_5[x]$ (b) $\mathbb{Z}[x^2 + 1]$

Fig. 2. The same XML example as in figure 1 but now reduced from $\mathbb{Z}[x]$ to the finite rings $\mathbb{F}_p[x]/(x^{p-1} - 1)$ and $\mathbb{Z}[x]/(r(x))$

are roots of $f(x)$. By Fermat's little theorem, for p prime all these $p - 1$ roots of $f(x)$ are also roots for $g(x)$. Thus the two polynomials are equal.

Lemma 2. *Let p be prime and $f(x) \in \mathbb{F}_p[x]$. If $f(x)$ is non-zero mod $x - (p-1)$ then $f(x)$ is also non-zero modulo $x^{p-1} - 1$.*

Proof. Since $f(x) \equiv 0 \pmod{x^{p-1} - 1} \Longleftrightarrow (x^{p-1} - 1)|f(x)$ and from lemma 1 it follows that $x - (p-1)|x^{p-1} - 1$ in $\mathbb{F}_p[x]$, we can conclude that $x - (p-1)|f(x)$ and thus also that $f(x) \equiv 0 \pmod{x - (p-1)}$. This proves that $f(x) \equiv 0 \pmod{x^{p-1} - 1} \Longrightarrow f(x) \equiv 0 \pmod{x - (p-1)}$, which is equivalent to the statement of the lemma.

Lemma 3. *Let p be prime, and let $f(x) \in \mathbb{F}_p[x]$ be defined as $f(x) = \prod_{i=1}^{p-2}(x - i)^{e_i}$. Then $f(x) \not\equiv 0 \pmod{x^{p-1} - 1}$.*

Proof. Consider the evaluation of $f(x)$ at $p - 1$:

$$f(p-1) = \prod_{i=1}^{p-2}((p-1) - i)^{e_i}$$

Because $\forall i \in \{1, \ldots, p-2\} : i \neq p-1$, $f(p-1) \neq 0$. Thus $x - (p-1)$ cannot be a factor of $f(x)$, and we have that $f(x) \not\equiv 0 \pmod{x - (p-1)}$. By lemma 2 this implies that $f(x) \not\equiv 0 \pmod{x^{p-1} - 1}$.

Now we are ready to prove that the mapped values can be retrieved uniquely:

Theorem 1. *Given a polynomial $f(x)$ in $\mathbb{F}_p[x]/(x^{p-1} - 1)$ (p prime) of an element node and all polynomials $(q_1, \ldots, q_n)$ of its children, the mapped value map(node) can be retrieved uniquely.*

Proof. Because of the way the polynomial $f(x)$ of the element *node* was constructed, we know at least one solution exists for the equation

$$f(x) \equiv q_1(x) \cdots q_n(x)(x - t),$$

where t is the mapped value to be retrieved. To prove that the solution is unique, suppose there are two solutions t_1 and t_2 to this equation: $f(x) \equiv$

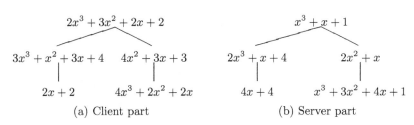

Fig. 3. The shared data over client and server. The sum of a polynomial at the client side with the corresponding polynomial at the server side equals the original polynomial of figure 2(a). All polynomials are elements of $\mathbb{F}_5[x]/(x^4 - 1)$

$q_1(x) \cdots q_n(x)(x - t_1)$ and $f(x) \equiv q_1(x) \cdots q_n(x)(x - t_2)$. Then $q_1(x) \cdots q_n(x)(x - t_1) \equiv q_1(x) \cdots q_n(x)(x - t_2)$. This can be rewritten to

$$q_1(x) \cdots q_n(x)(t_1 - t_2) \equiv 0 \pmod{p}.$$

Thus either $q_1(x) \cdots q_n(x) \equiv 0 \pmod{p}$ or $(t_1 - t_2) \equiv 0 \pmod{p}$. Since we know that $q_1(x) \cdots q_n(x) \not\equiv 0 \pmod{p}$ by lemma 3 (the q_i's match the required form by construction), we can conclude that $t_1 \equiv t_2 \pmod{p}$.

Theorem 2. *Given a polynomial $f(x)$ in $\mathbb{Z}[x]/(r(x))$ of an element node and all polynomials $(q_1, \ldots, q_n)$ of its children, the mapped value map(node) can uniquely be retrieved.*

Proof. As in theorem 1 due to construction there exists at least one t that satisfies $f(x) \equiv q_1(x) \cdots q_n(x)(x - t) \pmod{p}$. To prove that the solution is unique suppose there are two solutions t_1 and t_2. Then $q_1(x) \cdots q_n(x)(t_1 - t_2) \equiv 0 \pmod{r(x)}$. Since $r(x)$ is irreducible, and none of the $q_i(x)$ are zero modulo $r(x)$ (by construction), we have that $t_1 - t_2 \equiv 0 \pmod{r(x)}$. Therefore $t_1 = t_2$.

Note that in both cases the actual solution for t can easily be found.

4.2 Data Sharing

Before the data can be stored on the server, it should be split into two parts: one for the server and one for the client. The client builds a tree structure similar to the tree structure of the original data. But instead of just copying the elements it chooses random polynomials. Also it builds the tree to be stored on the server. The sum of the corresponding polynomials should be equal to the polynomial of the original tree. Look for example to the top nodes of figure 4. The sum $(9x - 12) + (256x + 57)$ equals the root node of figure 2(b) $(265x + 45)$.

If the client does not have the storage capacity to store the whole tree, it could store only the random seed with which the random polynomials were generated and recompute the needed entries of the tree for each query.

Note that this is a direct application of a basic secret sharing scheme (as is often used in secure multi-party computations). This can easily be extended to a model with multiple servers, in which the client together with k out of n servers (or any other access structure) can reconstruct the shared secret polynomial.

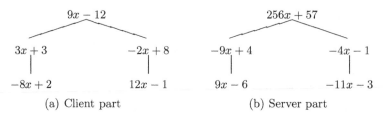

(a) Client part   (b) Server part

Fig. 4. Another sharing with the same principles as in figure 3 but now with polynomials in $\mathbb{Z}[x]/(x^2 + 1)$

4.3 Querying

Now that the data has been shared on both the client and the server, we will describe how to query the data. First we will discuss simple element lookups: find an element given its tag name. In section 4.3 we will look at more difficult XPath queries.

Element Lookup. We assume that the document of figure 1 has been shared as described in section 4.2. Let's further assume that we would like to evaluate the query //client. This XPath expression means that we want to find 'client' elements somewhere in the tree. Normally (even in the non-encrypted case) this boils down to traversing the whole tree and comparing the tag names with the name 'client'. We will do it smarter than that.

First we use the mapping function to translate the tag name 'client' to $x = 2$ (see figure 1(b)). The client sends this value of x to the server. If we want to keep the query secret for the server the mapping function should be private to the client.

The server evaluates the polynomials in the given point ($x = 2$). Each time a polynomial has been evaluated the calculated value is sent back to the client.

The client does the same thing on its own side. Furthermore it calculates the sum of the client element and the server element. If this sum equals zero than the element contains a factor $(x - 2)$, meaning either that the element has tag name 'client' or that it contains a descendant named 'client'. A sum different from zero means that the branch is dead. If this is the case the client informs the server so that the server can stop evaluating polynomials for elements in the tree starting with that branch.

Each zero element in the sum tree that does not have a zero sub element represents an answer to the query. All other zero's in the sum tree may or may not represent correct answers. To find out whether the element itself or one of its descendants is named 'client', the non-shared polynomials of both the element and all its direct children have to be reconstructed.

To reconstruct the element value, let f be the sum of the polynomials on the server and the client of an element and $q_1, \ldots, q_n$ the combined polynomials of all its direct children.

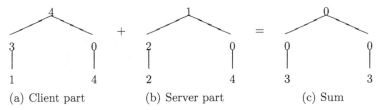

Fig. 5. Query result for the query '$x = 2$'. Both the server and the client evaluates the polynomials for the given value of x modulo p. The server sends its values to the client which adds it to its own calculated value. A branch is a dead end if the sum is not 0

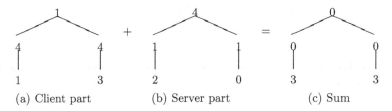

Fig. 6. Query result for the query '$x = 2$' for the case $\mathbb{Z}[x]/(x^2 + 1)$. everything is calculated modulo $r(2) = 2^2 + 1 = 5$

By construction we know that f can be written as

$$f = (x - t) \prod_{i=1}^{n} q_i \quad (\text{mod } r) \tag{1}$$

To check the correctness of an answer we have to solve t in $f(x) = 0$. In our example t should be 2.

Theorem 2 proves that there is just a single solution for t. It is solved by:

$$\left.\begin{array}{l} d = d(r) \\ f - q_1 \cdots q_n (x - t) = 0 \quad (\text{mod } r) \\ a_{d-1}x^{d-1} + a_{d-2}x^{d-2} + \cdots + a_1 x + a_0 = 0 \end{array}\right\} \Longrightarrow \tag{2}$$

Where each a_i is a function in t. Note that the same scheme can be used for the field $\mathbb{F}_p/(x^{p-1} - 1)$.

$$\begin{cases} a_{d-1}(t) = 0 \\ \cdots \\ a_0(t) = 0 \end{cases} \tag{3}$$

A single (non-trivial) equation in 3 is enough to solve t. The other equations may be used to verify the result. Remember that we did not trust the server. We now have at least a way to check the answer. If, however, we trust the server to give correct answers, only the last equation is enough. In that case only the constant factor (without x) of each polynomial stored on the server has to be transmitted. This reduces bandwidth and increases efficiency but decreases security.

Advanced Querying. So far we evaluated only queries like //tagname. But also more elaborate XPath queries can be performed. It is of course possible to evaluate a query like //a/b//c/d/e from left to right. That is, search the tree for occurences of 'a', then search within the found branches for 'b', etc. But it is more efficient to evaluate the whole query at once. Since every polynomial in the tree consists of the roots of all its descendants, a single query can find all elements that contains the elements a, b, c, d and e (in any order). In this case a search consists of the following steps:

1. from the root node find all 'a' elements that have b, c, d and e elements somewhere deeper in the tree
2. from the found nodes find all direct children 'b' that have elements c, d and e as descendants
3. . . .

Using this strategy elements are filtered out in a very early stage and therefore increases efficiency.

5 Conclusion and Future Work

We have seen a method to store a tree of XML elements as a tree of polynomials and two reduction schemes, one in $\mathbb{Z}[x]/(r(x))$ and one in $\mathbb{F}_p[x]/(x^{p-1} - 1)$. These trees are split in a server and a client part. Both parts are needed to retrieve the original data. The created trees can be used to query the data in a secure way. Our scheme has only a small penalty in storage space compared to the unencrypted case. To store an XML tree with n elements and p different tagnames in an unencrypted way we need a storage space in the order of $n \log p$. In the encrypted case the orders for the cases $\mathbb{Z}[x]/(r(x))$ and $\mathbb{F}_p[x]/(x^{p-1} - 1)$ are $n(d + 1) \log p^n = n^2(d + 1) \log p$ respectively $n(p - 1) \log p$, where d is the degree of $r(x)$.

The extra amount of storage space is used as a smart index which enables an efficient search strategy. Each element has some knowledge of its descendants. When searching the tree for an element, a branch can be marked as a dead-end in a very early stage. Thus, only a small portion of the tree has to be examined.

In this paper we only looked at storing and retrieving trees of tag names. We did not take into account the actual data between the tags. We cannot straightforwardly use the same method for the actual data because, in order to keep the mapping function invertible, p and therefore the storage capacity becomes unreasonably large. We can use a hash function to map the data to an element of $\mathbb{Z}_p$ but in that case the mapping function is no longer invertible. In this case the data polynomials can be used as an index to the encrypted data. Another approach would be to choose a totally different approach like Song et al [2], Feng and Jonker [16] or using bloomfilters [18]. The storage and retrieval of the actual data is still subject to ongoing research.

References

1. E. Bertinoro. Secure and selective dissemination of XML documents. *ACM Transactions on Information and System Security*, 5(3):390–331, 2002.
2. Dawn Xiaodong Song, David Wagner, and Adrian Perrig. Practical techniques for searches on encrypted data. In *IEEE Symposium on Security and Privacy*, pages 44–55, 2000. http://citeseer.nj.nec.com/song00practical.html.
3. R. Brinkman, L. Feng, J.M. Doumen, P.H. Hartel, and W. Jonker. Efficient tree search in encrypted data. *Information Systems Security Journal*, pages 14–21, May/June 2004. http://www.ub.utwente.nl/webdocs/ctit/1/000000f3.pdf.
4. D. Boneh, G. Di Crescenzo, R. Ostrovsky, and G. Persiano. Public key encryption with keyword search. In *Proceedings of Eurocrypt*, pages 506–522, 2004. http://crypto.stanford.edu/ dabo/abstracts/encsearch.html.
5. R. Agrawal, J. Kieman, R. Srikant, and Y. Xu. Order-preserving encryption for numeric data. In *Proc. of the ACM SIGMOD 2004 Conference*, Paris, France, June 2004.
6. H. Hacıgümüş, Balakrishna R. Iyer, Chen Li, and Sharad Mehrotra. Executing SQL over encrypted data in the database service provider model. In *SIGMOD Conference*, 2002.
7. H. Hacıgümüş, B. Iyer, and S. Mehrotra. Efficient execution of aggregation queries over encrypted relational databases. In *Proc. of the 9th International Conference on Database Systems for Advanced Applications*, Jeju Island, Korea, March 2004.
8. E. Damiani, S. De Capitani di Vimercati, S. Jajodia, S. Paraboschi, and P. Samarati. Balancing confidentiality and efficiency in untrusted relational DBMSs. In *Proc. of the 10th ACM Conference on Computer and Communications Security*, Washington, DC, USA, October 2003.
9. B. Chor, O. Goldreich, E. Kushilevitz, and M. Sudan. Private information retrieval. In *FOCS*, pages 41–50, 1995.
10. B. Chor and N. Gilboa. Computationally private information retrieval. In *ACM Symposium on the Theory of Computing*, 1997.
11. E. Kushilevitz and R. Ostrovsky. Replication is not needed: single database. In *IEEE Symposium on Foundations of Computer Science*, pages 364–373, 1997. citeseer.ist.psu.edu/kushilevitz97replication.html.
12. P. Lin and K.S. Candan. Ensuring privacy of tree structured data and queries from untrusted data stores. *Information Systems Security Journal*, May/June 2004.
13. O. Goldreich. *Foundations of Cryptography*, volume 2. Cambridge University Press, May 2004. ISBN 0-521-83084-2.
14. Adi Shamir. How to share a secret. *Communications of the ACM*, 22(11):612–613, November 1979.
15. R. Brinkman, L. Feng, S. Etalle, P. H. Hartel, and W. Jonker. Experimenting with linear search in encrypted data. Technical report TR-CTIT-03-43, Centre for Telematics and Information Technology, Univ. of Twente, The Netherlands, Sep 2003. http://www.ub.utwente.nl/webdocs/ctit/1/000000d9.pdf.
16. Ling Feng and Willem Jonker. Efficient processing of secured XML metadata. In *Proceedings of Intl. Workshop on Security for Metadata*, Catania, Italy, Nov 2003.
17. E. Damiani, S. de Capitani di Vimercati, S. Paraboschi, and P. Samarati. Computing range queries on obfuscated data. In *Proc. of IPMU 2004*, Perugia, Italy, 2004.
18. Eu-Jin Goh. Building secure indexes for searching efficiently on encrypted compressed data. Cryptology ePrint Archive, Report 2003/216, 2003. http://eprint.iacr.org/2003/216/.

A Structure Preserving Database Encryption Scheme

Yuval Elovici[1], Ronen Waisenberg[1], Erez Shmueli[1], and Ehud Gudes[2]

[1] Ben-Gurion University of the Negev, Faculty of Engineering,
Department of Information Systems Engineering, Postfach 653,
84105 Beer-Sheva, Israel
{elovici,ronenwai,erezshmu}@bgu.ac.il
[2] Ben-Gurion University of the Negev, Department of Computer Science, Postfach 653,
84105 Beer-Sheva, Israel
ehud@cs.bgu.ac.il

Abstract. A new simple and efficient database encryption scheme is presented. The new scheme enables encrypting the entire content of the database without changing its structure. In addition, the scheme suggests how to convert the conventional database index to a secure index on the encrypted database so that the time complexity of all queries is maintained. No one with access to the encrypted database can learn anything about its content without having the encryption key.

1 Introduction

Database is an integral part of almost every information system. According to [1] the key features that databases propose are shared access, minimal redundancy, data consistency, data integrity and controlled access.

The case where databases hold critical and sensitive information is not rare, therefore an adequate level of protection to database content has to be provided. Database security methods can be divided into four layers [2]: physical security [3], operating system security [4, 5, 6], DBMS security [7, 8, 9] and data encryption [10, 11, 12]. The first three layers alone are not sufficient to guarantee the security of the database since the database data is kept in a readable form [13]. Anyone having access to the database including the DBA (Database Administrator), is capable of reading the data. In addition, the data is backed up frequently so access to the backed up data also needs to be controlled [14]. Moreover, a distributed database system makes it harder to control the disclosure of the data.

Database encryption introduces an additional security layer to the first three layers mentioned above. It conceals the readable form of sensitive information even if the database is compromised. Thus, anyone who manages to bypass the conventional database security layers (e.g., an intruder) or a DBA, is unable to read the sensitive information without the encryption key. Furthermore, encryption can be used to maintain data integrity so that any unauthorized changes of the data can easily be detected.

Database encryption can be implemented at different levels [14]: tables, columns, rows and cells. Encrypting the whole table, column or row entails the decryption of the whole table, column or row respectively when a query is executed. Therefore, an implementation which decrypts only the data of interest is preferred.

W. Jonker and M. Petković (Eds.): SDM 2004, LNCS 3178, pp. 28–40, 2004.

The database encryption scheme presented in [13] is based on the Chinese-Reminder theorem where each row is encrypted using different sub-keys for different cells. This scheme enables encryption at the level of rows and decryption at the level of cells. The database encryption scheme presented in [14] extends the encryption scheme presented in [13] by supporting multilayer access control. It classifies subjects and objects into distinct security classes. The security classes are ordered in a hierarchy such that an object with a particular security class can be accessed only by subjects in the same or a higher security class. In this scheme, each row is encrypted with sub-keys according to the security class of its cells. One disadvantage of both schemes is that the basic element in the database is a row and not a cell, thus the structure of the database needs to be changed. In addition, both schemes require re-encrypting the whole row when a cell value is modified.

The conventional way to provide an efficient execution of database queries is by using indexes, but indexes in an encrypted database raise the question of how to construct the index so that no information about the database content is revealed [15, 16].

The indexing scheme provided in [17] is based on encrypting the whole row and assigning a set identifier to each value in this row. When searching a specific value its set identifier is calculated and then passed to the server which in turn returns to the client a collection of all rows with values assigned to the same set. Finally, the client searches the specific value in the returned collection and retrieves the desired rows. However, in this scheme, equal values are always assigned to the same set, thus some information is revealed when applying statistical attacks.

The indexing scheme provided in [18] is based on constructing the index on the plaintext values and encrypting each page of the index separately. Whenever a specific page of the index is needed for processing a query, it is loaded into memory and decrypted. Since the uniform encryption of all pages is likely to provide many cipher breaking clues, the indexing scheme provided in [19] suggests encrypting each index page using a different key depending on the page number. However, these schemes being implemented at the level of the operating system are not satisfactory.

Assuming the index is implemented as a B+-Tree, encrypting each of its fields separately would reveal the ordering relationship between the ciphertext values. The indexing scheme provided in [15] suggests encrypting each node of the B+-Tree as a whole. However, since references between the B+-Tree nodes are encrypted together with the index values, the index structure is concealed.

In order to overcome the shortcomings of existing database encryption schemes, a new simple and efficient scheme for database encryption is proposed which suggests how to encrypt the entire content of the database without changing its structure. This property allows the DBA to continue managing the database without being able to view or manipulate the database content. Moreover, anyone gaining access to the database can learn nothing about its content without the encryption key. The new scheme suggests how to construct a secure index on the encrypted database so that the time complexity of all queries is maintained. Since the database structure remains the same no changes are imposed on the queries.

The remainder of the paper is structured as follows: in section 2 the desired properties of a database encryption scheme are outlined; in section 3 the new database encryption scheme is illustrated; in section 4 the desired properties of a secure indexing scheme are described; in section 5 a new indexing scheme for the encrypted database is proposed; in section 6 performance and implementation issues are discussed, and section 7 presents our conclusions.

2   The Desired Properties of a Database Encryption Scheme

According to [13], a database encryption scheme should meet the following requirements:

1) The encryption scheme should either be theoretically or computationally secure (require a high work factor to break it).
2) Encryption and decryption should be fast enough so as not to degrade system performance.
3) The encrypted data should not have a significantly greater volume than the unencrypted data.
4) Decryption of a record should not depend on other records.
5) Encrypting different columns under different keys should be possible.
6) The encryption scheme should protect against patterns matching and substitution of encrypted values attacks.
7) Modifying data by an unauthorized user should be noticed at decryption time.
8) Recovering information from partial records (records where some cells have null values) should be the same as from full records.
9) The security mechanism should be flexible and not entail any change in the structure of the database.

A naïve approach for database encryption is to encrypt each cell separately but this approach has several drawbacks. First, two equal plaintext values are encrypted to equal ciphertext values.

$$V_1 = V_2 \longleftrightarrow E_k(V_1) = E_k(V_2) \tag{1}$$

Therefore, it is possible, for example, to collect statistical information as to how many different values a specified column currently has, and what are their frequencies. The same holds for the ability to execute a join operation between two tables and collect information from the results. Second, it is possible to switch unnoticed between two ciphertext values. Different ciphertext values for equal plaintext values can be achieved using a polyalphabetic cipher (e.g. Vernam). However, in this solution decryption of a record depends on other records and thus requirement 4 is violated.

In the next section a new database encryption scheme complying with all the above requirements is presented.

3   A New Database Encryption Scheme

The position of a cell in the database is unique and can be identified using the triplet that includes its Table ID, Row ID, and Column ID. We will refer to this triplet as the cell coordinates.

We suggest a new database encryption scheme where each database value is encrypted with its unique cell coordinates. These coordinates are used in order to break the correlation between ciphertext and plaintext values in an encrypted database. The new scheme has two immediate advantages. First, it eliminates substitution attacks attempting to switch encrypted values. Second, patterns matching attacks attempting to gather statistics based on the database encrypted values would fail.

a) Table T before Encryption		b) Encryption of Table T Using the Naive Approach		c) Encryption of Table T Using the New Scheme	
Row	C	Row	C	Row	C
0	16	0	#$	0	!#
1	85	1	]{	1	:]
2	37	2	&*	2	&*
3	16	3	#$	3	"/
4	16	4	#$	4	~?
5	92	5	^%	5	|^
6	37	6	&*	6	>\
7	50	7	0-	7	@=
8	24	8	+=	8	){
9	86	9	@!	9	-+

Fig. 1. Database encryption using two approaches.

Figure 1 illustrates database encryption using two approaches. Figure 1a describes a database table (T) with one data column (C). Figure 1b describes encryption of table T using the naïve approach. Figure 1c describes encryption of table T using the new approach where each cell is encrypted with its cell coordinates. It is easy to see that equal plaintext values in figure 1a are encrypted to different ciphertext values in figure 1c as opposed to the ciphertext values in figure 1b.

3.1 Encryption/Decryption in the New Scheme

Let us define:

V_{trc} - A plaintext value located in table t, row r and column c.

$\mu : (N \times N \times N) \to N$ - a function that generates a number based on the database coordinates.

Enc_k - A function which encrypts a plaintext value with its coordinates.

$$Enc_k (V_{trc}) = E_k (V_{trc} \oplus \mu(t, r, c)) \tag{2}$$

Where k is the encryption key and E_k is a symmetric encryption function (e.g. DES, AES).

X_{trc} - A ciphertext value located in table t, row r and column c.

$$X_{trc} = Enc_k (V_{trc})$$ (3)

Dec_k - A function which decrypts a ciphertext value (X_{trc}) and discards its coordinates.

$$Dec_k (X_{trc}) = D_K (X_{trc}) \oplus \mu(T, R, C) = V_{trc}$$ (4)

Where k is the decryption key and D_k is a symmetric decryption function.

3.2 Data Integrity

Encryption ensures that a user not possessing the encryption key cannot modify a ciphertext value and predict the change in the plaintext value. Usually the range of valid plaintext values is significantly smaller than the whole range of possible plaintext values. Thus, the probability that an unauthorized change to a ciphertext value would result in a valid plaintext value is negligible. Therefore, unauthorized changes to ciphertext values are likely to be noticed at decryption time.

Substitution attacks as opposed to patterns matching attacks can not be prevented simply by using encryption. In the new scheme, each value is encrypted with its unique cell coordinates. Therefore, trying to decrypt a value with different cell coordinates (e.g. as a result of a substitution attack) would probably result in an invalid plaintext value.

If the range of valid plaintext values is not significantly smaller than the whole possible range, or invalid plaintext values cannot be distinguished from valid plaintext values, encryption has to be carried out as follows:

$$Enc_K (V_{trc}) = E_k (V_{trc} \| \mu(t, r, c))$$ (5)

Since $\mu(t, r, c)$ is concatenated to the plaintext value before encryption, attempting to change the ciphertext value or trying to switch two ciphertext values would result in a corrupted $\mu(t, r, c)$ [1] after decryption. Obviously, concatenating $\mu(t, r, c)$ results in data expansion.

3.3 Scheme Analysis

The new database encryption scheme satisfies the requirements mentioned in section 2:

1) The scheme security relies on the security of the encryption algorithm used. In order to reveal some database value it has to be decrypted using the correct key.
2) Encryption and decryption are fast operations and are mandatory in any database encryption scheme. The proposed implementation adds the overhead of a Xor operation and μ computation which are negligible compared to encryption.
3) Using encryption algorithms such as DES or AES which are based on encrypting blocks of data results in value expansion (in many cases this expansion is negligible).

---

[1] μ implementation is discussed in section 6.2.

4) The basic element of reference is a database cell. Operations on a cell do not depend on or have any effect on other cells.
5) The proposed scheme facilitates subschema implementation. Since each cell is encrypted separately, each column can be encrypted under a different key[2].
6) The new scheme prevents patterns matching attacks since there is no correlation between a plaintext value and a ciphertext value (achieved by using encryption) and there is no correlation between ciphertext values (achieved by using μ before encryption). Substitution attacks are also prevented as discussed in section 3.2.
7) Unauthorized manipulation on the encrypted data without the encryption key would be noticed at decryption time. (see section 3.2)
8) As the basic element of reference is a database cell, it is possible to recover information from partially completed records (records with null values) in the same way as it is recovered from full records.
9) The new scheme complies with the structure preserving requirements as the basic element of reference is a database cell.

4   The Desired Properties of a Secure Indexing Scheme

An index is a data structure supporting efficient access to data and indexes are frequently used in databases. Most commercial databases even create a default index on the primary-key columns. Most databases implement indexes using a B+-Tree which is a data structure maintaining an ordered set of values and supporting efficient operations on this set such as search, insert, update and delete.

Figure 2 illustrates a database index which is constructed on column C in table T and is implemented as a B+-Tree. A graphical representation of the B+-Tree is given in figure 2a; a table representation of the B+-Tree is given in figure 2b and table T is given in figure 2c. Figure 2b sharpens the separation between the index structure and its data.

A secure index in an encrypted database has to comply with the following requirements:

1) No information about the database plaintext values can be learned from the index.
2) The secure index should not reduce the efficiency of data access.
3) The secure index should not reduce the efficiency of insert, update and delete operations.
4) The secure index should not have a significantly greater volume than an ordinary index.
5) The secure index structure should not differ from a standard index. In this way, a DBA can manage the index without the encryption key.

A trivial approach which constructs an index over the plaintext values would reduce security since the plaintext values are exposed. Another approach would construct the

---

[2] Key management is discussed in section 6.3.

index over the database ciphertext values. In this approach, executing equality queries is possible but executing range queries is a problem. This approach would expose the index to patterns matching attacks since equal plaintext values are encrypted to equal ciphertext values. Moreover, since executing range queries is a problem, Oracle does not support encrypting indexed data [20].

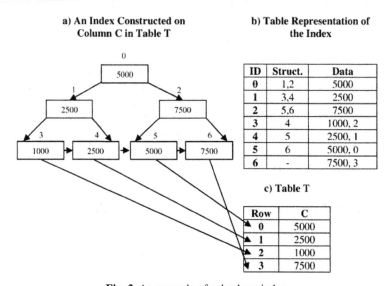

a) An Index Constructed on Column C in Table T

b) Table Representation of the Index

ID	Struct.	Data
0	1,2	5000
1	3,4	2500
2	5,6	7500
3	4	1000, 2
4	5	2500, 1
5	6	5000, 0
6	-	7500, 3

c) Table T

Row	C
0	5000
1	2500
2	1000
3	7500

Fig. 2. An example of a database index.

In the next section, a new indexing scheme which overcomes the shortcomings of existing indexing schemes is presented.

5   A New Database Indexing Scheme

Several indexing schemes for encrypted databases were proposed [15, 18, 17, 21] that fulfill most of the requirements described in section 4 but none preserve the index structure. We claim that there should be a separation between data and structure. For example, A DBA should be able to manage database indexes without the need of decrypting its values.

We suggest a new database indexing scheme which preserves the index structure where each index value is the result of encrypting a plaintext value in the database concatenated with its row-id. This ensures that there is no correlation between the index values and the database ciphertext values[3]. Furthermore, the index does not reveal the statistics or order of the database values.

---

[3] If the database is encrypted as described in section 3.2, then μ should not be implemented as $\mu(t, r, c) = r$ since there will be a strong correlation between the index values and the database encrypted values.

5.1 Index Construction in the New Scheme

In order to construct an index, a set of values and a function determining the order[4] of these values are needed.

Let us define:

C - An encrypted database column that was encrypted as defined in section 3.1.

C_p - The column obtained from decrypting column C:

$$Dec_k(x_{trc}) \in C_p \longleftrightarrow x_{trc} \in C \tag{6}$$

Where Dec_k is the decryption function defined in section 3.1.

C_i - The column obtained from encrypting values in C_p concatenated with their row-ids:

$$E_k(V_{trc} \| r) \in C_i \longleftrightarrow V_{trc} \in C_p \tag{7}$$

Where k is the encryption key, E_k is an encryption function and r is the row id.

$\lambda_k : C_i \to C_p$ - A function which decrypts a value in C_i (using key k) and discards its row-id:

$$\lambda_k(x) = Discard(D_k(x), |r|) \tag{8}$$

Where k is the decryption key, D_k is a decryption function, r is the row-id, $|r|$ is the length of r in bits, and $Discard(v,n)$ stands for discarding the n rightmost bits of v.

R_p - The values in C_p are ordered by the relation R_p:

$$(x, y) \in R_p \longleftrightarrow x, y \in C_p \, And \, (x \le y) \tag{9}$$

R_i - The values in C_i are ordered by the relation R_i:

$$(x, y) \in R_i \longleftrightarrow x, y \in C_i \, And \, (\lambda_k(x), \lambda_k(y)) \in R_p \tag{10}$$

The new index will be constructed based on the values in C_i, using the relation R_i as an order function.

Figure 3 illustrates encryption of the table and the index which were illustrated in figure 2 using the new schemes. Figure 3a describes the encryption of the table in the new scheme where each cell is encrypted with its coordinates. Figure 3b describes the encryption of the index where each index value is the result of encrypting a database plaintext value concatenated with its row-id. It is easy to see that the table and index structure are not changed by the encryption process.

---

[4] Some indexes require only an equality function and not an order function to be constructed. In this case, the term "order" in this section can be replaced by the term "equality".

| a) Encryption of Table T in the New Scheme | | b) Encryption of the Index in the New Scheme | | |

Row	C
0	$E_k(5000 \oplus \mu(T,0,C))$
1	$E_k(2500 \oplus \mu(T,1,C))$
2	$E_k(1000 \oplus \mu(T,2,C))$
3	$E_k(7500 \oplus \mu(T,3,C))$

ID	Struct.	Data
0	1,2	$E_k(5000 \parallel 0)$
1	3,4	$E_k(2500 \parallel 1)$
2	5,6	$E_k(7500 \parallel 3)$
3	4	$E_k(1000 \parallel 2)$
4	5	$E_k(2500 \parallel 1)$
5	6	$E_k(5000 \parallel 0)$
6	-	$E_k(7500 \parallel 3)$

Fig. 3. Encryption in the new scheme.

5.2 Executing a Query in the New Scheme

The following SQL query illustrates the retrieval of all rows in table T, which their values in column C are greater or equal to V:

$$\text{SELECT * FROM T WHERE T.C>=V} \tag{11}$$

The following pseudo code illustrates the retrieval of row-ids of rows which answer the above query. The pseudo code assumes that the index is implemented as a binary B+-Tree.

```
INPUT: A table T, a column C and a value V.
OUTPUT: A collection of row-ids.

X := getIndex(T, C).getRootNode();

While X is not a leaf Do
    If X.getData().getValue()<V Then
        X := X.getRightSonNode();
    Else
        X := X.getLeftSonNode();
    End If;
End While;

RESULT := ∅;

While X.getData().getValue()<V Do
    X := X.getRightSiblingNode();
End While;

While X is not null Do
    RESULT := RESULT ∪ {X.getData().getRowId()};
    X := X.getRightSiblingNode();
End While;

Return RESULT;
```

Each *node* in the index which is not a *leaf* has a *left son node*, a *right son node* and a *data* which stores a value. Each *leaf* in the index has a *right sibling node* and a *data* which stores a value and a row-id.

In the new scheme the data in each index node is an encryption of a database value concatenated with its row-id. Thus, the functions getValue() and getRowId() need to be given a new implementation in order to support the new indexing scheme. However, the above pseudo code stands without any change.

5.3 Index Integrity

In the new scheme, a substitution attack which attempts to substitute index values can be carried out without being noticed at decryption time. If it is possible to maintain a unique position for each value in the index, this kind of attack can be eliminated using a technique similar to the one proposed in section 3 where each value is encrypted with its unique position.

Figure 4 illustrates data integrity maintenance of the table and the index which were illustrated in figure 2. Figure 4a describes data integrity maintenance of the table as suggested in section 3.2. Figure 4b describes data integrity maintenance of the index where each index value is concatenated to its unique position in the index (ID) and then encrypted.

We argue that without changing the index structure and affecting its efficiency, maintaining a unique position for each value in the index is not a trivial matter.

<table>
<tr><td colspan="2" align="center">a) Maintaining Data Integrity of
Table T</td><td colspan="3" align="center">b) Maintaining Data Integrity of
the Index</td></tr>
<tr><td>Row</td><td>C</td><td>ID</td><td>Struct.</td><td>Data</td></tr>
<tr><td>0</td><td>$E_k(5000 \parallel \mu(T,0,C))$</td><td>0</td><td>1,2</td><td>$E_k(5000 \parallel 0)$</td></tr>
<tr><td>1</td><td>$E_k(2500 \parallel \mu(T,1,C))$</td><td>1</td><td>3,4</td><td>$E_k(2500 \parallel 1)$</td></tr>
<tr><td>2</td><td>$E_k(1000 \parallel \mu(T,2,C))$</td><td>2</td><td>5,6</td><td>$E_k(7500 \parallel 2)$</td></tr>
<tr><td>3</td><td>$E_k(7500 \parallel \mu(T,3,C))$</td><td>3</td><td>4</td><td>$E_k((1000,2) \parallel 3)$</td></tr>
<tr><td></td><td></td><td>4</td><td>5</td><td>$E_k((2500,1) \parallel 4)$</td></tr>
<tr><td></td><td></td><td>5</td><td>6</td><td>$E_k((5000,0) \parallel 5)$</td></tr>
<tr><td></td><td></td><td>6</td><td>-</td><td>$E_k((7500,3) \parallel 6)$</td></tr>
</table>

Fig. 4. Maintaining data integrity.

5.4 Scheme Analysis

The new index implementation on an ordered set of values is identical to the ordinary index implementation. The only differences between the ordinary index and the new one are the set of values and the order function defined on them.

The new index complies with the requirements mentioned in section 4:

1) Since the values in the index are encrypted and unique (achieved by concatenating row-id) there is no correlation between them as to the column ciphertext values, or the column plaintext values. Therefore, no information is revealed on the database data by the new index.

2) The order function is implemented in a time complexity of $O(1)$ since decryption and discarding bits are implemented in a time complexity of $O(1)$. Therefore, data access using the proposed index is as efficient as with an ordinary index.

3) Determining the order of two values is implemented in a time complexity of $O(1)$. Therefore, the delete operation is as efficient as in an ordinary index. Encrypting a new value is implemented in a time complexity of $O(1)$, thus the efficiency of insert and update operations is not changed.
4) Each value in the new index is a result of encrypting a database plaintext value concatenated with its row-id, therefore the space added for each node in the new index is fixed. Thus, the index space complexity remains the same.
5) The new index structure remains the same and only its data is modified. Thus, any administrative work on the index can be carried out without the need of decrypting the index values.

6   Performance and Implementation Issues

Implementing the new schemes requires careful consideration. Several performance and implementation issues are discussed in this section.

6.1   Stable Cell Coordinates

The proposed scheme assumes that cell coordinates are stable. That is, insert, update and delete operations do not change the coordinates of existing cells. However, if a database reorganization process changes cell coordinates, all affected cells are to be re-encrypted with their new coordinates and the index updated respectively.

A naïve implementation which uses the row number in the table as the row-id, proves to be limited in this respect as row numbers are affected by insert and delete operations. In the Oracle database, for example, cell coordinates are stable.

6.2   Implementing a Secure μ Function

As defined in section 3.2, the values in the database are encrypted as follows:

$$Enc_K(V_{trc}) = E_k(V_{trc} \parallel \mu(t,r,c)) \tag{12}$$

A secure implementation of μ would generate different numbers for different coordinates:

$$(t_1,r_1,c_1) \neq (t_2,r_2,c_2) \longleftrightarrow \mu(t_1,r_1,c_1) \neq \mu(t_2,r_2,c_2) \tag{13}$$

Unfortunately, generating a unique number for each database coordinates may result in considerable data expansion. An alternative implementation reducing the data expansion may result in collisions. Assume that there are two cells, which μ generates two equal values for their coordinates:

$$\exists t_1,r_1,c_1,t_2,r_2,c_2 \mid$$
$$[(t_1,r_1,c_1) \neq (t_2,r_2,c_2)] \wedge [\mu(t_1,r_1,c_1) = \mu(t_2,r_2,c_2)] \tag{14}$$

It is possible to substitute the ciphertext values of these cells ($x_{t_1r_1c_1}$ and $x_{t_2r_2c_2}$) without μ being corrupted at decryption time. If it is difficult to find two cells such as those mentioned above, this kind of attack can be prevented. This can be achieved by using a collision free hash function.

6.3 Key Management

Databases contain information of different sensitivity degrees that have to be selectively shared between a large numbers of users. The proposed scheme facilitates subschema implementation since each column can be encrypted with a different key. Encrypting each column with a different key, results in a large number of keys for each legitimate user. However, using the approach proposed in [22] can reduce the number of keys. It is suggested in [22] how the smallest elements which can be encrypted using the same key according to the access control policy can be found. Thus, the keys are generated according to the access control policy in order to keep their number minimal. This approach can be incorporated in the proposed scheme in order to encrypt sets of columns with the same key in accordance with the database access control policy.

6.4 Performance

In the new scheme, all conventional algorithms remain the same since the structure of the database remains the same. This ensures that the only overhead of the new scheme is that of encryption and decryption operations.

7 Conclusions

In this paper, a new structure preserving scheme for database encryption has been presented. In the new scheme, each database cell is encrypted with its unique position and this guarantees that patterns matching and substitution attacks cannot succeed, thus, guaranteeing information confidentiality and data integrity.

A new database indexing scheme that does not reveal any information on the database plaintext values was proposed. In the new scheme index values are encrypted with a unique number (the row-id of the database value) in order to eliminate patterns matching attacks and any correlation between index and database values. Ensuring index integrity is possible if an index position can be attached to each index value by simply using a technique similar to the one used for table encryption.

The new schemes do not impose any changes on the database structure, thus enabling a DBA to manage the encrypted database as any other non-encrypted database. Furthermore, implementing the new scheme in existing applications does not entail modifying the queries.

References

1. Date, C.J.: An Introduction to Database Systems. Vol. 1, Fifth Edition. Addison Wesley, Massachusetts (1990)

2. Fernandez , E.B., Summers, R.C. and Wood C.: Database Security and Integrity. Addison-Wesley, Massachusetts, (1980)
3. Coper, J.A.: Computer & Communication Security: Strategies for the 1990s. McGraw-Hill, New York (1989)
4. Conway, R.W., Maxwell, W.L. and Morgan, H.L.: On the implementation of security measures in information systems. Communications of the ACM 15(4) (1972) 211-220
5. Graham, G.S. and Denning, P.J.: Protection - Principles and practice. Proc. Spring Jt. Computer Conf., Vol. 40, AFIPS 417-429, Montrale, N.J. (1972)
6. Hwang, M.S. and Yang, W.P.: A new dynamic access control scheme based on subject-object-list. Data and Knowledge Engineering 14(1) (1994) 45-56
7. Garvey, C. and Wu, A.: ASD-Views. Proc. IEEE Symposium on Security and Privacy, Oakland, California (1988) 85-95
8. Lunt, T.F., Denning, D.E., Schell, R.R., Heckman, M. and Shockley, W.R.: The SeaView security model. IEEE Trans. on Software Engineering, SE-16(6) (1990) 593-607
9. Stachour, P.D. and Thuraisingham, B.: Design of LDV: A multilevel secure relational database management system, IEEE Trans. on Knowledge and Data Engineering 2(2) (1990) 190-209
10. National Bureau of Standards. Data Encryption Standard. FIPS, NBS (1977)
11. Rivest, R.L., Shamir, A. and Adleman, L.: A method for obtaining digital signatures and public key cryptosystems. Communications of the ACM 21(2) (1978) 120-126
12. Smid, M.E. and Branstad, D.K.: The data encryption standard: past and future. Proc. IEEE 76(5) (1988) 550-559
13. Davida, G.I., Wells, D.L., and Kam, J.B.: A Database Encryption System with Subkeys. ACM Trans. Database Syst. 6 (1981) 312-328
14. Min-Shiang, H. and Wei-Pang, Y.: Multilevel secure database encryption with subkeys. Data and Knowledge Engineering 22 (1997) 117-131
15. Damiani, E., De Capitani diVimercati, S., Jajodia, S., Paraboschi, S. and Samarati, P.: Balancing Confidentiality and Efficiency in Untrusted Relational DBMSs. CCS'03, Washington (2003) 27–31
16. Denning, D.E.: Cryptography and Data Security. Addison-Wesley, Massachusetts (1982)
17. Hacigümüs, H., Iyer, B., Li, C., and Mehrotra, S.: Executing SQL over encrypted data in the database-service-provider model. In Proc. of the ACM SIGMOD'2002, Madison, Wisconsin, USA (2002)
18. Iyer, B., Mehrotra, S., Mykletun, E., Tsudik, G. and Wu, Y.: A Framework for Efficient Storage Security in RDBMS. E. Bertino et al. (Eds.): EDBT 2004, LNCS 2992 (2004) 147–164
19. Bouganim, L. and Pucheral, P.: Chip-secured data access: Confidential data on untrusted servers. In Proc. of the 28th International Conference on Very Large Data Bases, Hong Kong, China (2002) 131–142
20. Database Encryption in Oracle9i™. An Oracle Technical White Paper (2001)
21. Bayer, R. and Metzger, J.K.: On the Encipherment of Search Trees and Random Access Files. ACM Trans Database Systems, Vol. 1 (1976) 37-52
22. Bertino, E. and Ferrari, E.: Secure and Selective Dissemination of XML Documents. ACM Transactions on Information and System Security Vol. 5 No. 3 (2002) 290–331
23. Hwang, M.S. and Yang, W.P.: A two-phase encryption scheme for enhancing database security. J. Systems and Software 31(12) (1995) 257-265

Modeling Integrity in Data Exchange

Gerome Miklau and Dan Suciu

Department of Computer Science and Engineering
University of Washington
Seattle, WA, USA
{gerome,suciu}@cs.washington.edu

Abstract. We provide a formal model of security guarantees offered by digital signature schemes when they are applied to structured data. This model is an important step towards managing the integrity of data that is shared, integrated, transformed, and exchanged on the World Wide Web. We express signature semantics using well-known database constraints, which can help authors decide what to sign, help recipients evaluate the integrity of signed data, and clarify the capabilities of different signature technologies.

1 Introduction

Data exchange on the World Wide Web is characterized by many original authors, many contributing or integrating agents, and many final recipients. For example, a report on scientific data exchange [16] finds that a major source of scientific discovery today is the *dry laboratory*, which takes previously published experimental data and processes, cleans, integrates, and republishes it. For some applications, including scientific data exchange, it is critical for users to be able to trace the original source of each data item and to prevent tampering. That is, users require *data integrity*, which means accurately attributing data to its author and preventing unauthorized modification of data items. Our goal is to provide integrity in large-scale data exchange by using digital signatures.

We do not propose a novel signature scheme here. Instead, our main contribution is a formalization of known signature schemes [7, 18, 9, 12, 13] in terms of logical constraints over database instances. We provide a formal model of integrity for signed data which we use to address a number of difficult open problems in adapting signatures to data exchange. For one, the original data author uses this formal model in choosing a specific signature scheme, which constrains how contributing agents downstream may modify the data while still attributing it to the original author. Second, end users can use this formal model – along with well-established database theory – to reason about the integrity of queries over signed data received from intermediate agents. Finally, the formal model provides a uniform treatment of disparate techniques, allowing them to be compared precisely and combined appropriately.

Basic setting. The basic setting for providing integrity in data exchange is illustrated in Figure 1. Alice is an author who publishes a database R. This data

W. Jonker and M. Petković (Eds.): SDM 2004, LNCS 3178, pp. 41–54, 2004.

Fig. 1. Simplified data exchange scenario. S_{Alice} is Alice's signature on R. S'_{Alice} is a (possibly different) signature object provided by Bob to Carol (but still in the name of Alice).

is received and processed by Bob, who may transform it, integrate it with other data sources, or provide some other service, and then publishes it in the form of a database R'. Carol is an end-user who wants to use Bob's enhanced data R', yet wants to verify that the content in R' that came from Alice has not been modified. To ensure the integrity of her data, Alice provides a digital signature of R to Bob, who uses it to derive a digital signature on the modified data R'. This, in turn, is verified by Carol.

The simplest way to sign R is to apply a conventional digital signature to the entire database. Any modification of R will cause verification to fail, but this signature strategy prevents Bob from making any meaningful changes to the data. Therefore it is often important for Alice to sign the data so as to allow extraction, integration, and sometimes controlled modifications of the data by Bob.

A formal model for signed data. In recent work, a number of signature schemes [18, 9, 12, 7, 13] have been devised that can be used to manage the balance between preventing unauthorized modification and allowing reuse of data (we describe their features in Sec. 2). However, there is currently no unified formal model for stating their properties, making them hard to use in complex data exchange scenarios. We propose here such a formal model, which describes the security properties offered by a signature as a set of constraints that hold between the original (but unavailable) source R and the received database R'.

We believe a formal model is critical to providing integrity in data exchange. It is the basis upon which Alice chooses the correct signature (to prevent unauthorized modification but allow innocuous modification). It also allows Carol to analyze the integrity of the data she receives. For example, Carol may want to evaluate a particular query over the data and be assured that the answer to the query could not have been modified by Bob. Finally, a formal model clarifies the capabilities of known signature schemes and suggests new signature schemes required for providing integrity in data exchange.

Constraints appear to be the right tool because they are capable of expressing the semantics of signatures, they are familiar to database practitioners, and because there is a rich theory whose results can be applied to our setting (see Section 4).

Application: scientific data exchange. The management of molecular biology data is an application scenario requiring the management of integrity for exchanged data. Primary sources contain original experimental data, from which hundreds of secondary biological sources [2] are derived. The secondary sources

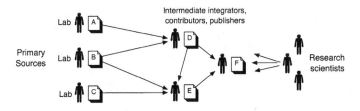

Fig. 2. Exchange scenario for scientific data.

export views over primary sources and/or other secondary sources, and usually add their own curatorial comments and modifications [14]. These databases are often published on the Web as structured text files – not stored in proprietary systems or servers that can provide security guarantees. The data consumers are scientists, and a significant fraction of research takes place in so-called "dry" laboratories using data collected and curated by others. An illustration of this scenario is provided in Figure 2.

The main security concerns in this setting are attributing and retaining authorship, permitting proper curatorial additions, and avoiding the careless modification of data through integrity controls. The risk of malicious tampering with the data is usually not a primary security concern in this setting. To the best of our knowledge, security properties are rarely provided in scientific data exchange. Although in some cases authorship may be traced, there is little verification or certification of accurate authorship.

Digital signatures alone cannot solve the challenges of providing integrity in such complex scenarios. The formal model presented below allows us to unify disparate signature technologies in terms of constraints that they enforce, and forms a basis for managing integrity in data exchange.

Paper organization. In Section 2 we present some simple integrity challenges, and then describe three types of known digital signature schemes that can be used to address them. In Section 3, we present a formal model of each signature scheme, and in Section 4 we apply the formal model to query answering. We summarize related work and conclude in Sections 5 and 6.

2   Signing Data to Provide Integrity

We begin this section with some simple examples of properties an author may want to enforce over published data. Then we describe informally three known classes of signature schemes (conventional, homomorphic, and tree-based signatures).

2.1   Integrity Challenges for Data Exchange

We illustrate here several properties that Alice may want to enforce when signing a data source, using a simple example consisting of a database relation Stock

Ticker	Rating	Industry
IBM	BUY	Technology
MSFT	HOLD	Technology
WFMI	HOLD	Consumer
JPM	SELL	Financial

(a)

(b)

IBM	BUY	Technology
MSFT	HOLD	Technology

(c)

IBM	BUY
MSFT	HOLD
WFMI	HOLD
JPM	SELL

Fig. 3. A database of stock recommendations Stock(ticker,rating,industry) shown in (a) along with sets of tuples (b) and (c) derived from (a).

describing attributes ticker, rating, and industry of stock recommendations. A sample database is illustrated in Fig. 3. While our interest is in richer domains like scientific data, we use this dataset to simplify the discussion. Further, we restrict ourselves to relational data even though semi-structured XML data is a more likely choice in large-scale data exchange.

Recall from Fig. 1 that Alice wants to sign the data so as to allow Bob to perform only certain transformations. We consider in this paper the following challenges:

1. Alice requires Stock to be complete and correct whenever it is attributed to her: every tuple must be present, and no forged tuples may be added by Bob.

2. Alice allows tuples to be removed from Stock, permitting Bob to publish a subset of the stock recommendations. However it should not be possible for Bob to introduce tuples not present originally.

3. Alice requires all tuples of Stock to be present, but Bob may add additional tuples.

4. Alice allows subsets of Stock tuples defined by a selection condition on the industry attribute, but all tuples must be provided for each such selection. Fig. 3(b) satisfies this requirement for condition industry='Technology'.

5. Alice permits Bob to update rating attribute of any tuple, but he cannot modify other columns. All tuples must be present in the collection.

6. Alice permits Bob to add a new attribute such as risk-premium to Stock. All tuples must be present in the collection.

7. Alice permits Bob to remove the industry attribute from Stock; that is, Bob can publish the relational projection of Stock on ticker and rating, which must be complete. Fig. 3(c) satisfies this requirement.

2.2   Existing Signature Techniques

While there are techniques which address individual integrity challenges, there is no general framework for signing structured data and evaluating the integrity of signed data. Here we briefly review existing technologies: conventional digital signatures, homomorphic signature schemes, and tree-based query certification schemes based on Merkle trees.

Conventional digital signatures. Aside from key generation, a conventional digital signature scheme consists of two operations, SIGN and VERIFY, which we apply to databases. These operations are employed in our basic setting as follows:

Alice : signs relation R by computing signature $S_{Alice} = \mathsf{SIGN}_{Alice}(R)$.

Bob : receives S_{Alice} from Alice. Publishes S_{Alice} and relation R'.

Carol : Verifies signature by computing $\mathsf{VERIFY}_{Alice}(S_{Alice}, R')$

Here $\mathsf{VERIFY}_{Alice}(S_{Alice}, R')$ returns yes if and only if $R = R'$; otherwise it returns no. Alice's private key is implicit in SIGN_{Alice} and her public key is implicit in VERIFY_{Alice}.

Ideally, it is computationally infeasible to compute a valid signature on a database without knowledge of the private key. A common digital signature scheme is built using the RSA public-key cryptosystem [17] and a message digest like SHA-1 [20]. The output of the message digest on the database (appropriately padded [19]) is signed by encrypting it under a private key. A recipient verifies a signature by retrieving the author's public key, using it to decrypt the signature, and checking that the result is equal to the padded digest of the database purportedly signed.

Obviously, conventional signatures are restricted, since they allow Bob to perform very limited operations on the data. We illustrate here on our running example.

Example 1 (Applying conventional signatures).

(a) A conventional signature applied to relation Stock can be used to implement Challenge (1). This is the typical use of a digital signature, just described.
(b) A conventional signature can implement Challenge (2) where Alice wishes only to ensure that authorized tuples are provided, but permits deletions. A danger exists however that Bob could collect tuples signed by Alice at different times or in different contexts, and mix tuples to construct a collection in which each tuple verifies. To avoid this, for each tuple t, and given an identifier τ unique for each instance R, Alice can sign the pair (τ, t). The identifier τ may simply be a date or timestamp, and Carol must check the consistency of each τ in the tuples she receives from Bob.
(c) A conventional signature can also implement Challenge (4), to support selections on industry. Alice will compute a view of the database for each industry. For instance, in Datalog notation, the following views return the sets of (ticker,rating,industry) triples for each of the Technology, Financial, and Consumer sectors. (The result of V_1 is pictured in Fig 3(b)).

$$V_1(t, r, i) : - Stock(t, r, i), \; i = \,'\text{Technology}'$$
$$V_2(t, r, i) : - Stock(t, r, i), \; i = \,'\text{Financial}'$$
$$V_3(t, r, i) : - Stock(t, r, i), \; i = \,'\text{Consumer}'$$

Alice must sign each view definition together with the view result. Bob may present any of the view results to Carol with a verifiable signature from Alice. Bob cannot tamper with the tuples in any view result. This technique is straightforward, but neither efficient nor feasible in general because Alice must predict which selections or views Carol may need, and generate signatures for each.

Homomorphic signatures. Recently, digital signature schemes have been proposed [18, 12, 9] that allow anyone (i.e. without knowledge of the private key) to compute new signatures for certain data values. The new signatures are computed from signed data items, and can be computed only for data items derived in certain limited ways from signed data items. Such a scheme is used to permit Bob to modify or extract data signed by Alice, and then compute Alice's signature on the derived data. The signatures on the derived objects are designed to be indistinguishable from signatures computed by the private key holder. Clearly, the basic security property of a digital signature does not hold for a homomorphic scheme because certain signatures are easily computed (i.e. forged).

Homomorphic signature schemes have been proposed for specific operations like subset, redaction [9] and transitive closure [12]. We define the homomorphic signature scheme for subset, and describe the other two briefly below.

Alice : Alice signs R by computing $HS_{Alice} = \mathsf{HSIGN}[subset]_{Alice}(R)$.

Bob : receives HS_{Alice} from Alice; uses HS_{Alice} to compute a new signature $HS'_{Alice} = \mathsf{HSIGN}[subset]_{Alice}(R')$ for any subset R' of R of his choice.

Carol : Verifies signature by computing $\mathsf{VERIFY}_{Alice}(HS'_{Alice}, R')$

Here $\mathsf{VERIFY}_{Alice}(HS'_{Alice}, R')$ returns yes if and only if $R' \subseteq R$. Alice's private key is implicit in $\mathsf{HSIGN}[subset]_{Alice}$ and her public key is implicit in VERIFY_{Alice}. It should be computationally infeasible for Bob to construct new signatures like HS'_{Alice} for sets that are not subsets of R. We omit the actual description of the subset signature scheme referring the reader to [9] instead.

Example 2 (Applying homomorphic signatures).

(a) Set operations – The subset signature scheme clearly allows us to address Challenge (2).

A *redaction* signature scheme applies primarily to a text. To redact a textual data element x means to replace any selection of the characters in x with a fixed symbol, say #, thereby hiding the selected portions. A signature scheme that permits redaction allows anyone to derive a signature of any redacted version of x from the signature of x. Such a scheme is proposed in [9]. For example, given a signed text "Dec. 1, 1972", a signature can be computed for the redacted version "Dec. 1, 19##".

A *transitive closure* signature scheme [12] allows an author to sign nodes and edges representing an undirected graph such that anyone can derive a signature of an edge between nodes for which there exists a signed path. For example, given tuples $(a, b), (b, c), (d, e)$ signed by Alice, Bob can efficiently compute signatures for (a, c), but cannot compute a signature for (a, d).

Tree-based signatures for query certification. We illustrate here the main idea behind the techniques [7, 6, 13] based on Merkle trees [10, 11]. To simplify the discussion we assume a binary relation $R(x, y)$. A *query certification* signature scheme allows Alice to sign R in such a way that it allows Bob to publish the answer to any query q of the form:

$$R'(x, y) : -R(x, y), x = a$$

for an arbitrary constant a. Notice that while $R' \subseteq R$, a subset signature scheme is not useful here, since R' may not be an arbitrary subset but must consist of precisely the tuple(s) with a certain value of x. As we discussed earlier, Alice could simply use a conventional signature and sign all possible answers (there are no more answers than tuples in R, plus one), but the query certification technique allows Alice to provide a much shorter signature object. Bob can use it to construct a new signature for R', for any specific a. Formally:

Alice : Alice signs R by computing $MS_{Alice} = \mathsf{MSIGN}_{Alice}(R)$.

Bob : receives MS_{Alice} from Alice; for any constant a, Bob uses MS_{Alice} to compute a new signature MS^q_{Alice} for the answer to the query $R'(x, y) : -R(x, y), x = a$.

Carol : Verifies signature by computing $\mathsf{VERIFY}_{Alice}(MS^q_{Alice}, R')$.

Here $\mathsf{VERIFY}_{Alice}(MS^q_{Alice}, R')$ returns yes if and only if R' is obtained from R by answering some query of the form $R'(x, y) : -R(x, y), x = a$.

We briefly illustrate the Merkle tree for our running example in Fig. 4. Alice uses a collision-resistant hash function f to build a binary tree of hash values as follows. First, she computes the hash for each tuple t_i. Then she pairs these values, computing the hash of their concatenation and storing it as the parent. She continues bottom-up, pairing values and hashing their combination until a root hash value h_ϵ is formed. Note that h_ϵ is a hash value that depends on all tuples in her database. Alice publishes a description of f and $S_{Alice} = \mathsf{SIGN}_{Alice}(h_\epsilon)$.

Bob can now produce a verification object for the query below:

$$R'(r, r) : -R(t, r), t = \mathsf{WFMI}$$

Bob provides $t_3 = (\mathsf{WFMI}, \mathsf{hold})$ as an answer and proves the accuracy of this answer by providing a path of hash values in the tree sufficient to compute h'_ϵ. In this case, Bob gives Carol h_{11} and h_0, in addition to Alice's original signature S_{Alice}. Carol computes $h_{10} = f(t_3)$ and uses the provided hash values to compute h'_ϵ which is verified against h_ϵ signed by Alice.

This basic technique can be extended to support selection queries and range queries over non-key attributes, and to some additional types of relational queries [7].

Example 3 (Applying query certification). A tree-based signature scheme can be used to efficiently implement Challenge (4) where Alice would like to allow authorized publication of selection queries on industry. She would sort her

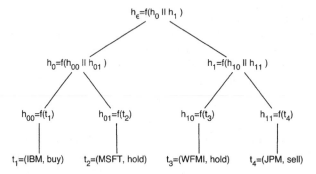

Fig. 4. A Merkle tree built over an abbreviated version of the relation **Stock**. The root value h_ϵ is computed bottom-up by repeated applications of f, a collision-resistant hash function. Concatenation is denoted $||$.

database of stock recommendations on industry, and generate a tree-based signature. Then for *any* industry ind, Bob can provide a verified answer for query $q(r, t, i) : -R(r, t, i), i = $ ind. Here Alice can construct the tree-based signature object without knowledge of the particular queries Carol may ask.

3   Modeling Signatures Using Constraints

Recall that Carol uses the mediated data R' received from Bob, in place of the original data R authored by Alice. A verified signature on R' provides Carol with a guarantee about a certain relationship between R and R'. We now explain how logical constraints can be used to formalize these guarantees. To do so, we will work with statements of the following form:

$$\text{VERIFY}(S_{Alice}, R') \quad \models \quad \textit{constraint-expression}$$
$$\text{VERIFY}(HS_{Alice}, R') \quad \models \quad \textit{constraint-expression}$$
$$\text{VERIFY}(MS_{Alice}^q, R') \quad \models \quad \textit{constraint-expression}$$

On the left-hand side we have a verification operation (conventional, homomorphic, or tree-based) performed by Carol on a signature object and data instance R' received from Bob. On the right is a constraint expression referring to R and R'. The meaning of a statement is that successful verification proves[1] that the constraint expression holds.

In the following subsections we describe a language for constraint expressions, provide correct constraint expressions for the signature schemes described above, and finally explain how to choose a signature scheme to enforce a desired constraint.

---

[1] Relative to the security assumptions of the signature scheme.

3.1   Constraints

We express a constraint as a logical formula called an *embedded dependency* [1], having the following form[2]:

$$\forall x_1 \ldots \forall x_n [\exists y_1, \ldots \exists y_m \varphi(x_1, \ldots x_n, y_1, \ldots y_m) \rightarrow \exists z_1, \ldots \exists z_k \psi(x_1, \ldots x_n, z_1, \ldots z_k)]$$

where both φ and ψ are conjunctions of positive relational atoms and equality/inequality predicates, and each of them uses all the variables $x_1, \ldots x_n$.

Constraints are a fundamental topic in databases, which are used to define properties that must hold for all database instances. In the relational model they are most commonly used to express key and foreign key relationships. A broad theory of constraints has been developed over time. Two of the most important theoretical problems are inference (deciding whether a new constraint is implied by existing constraints), and query optimization (improving query execution using constraints known to hold over the data).

An example of a basic embedded dependency expresses completeness by asserting that R' contains every tuple in R, i.e. $R \subseteq R'$:

$$c_c : \forall x_1 \ldots \forall x_n [R(x_1, \ldots x_n) \rightarrow R'(x_1, \ldots x_n)] \qquad \text{(completeness)}$$

If every tuple of R' is present in R, i.e. $R' \subseteq R$, then we write the constraint:

$$c_s : \forall x_1 \ldots \forall x_n [R'(x_1, \ldots x_n) \rightarrow R(x_1, \ldots x_n)] \qquad \text{(soundness)}$$

We define C_{eq} to be the set of constraints $\{c_c, c_s\}$ and note that C_{eq} holds iff $R = R'$.

3.2   Constraints Enforced by Signatures

We now review each of the signature schemes described in Section 2 and formalize their security guarantees with constraint expressions.

Conventional signatures. If Alice uses a conventional signature to sign a relation R, that signature will verify on R' if and only if $R = R'$. Thus the following statement holds:

$$\mathsf{VERIFY}(S_{Alice}, R') \models C_{eq}$$

Suppose, as in Example 1(c), that Alice signs the view:

$$V_1(t, r, i) :- \mathsf{Stock}(t, r, i), i = \text{'Tech'}$$

over Stock so that $S_{Alice} = \mathsf{SIGN}_{Alice}(V_1(\mathsf{Stock}))$. Then the following statement holds:

$$\mathsf{VERIFY}(S_{Alice}, R') \models \forall t \forall r [\mathsf{Stock}(t, r, \text{'Tech'}) \rightarrow R'(t, r, \text{'Tech'})]$$
$$\forall t \forall r \forall i [R'(t, r, i) \rightarrow \mathsf{Stock}(t, r, i) \wedge (i = \text{'Tech'})]$$

---

[2] The variables $y_1, \ldots y_m$ are not technically needed, but convenient for the examples in this section.

Homomorphic signatures. Signing R as a subset of tuples with a homomorphic signature scheme supporting subsets, we have $HS_{Alice} = \mathsf{HSIGN}[subset]_{Alice}$ (R) and the following statement holds:

$$\mathsf{VERIFY}(HS_{Alice}, R') \quad \models \quad \forall x_1 \ldots \forall x_n [R'(x_1, \ldots x_n) \to R(x_1, \ldots x_n)]$$

To model the redaction signature, we represent a document as a binary relation $R(x, y)$, where the first attribute is a position number and the second is a character. For example a text document like "This is a message..." is represented as $R = \{(1, 'T'), (2, 'h'), (3, 'i'), (4, 's'), \ldots\}$. Then the redaction signature scheme enforces the following constraint:

$$\mathsf{VERIFY}(HS_{Alice}, R') \quad \models \quad \forall x \, [\exists y \, R(x, y) \to \exists y' \, R'(x, y')] \wedge$$
$$\forall x \, [\exists y' \, R'(x, y') \to \exists y \, R(x, y)] \wedge$$
$$\forall x \, [\exists y \, \exists y' \, R(x, y) \wedge R(x, y') \wedge y \neq y' \to y' = '\#']$$

Tree-based signatures. Let $MS_{Alice} = \mathsf{MSIGN}_{Alice}(R)$ be a tree-based signature on R, and let MS^q_{Alice} be the certification object. As before, we assume R to be a binary table, to simplify our discussion.

$$\mathsf{VERIFY}_{Alice}(MS^q_{Alice}, R') \quad \models \quad \forall x \forall y \, (R'(x, y) \to R(x, y)) \wedge$$
$$\forall x \forall y \forall y' \, (R'(x, y) \wedge R(x, y') \to R'(x, y'))$$

By writing the constraint this way we do not enforce that $R'(x, y)$ contain a *single* value a on the x position, but we enforce the fact that whenever it contains some tuple (a, b) then it contains all tuples where $x = a$. For example if $R = \{(a_1, b), (a_2, c), (a_2, d), (a_3, e)\}$ then the constraint holds for $R' = \{(a_2, c), (a_2, d)\}$ and it holds similarly for $R' = \{(a_1, b), (a_2, c), (a_2, d)\}$. But the constraint does not hold for $R' = \{(a_1, b), (a_2, c)\}$. One could write a more complex constraint that requires a single value for x in R', but this is unnecessary since Carol can check it herself by examining all tuples in R'.

By abuse of notation we write this constraint as:

$$\mathsf{VERIFY}_{Alice}(MS^q_{Alice}, R') \quad \wedge \quad \models \quad q(R) = R'$$

where q is the query $R'(x, y) : -R(x, y), x = a$. Notice that the query needs to specify a certain constant a, while the actual constraint is independent of any constant.

A subtle but important aspect of this formalism is that it allows us to express precisely what Carol knows about the original source. For example, suppose that Carol asks Bob two different queries, q_1 and q_2, and Bob provides her with two answers R_1 and R_2 plus two certification objects $MS^{q_1}_{Alice}$ and $MS^{q_2}_{Alice}$. Then Carol can verify that these come from *the same* database signed by Alice, i.e.:

$$\mathsf{VERIFY}_{Alice}(MS^{q_1}_{Alice}, R_1) \wedge \mathsf{VERIFY}_{Alice}(MS^{q_2}_{Alice}, R_2) \models q_1(R) = R_1 \wedge q_2(R) = R_2$$

This is because Carol can check that the two verification objects carry the same original signature by Alice, hence they refer to the same instance of the database.

3.3   Constraints for Other Integrity Challenges

The remaining challenges from Sec. 2 are listed below. We express each as a constraint.

(3) Alice requires all tuples of Stock to be present, but Bob may add additional tuples. This is the completeness constraint:

$$c_c : \forall x_1 \ldots \forall x_n \, [R(x_1, \ldots x_n) \rightarrow R'(x_1, \ldots x_n)]$$

A conventional signature can enforce the combined constraints $\{c_c, c_s\}$, but there is a subtlety in enforcing c_c alone. Although it is not difficult to enforce that each of Alice's tuples are present in any collection Bob publishes, those tuples would have to be distinguished from tuples later added by Bob. It's not clear how to enforce this challenge while hiding this distinction from Carol.

(5) Alice permits Bob to update rating, but he cannot modify other columns. All tuples must be present in the collection.

$$\forall t \forall r \forall i \, [\mathsf{Stock}(t, r, i) \rightarrow \exists r' \, R'(t, r', i)]$$
$$\forall t \forall r' \forall i \, [R'(t, r', i) \rightarrow \exists r \, \mathsf{Stock}(t, r, i)]$$

(6) Alice permits Bob to add a new column such as risk premium to Stock. All tuples must be present in the collection.

$$\forall t \forall r \forall i \, [\mathsf{Stock}(t, r, i) \rightarrow \exists z \, R'(t, r, i, z)]$$
$$\forall t \forall r \forall i \forall z \, [R'(t, r, i, z) \rightarrow \mathsf{Stock}(t, r, i)]$$

(7) Alice permits Bob to remove industry from Stock; that is, Bob can publish the projection of Stock on ticker and rating, which must be complete.

$$\forall t \forall r \forall i \, [\mathsf{Stock}(t, r, i) \rightarrow R'(t, r)]$$
$$\forall t \forall r \, [R'(t, r) \rightarrow \exists i \, \mathsf{Stock}(t, r, i)]$$

4   Applying the Formal Model

Signatures modeled with constraints are a critical tool that Carol can use to evaluate the integrity of the data R' provided by Bob. In data exchange scenarios, Carol usually needs to access the data in terms of queries. We consider two such scenarios. First, provided with R', Carol may have in mind a query q' over R'. In order to assess the integrity of the query answer $q'(R')$, she would like to relate it to R, and she does so by using the constraints provided by the signatures. She characterizes the integrity of the result by computing the query q over R such that the query results match:

Problem 1 (Characterizing integrity of query result). Given Alice's signature object S_{Alice} and a query q' over R' what is a query q over R such that $\mathsf{VERIFY}_{Alice}(S_{Alice}, R') \models q(R) = q'(R')$?

A dual problem results if we suppose Carol's goal is to answer a query q over R. She must use R' to answer q and to do so, she must understand the impact of the constraints that hold between R and R'. We formalize this answerability problem as follows:

Problem 2 (Exact answerability over signed data). Given Alice's signature object S_{Alice} and a query q over R, does there exist a query q' over R' such that $\mathsf{VERIFY}_{Alice}(S_{Alice}, R') \models q'(R') = q(R)$?

Common to both problems is a basic decision problem:

Problem 3 (Equivalence decision problem). Given Alice's signature object S_{Alice}, a query q over R, and a query q' over R', decide whether $\mathsf{VERIFY}_{Alice}(S_{Alice}, R') \models q(R) = q(R')$.

These problems seem nearly impossible to solve without reference to the formal model we have presented. However, if we invoke the constraint statements of Sec. 3 then it is clear that Carol must verify each signature object, and collect the implied constraints into a set of constraints C. We can then use well-understood techniques of query answerability [8] or chase/backchase [15] to solve these problems. We illustrate here with one special case, which is a direct application of a result in [15].

Theorem 1. *Let C be the embedded dependencies enforced by Alice's signature S_{Alice}. For a query q, let $chase_C(q)$ denote the result of applying the chase technique of [15], if it exists. Then:*

1. *Suppose $chase_C(q')$ exists. Then one can solve Problem 1 by performing a backchase on $chase_C(q')$. This problem is NP-complete.*
2. *Suppose $chase_C(q)$ exists. Then one can solve Problem 2 by performing a backchase on $chase_C(q)$. This problem is NP-complete.*
3. *Suppose $chase_C(q)$ and $chase_C(q')$ exists. Then one can solve Problem 3 by checking the query equivalence $chase_C(q) \equiv chase_C(q')$. This problem is NP-complete.*

5   Related Work

Throughout the paper we have referred to the homomorphic signature schemes [18, 12, 9] and tree-based signature schemes [10, 11, 7, 6] on which this work depends. The authors of [4] use the W3C XML Signature as a format for implementing "content extraction signatures" which allow an author to sign a document along with a definition of permissible operations of blinding (similar to redaction) and extraction. An authorized recipient can blind or extract the document and generate a signature without contacting the author. However, verification of the signature by a third-party requires contacting the author who will verify the extractions were legal and verify the new signature. The authors of [3] propose a framework of cooperative updates to a document which are controlled according to confidentiality and integrity processes. The drawback of their scheme is that the flow of the document through a sequence of collaborating parties must be predetermined by the first author.

The BAN logic is a formalism for reasoning about the beliefs of parties in a cryptographic protocol [5]. The model captures parties' knowledge and beliefs and how they evolve over time as the result of communication. To the best of our knowledge, ours is the first attempt to formally model signatures applied to structured data, and in particular to relate the semantics of signatures to traditional database constraints.

6   Conclusion and Future Work

Conclusion. Conventional digital signatures and recent extensions to signature techniques are a promising tool for providing integrity in data exchange when enforcing conventional access control is not possible. We have introduced a formal model for signature semantics based on relational constraints. This model can guide the choice of signatures, and is the basis for evaluating queries over signed data. In addition, our model unifies disparate signature techniques, providing insight into their application, combination and their distinguishing features.

Future work. It is clear much work remains to complete a practical, expressive formalization of signature semantics. In particular, the best data model for exchange scenarios is likely to be semi-structured. Some of the signature techniques above can be applied to XML, and it remains to extend our present insights to a constraint language over XML like that proposed in [15]. The existing signature techniques we have described provide a basic set of primitives. To support real data exchange scenarios, new signature techniques need to be developed.

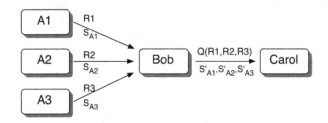

Fig. 5. Integrity for data integrated from multiple parties.

Furthermore, throughout the discussion we have concentrated on managing the integrity of data authored by Alice alone. Our eventual goal is to characterize the integrity of data authored by multiple parties and integrated by Bob. Such a scenario is pictured in Fig. 5 where distinct data sources publish databases R_1, R_2, and R_3, and Bob publishes $Q(R_1, R_2, R_3)$ along with some signatures. Here the challenge is for Carol to verify the integrity of the integrated results offered by Bob. A formal model of signatures is a basic prerequisite to tackling this generalization of the single-author case.

References

1. Serge Abiteboul, Richard Hull, and Victor Vianu. *Foundations of Databases.* Addison-Wesley, 1995.
2. Andreas D. Baxevanis. Molecular biology database collection. Nucleic Acids Research, available at www3.oup.co.uk/nar/database/, 2003.
3. Elisa Bertino, Giovanni Mella, Gianluca Correndo, and Elena Ferrari. An infrastructure for managing secure update operations on xml data. In *Symposium on Access control models and technologies*, pages 110–122. ACM Press, 2003.
4. Laurence Bull, Peter Stanski, and David McG. Squire. Content extraction signatures using xml digital signatures and custom transforms on-demand. In *Conference on World Wide Web*, pages 170–177. ACM Press, 2003.
5. Michael Burrows, Martin Abadi, and Roger Needham. A logic of authentication. *ACM Trans. Comput. Syst.*, 8(1):18–36, 1990.
6. P. Devanbu, M. Gertz, A. Kwong, C. Martel, G. Nuckolls, and S. G. Stubblebine. Flexible authentication of xml documents. In *Proceedings of the 8th ACM conference on Computer and Communications Security*, pages 136–145. ACM Press, 2001.
7. Premkumar T. Devanbu, Michael Gertz, Chip Martel, and Stuart G. Stubblebine. Authentic third-party data publication. In *IFIP Workshop on Database Security*, pages 101–112, 2000.
8. Alon Halevy. Answering queries using views: A survey. *VLDB Journal*, 10(4):270–294, 2001.
9. Robert Johnson, David Molnar, Dawn Xiaodong Song, and David Wagner. Homomorphic signature schemes. In *RSA Conference on Topics in Cryptology*, pages 244–262. Springer-Verlag, 2002.
10. Ralph C. Merkle. Protocols for public key cryptosystems. In *IEEE Symposium on Security and Privacy*, pages 122–134, 1980.
11. Ralph C. Merkle. A certified digital signature. In *CRYPTO*, pages 218–238, 1989.
12. Silvio Micali and Ronald L. Rivest. Transitive signature schemes. In *RSA Conference on Topics in Cryptology*, pages 236–243. Springer-Verlag, 2002.
13. Rafail Ostrovsky, Charles Rackoff, and Adam Smith. Efficient consistency proofs on a committed database, 2003.
14. Peter Buneman and Sanjeev Khanna and Wang-Chiew Tan. Data Provenance: Some Basic Issues. In *Foundations of Software Technology and Theoretical Computer Science*, 2000.
15. Lucian Popa and Val Tannen. An equational chase for path-conjunctive queries, constraints, and views. In *ICDT*, pages 39–57, 1999.
16. A question of balance: Private rights and the public interest in scientific and technical databases. National Academy Press, 1999. National Research Council.
17. R. L. Rivest, A. Shamir, and L. Adleman. A method for obtaining digital signatures and public-key cryptosystems. *Commun. ACM*, 21(2):120–126, 1978.
18. Ron Rivest. Two new signature schemes. Presented at Cambridge seminar, March 2001.
    See http://www.cl.cam.ac.uk/Research/Security/seminars/2000/rivest-tss.pdf.
19. RSA Data Security, Inc. *PKCS #1 v2.1: RSA Public Key Cryptography Standard*, June 2002.
20. Secure hash standard. *Federal Information Processing Standards Publication (FIPS PUB)*, 180(1), April 1995.

Experimental Analysis
of Privacy-Preserving Statistics Computation[*]

Hiranmayee Subramaniam[1], Rebecca N. Wright[2], and Zhiqiang Yang[2]

[1] Stevens Institute of Technology graduate
hiran@polypaths.com
[2] Department of Computer Science, Stevens Institute of Technology
Hoboken, NJ, 07030, USA
{rwright,zyang}@cs.stevens-tech.edu

Abstract. The recent investigation of privacy-preserving data mining and other kinds of privacy-preserving distributed computation has been motivated by the growing concern about the privacy of individuals when their data is stored, aggregated, and mined for information. Building on the study of *selective private function evaluation* and the efforts towards practical algorithms for privacy-preserving data mining solutions, we analyze and implement solutions to an important primitive, that of computing statistics of selected data in a remote database in a privacy-preserving manner. We examine solutions in different scenarios ranging from a high speed communications medium, such as a LAN or high-speed Internet connection, to a decelerated communications medium to account for worst-case communication delays such as might be provided in a wireless multihop setting.

Our experimental results show that in the absence of special-purpose hardware accelerators or practical optimizations, the computational complexity is the performance bottleneck of these solutions rather than the communication complexity. We also evaluate several practical optimizations to amortize the computation time and to improve the practical efficiency.

1 Introduction

Privacy-preserving data mining, as well as other kinds of privacy-preserving distributed computation, is intended to address conflicting goals. On the one hand, it is often desirable to extract information from collected data. On the other hand, there are often legitimate concerns about the privacy of personal data, proprietary data, and other sensitive information. Privacy-preserving data mining, in which certain computations are allowed, while other information is to remain protected, was first introduced in 2000 by Agrawal and Srikant [2]

[*] This research was partially supported by the National Science Foundation (CCR-0331584), the Wireless Network Security Center (WiNSeC) at Stevens Institute of Technology, the New Jersey Commission on Science and Technology, and the NJ Center for Wireless Networking and Internet Security.

W. Jonker and M. Petković (Eds.): SDM 2004, LNCS 3178, pp. 55–66, 2004.

and Lindell and Pinkas [13]. Since then, extensive research has been devoted to privacy-preserving data mining and other privacy-preserving computations efficient enough to be used on extremely large data sets (e.g., [3, 9, 5, 8, 17, 12, 7, 18, 10, 1, 19]).

In general, this research has been divided into solutions that provide strong cryptographic privacy protection, which require more computational overhead and have so far been limited to extremely simple (but useful) functions, and those that use perturbation, which provide weaker privacy properties, but allow much more efficient solutions and allow computation of more sophisticated data mining functions.

Our work provides an experimental evaluation of a cryptographic solution presented by the second author and others [5]. They introduced *selective private function evaluation*, a general methodology for efficient privacy-preserving solutions of computations by a client over data in a remote database. Their general solutions can provide efficiency improvements whenever the number of data elements involved in the computation is significantly fewer than the total number of data elements. As a particular instance, they consider a client/server environment in which the client and the server engage in a secure computation to evaluate a statistical function. Their solutions provide strong privacy guarantees, and involve encryption as a primary component.

As a specific selective private function computation, they consider private sum computation. In this setting, a client privately performs a sum or weighted sum of selected database elements held by the server. This is an important example because such protocols immediately yield private solutions for computing means, variances, and weighted averages, which can be useful on their own or as part of a larger privacy-preserving distributed data mining protocol. In our work, we implement a particular privacy-preserving solution to the private sum computation [6]; this protocol is described in more detail below. This protocol, as well as some of the others of Canetti et al. [5], can easily be extended to work for multiple distributed databases.

Our results show that the total running time needed is quite high, but it becomes feasible if certain straightforward optimizations are done, such as some client precomputation before the actual computation is to be done. Unless special hardware accelerators or practical optimizations are used, the computational delay caused by the encryption operations is the bottleneck, while the communication delay is significantly less.

To our knowledge, our implementation is one of the first implementations of privacy-preserving database computations. Relatedly, Malkhi et al.'s recent implementation [14] of Yao's general secure two-party computation solution [20] provides the first general secure multiparty computation results, and demonstrates that many computations on relatively small data sets can be done extremely efficiently. Indeed, secure multiparty computation and cryptographically strong privacy-preserving database computations, largely considered only theoretical, seem to be on the cusp of practicality as both theoretical and technological advances have improved their performance. Therefore, this kind of initial experimental work is an important contribution to understanding where such results are within the realm of practice and where further improvements are still needed.

In Section 2, we describe the private selected sum problem and our implemented solution in more detail. We present our experimental results, including various practical optimizations that reduce the execution time, in Section 3.

2   Private Selected Sum Computation

We consider the simple problem of privately evaluating the sum of a subset of numbers. The server holds a database of n numbers. The client is interested in the sum of m selected numbers in the database (whose indices it is assumed to know, e.g., from some publicly available source), but the client does not wish to reveal its selection criteria. The database owner on the other hand wants to reveal to the client only the sum and not the individual elements that contribute to the sum.

A privacy-preserving client/server computation must satisfy three requirements [5]. *Correctness* states that as long as the client and server follow the protocol then the client's output is the correct value. *Client Privacy* requires that a malicious server cannot learn anything from the interaction about which values the client has selected to be involved in the computation. *Database Privacy* requires that the client learn only a predefined amount of information about the data.

A trivial but nonprivate solution to this problem is to let the client send the m indices in which it is interested to the database server. The server then computes the sum of the values at the specified indices and returns the sum to the client. While this solution preserves the privacy of the server, the server learns the set of indices the client is interested in, thus compromising the client privacy requirement. Conversely, another alternative would be for the server to expose the database to the client and have the client compute the sum of the numbers it is interested in. In this solution, the client's privacy is preserved but the client learns the entire contents of the server's database, and hence the goal of database privacy is not met.

Secure multiparty computation (SMC) is a powerful cryptographic primitive in which two or more parties can jointly compute a specified function of their input while hiding their inputs from one another. The problem of securely evaluating the selected sum is a specific example of SMC: the client and server wish to jointly evaluate the sum of a selected subset of numbers without the server revealing the individual elements or the client revealing the indices of interest. General SMC solutions [4, 11, 20] can provide solutions to the database sum problem providing both client and database privacy, but these solutions have communication overhead that is at least quadratic in the size of the database, which will generally be impractical for large databases. For example, initial results of the Fairplay system [14] suggest that straightforward implementation of Yao's solution would require an execution time of at least 15 minutes for a database of only 10,000 elements [16].

Canetti et al. [5] present cryptographic privacy-preserving solutions that in particular focus on reducing the communication. This focus is justified because strong privacy requires at least linear computation, as at a minimum every data element must be accessed in order to avoid leaking any information to the server. They present both linear-communication and sublinear-communication solutions.

As a starting point for our investigations of the practical performance of selective private function evaluation, we investigate a simple linear-communication solution that provides database privacy and client privacy using semantically secure homomorphic encryption [6]. Semantic security means that ciphertexts yield no information about their plaintexts. (In particular, encryption is randomized, and it is not possible to tell from two ciphertexts whether they encrypt the same plaintext or different plaintexts.) A homomorphic encryption scheme is an encryption scheme in which certain efficient computations on ciphertexts, which can be computed without knowledge of the plaintexts or the secret key, correspond to certain computations on plaintexts. For our protocol, we require a homomorphic encryption scheme satisfying: $E(a) \cdot E(b) = E(a + b)$, where $\cdot$ and $+$ denote modular multiplication and addition, respectively. It also follows that $E(a)^c = E(a \cdot c)$ for $c \in \mathbb{N}$. The Paillier cryptosystem [15] satisfies this property and is the cryptosystem of our choice in our implementation.

In the database sum setting, the server holds a database of n numbers $x_1, \ldots, x_n$. The client holds the set of indices $I_1, \ldots, I_n$, which represent the subset of numbers it is interested in. That is, I_i is 0 if x_i is to be included in the sum computation, and 1 otherwise. (If desired, integer weights in some larger range could be used to produce a weighted sum, which in turn could be used for a weighted average.) The client has a public encryption key E and the corresponding private decryption key D of a homomorphic encryption scheme.

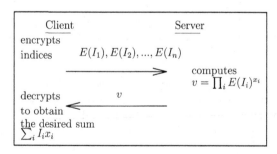

Fig. 1. Selected Sum Protocol

The private protocol, illustrated in Figure 1, executes as follows. The client encrypts its array of indices using the homomorphic cryptosystem and sends the encryptions $E(I_1), E(I_2), \ldots, E(I_n)$ to the server. The server then computes the product $\prod_{i=1}^{n} E(I_i)^{x_i}$. That is, the server takes the ith received encrypted value and raises it to the value of its ith data element x_i. Then the server multiplies all these values together modulo M, where M is a parameter of the encryption scheme. Note that this operation is applied directly to the received encrypted values, and does not require decryption nor does it yield any information about the cleartexts to the server. By the properties of homomorphic encryption, the resulting product is equal to the sum of numbers in the locations specified by the client's indices; that is,

$$\prod_{i=1}^{n} E(I_i)^{x_i} = E\left(\sum_{i=1}^{n} I_i x_i\right),$$

as desired. The server sends the product to the client, which decrypts it using the private key D to learn the desired sum. All operations are performed modulo M, where M is a parameter of the homomorphic encryption cryptosystem used. The client's privacy is protected by the encryption of the indices, while the database's privacy is protected because the result sent back is the encryption of the desired sum, and does not contain any information about the other database values.

3 Experimental Results

We implemented the client/server protocol shown in Figure 1 and measured the computation and communication performance. We implemented the protocol in Java and C^{++}. The Java version uses the Java security package to perform cryptographic operations and the C^{++} implementation uses the OpenSSL libraries. Cryptographic keys are 512 bits. We experimented across various database sizes from 10,000 numbers to 100,000 numbers, with numbers of 32 bits each. On average, the performance results from our Java experiments were around five times slower than those of similar C^{++} experiments; except in Section 3.5, we report only the C^{++} numbers here.

The experimental data was measured on a High Performance Cluster at Stevens Institute of Technology in Hoboken, NJ and on a High Performance Cluster at Illinois Institute of Technology in Chicago, IL to measure communication complexity over short and long distances, respectively. Communication between the client and server was enabled by a 64Gbps switch within the High Performance Computing facility at Stevens; communication between the client in Chicago and the server in Hoboken used a 56Kbps modem. Our results show that despite the longer distance between the client and server and the decelerated communication medium, computation time still prevails over the communication time, accounting for the bulk of the total running time.

3.1 Performance Results Without Any Optimizations

Figures 2 and 3 show experimental results of the direct implementation of the solution described in Section 2, without any optimizations.

In Figure 2, both the client and the server processes ran on 2GHz Pentium-III processors with 3GB memory, connected by a high-performance gigabit network

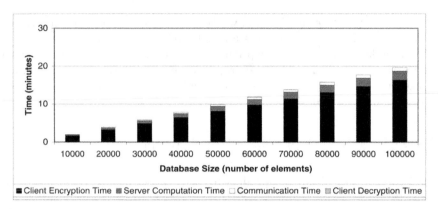

Fig. 2. Components of Overall Runtime without Any Optimizations over a Short Distance

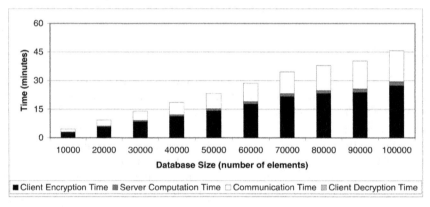

Fig. 3. Components of Overall Runtime without Any Optimizations Measured over a Long Distance

switch. Our results illustrate linear time performance, as expected. In this case, the bulk of the execution time is attributable to the client computation of the n public key encryptions of its index vector. The time for the server's computation is significantly less, followed by the communication time. The client's decryption time is constant (independent of the database size) and negligible since it is simply the time taken to decrypt a single encryption (of the desired sum). For a database of 100,000 elements, approximately 20 minutes is required for the execution.

Figure 3 shows the results of the experiment carried out over a long distance. In these experiments, the client process ran on a 500 MHz UltraSparc processor machine in Chicago, IL, and the server ran on a 1GHz Intel Pentium processor in Hoboken, NJ. Communication between client and server was via a 56Kbps dialup connection. As before, the client's encryption time increases linearly with increase in database size, as does the server's computation time and

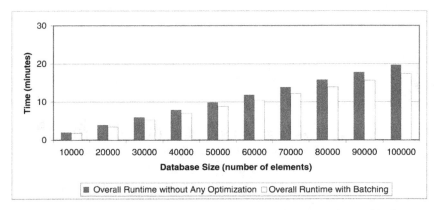

Fig. 4. Comparison of Overall Runtimes with and without Batching of Index Vector over a Short Distance

the communication time. As expected, the server's communication time now becomes a more substantial part of the execution time. However, despite the slow communication rate, the computation delay remains more significant than the communication delay.

Our results show that in the absence of any practical optimizations or specialized hardware to accelerate client encryption, computation time is the bottleneck for the algorithm's performance. In Sections 3.2–3.5, we evaluate several straightforward practical optimizations.

3.2   Single-Pass and Pipeline Parallelism

Noting that both the client computation and the server computation can be done in a single pass through their inputs, we implemented "batching" of the client processing, in which the client batches its processing of indices into smaller sized chunks, performing and sending the encryptions of the indices in each chunk before proceeding to the next chunk. On receiving each chunk, the server can continue computing the partial product.

In addition to taking advantage of pipeline parallelism, this approach also reduces the memory requirements of both the client and server. At any point in time, the client has to allocate memory needed to hold only one chunk of its indices rather than the whole index vector. Similarly, the server need only hold a single database chunk in memory at one time. The optimal chunk size will depend on the relative communication and computation speeds, as well as the overhead in processing messages and memory access. In order to achieve maximum parallelization, ideally all three activities (communication of one batch, client processing of the next batch, and server processing of the previous batch) will require approximately the same amount of time.

Figure 4 compares the overall runtime of the protocol with and without batching of index vector. In our experiments, we took a batch size of 100 elements, resulting in approximately a 10% reduction in overall runtime.

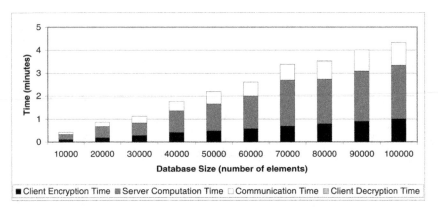

Fig. 5. Components of Overall Runtime after Preprocessing the Index Vector over a Short Distance

3.3 Preprocessing the Index Vector

This optimization aims at reducing the computation complexity of the client by encrypting the indices offline in advance and storing the encrypted indices. Even if the client does not yet know which indices will be 0 and which will be 1, it can simply encrypt a large number of 0's and a large number of 1's to use later. When the client needs to send encrypted indices to the server, it can just retrieve the appropriate encryptions. The optimization is useful for mobile devices, e.g. PDAs, that have limited computing power but reasonable amounts of storage.

The results of this optimization are shown in Figure 5, with overall on-line execution times reduced to about $3\frac{1}{2}$ minutes for a database of 100,000 elements. The client's processing time, now simply to read the stored encryptions and send them to the server, is much smaller. All other components remain unchanged; the server's computation time becomes the dominant factor. This experiment was conducted on the high performance cluster with a 64Gbps bandwidth switch as the communications medium. Hence the delay in communication does not assume significant proportions. The reduction in overall runtime is about 82%.

Figure 6 shows the results observed over a 56Kbps dialup connection with the client at Chicago, IL and the server at Hoboken, NJ. In this case, the communication delay becomes the significant factor.

3.4 Combination of Optimizations

The batching of index vector optimization reduces the server's idle time while preprocessing the vector of indices reduces the client's on-line encryption time. Combining these optimizations results in an overall on-line runtime reduction of about 94%, as shown in Figure 7.

3.5 Using Multiple Clients in Parallel

This alternative aims at reducing the time spent by the client in encrypting the index vector by partitioning the task of encryption among multiple clients. The challenge is how to protect the privacy of the server while using multiple clients.

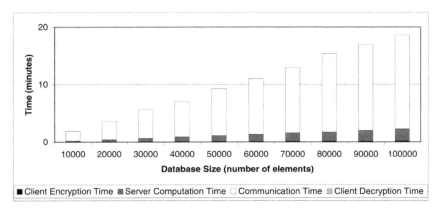

Fig. 6. Components of Overall Runtime after Preprocessing the Index Vector Measured over a Long Distance

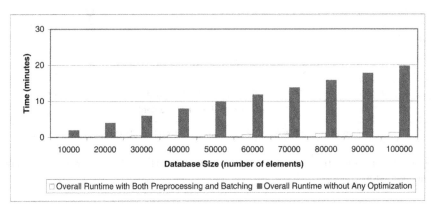

Fig. 7. Performance Gain Due to Combination of Optimizations over a Short Distance

In this setting, k clients work in cooperation. Each client is responsible for $1/k$th of the database, and will interact with the server to learn a partial sum corresponding to the chosen indices in that part of the database. However, learning these partial sums violates database privacy. Accordingly, the server uses a randomized blinding to protect the partial sums; the blinding is removed by the clients only after the partial sums are combined into a single sum, as shown in Figure 8 for $k = 3$.

In phase one, k clients C_1, C_2, ..., C_k are involved each holding an index vector of size n/k elements. (We assume for simplicity that the database size n is a multiple of k.) The clients independently and in parallel choose their own encryption keys and interact with the server to learn a blinded encryption of the appropriate partial sum. That is, the server chooses random numbers R_1, R_2, .., R_k such that $\sum_{i=1}^{k} R_i = 0 \pmod{M}$ (where again M is a parameter of the encryption scheme). When computing the product to return to client C_i,

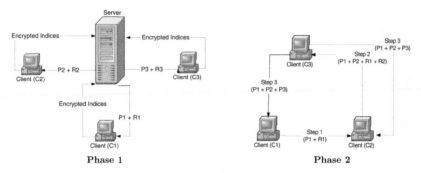

Fig. 8. Multiple Clients ($k = 3$)

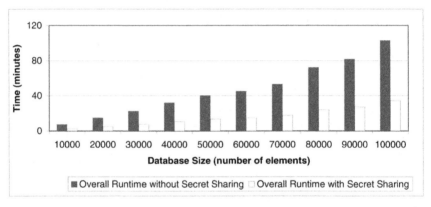

Fig. 9. Performance Improvement Due to Secret Sharing with Three Clients (Java implementation)

the server also computes $E(R_i)$ and multiplies it into the product. This has the effect of adding R_i to the partial sum P_i.

In phase two, the clients combine their partial sums and remove the blinding factor:

1. Client C_1 sends its blinded partial sum to client C_2.
2. In turn, each client C_i adds the value received from client C_{i-1} to its own blinded sum and sends the result to client C_{i+1}.
3. Client C_k receives the blinded partial sum from client C_{k-1}, adds it to its blinded partial sum to generate the total unblinded sum, and broadcasts the result to all the other clients.

The results in Figure 9 show performance results for $k = 3$. The overall execution time is reduced by a factor of approximately 2.99, which represents a 3-fold improvement, minus a small overhead for the combining phase. Note that we implemented multiple clients only for our Java implementation, so these performance numbers are significantly higher than those in earlier graphs. They are shown only to indicate the close to 3-fold improvement. The use of k clients would result in approximately a k-fold reduction in execution time.

4   Conclusions

We have analyzed and implemented an instance of selective private function evaluation that privately computes the sum of a subset of numbers held by a remote database, where the selection of the subset is done by the client. The database does not learn anything about which values the client's computation involves, and the client does not learn anything about the values in the database other than what is implied by the value of the given sum.

Our experimental results show that the running time needed is quite high, though perhaps feasible in some settings where privacy is considered sufficiently important. In a direct implementation, overall running times are around 20 minutes for a database of 100,000 elements in a high-speed communication environment. With straightforward optimizations, the running times are only a few minutes, and may be within the realm of practice. Unless practical optimizations or specialized hardware are used to accelerate encryptions, computation delay is the major bottleneck of performance of our implementation.

It remains open to improve the execution times to scale efficiently to realistically-sized databases. As directions for future work, we plan to investigate the use of special-purpose cryptographic hardware, as well as methods that give up some quantifiable amount privacy in order to achieve significant performance improvements.

Acknowledgments

This research was supported in part by the National Science Foundation (CCR-0331584), the Wireless Network Security Center (WiNSeC) at Stevens Institute of Technology, the New Jersey Commission on Science and Technology, and the NJ Center for Wireless Networking and Internet Security. Additional resources were provided by the Stevens High Performance Computing Facility. We also thank Scalable Computing Software laboratory at Illinois Institute of Technology, Chicago, IL for granting us access to their computing facility.

References

1. G. Aggarwal, N. Mishra, and B. Pinkas. Secure computation of the kth-ranked element. In *Proc. Eurocrypt 2004*, LNCS 3027, pages 40–55. Springer-Verlag, 2004.
2. R. Agrawal and R. Srikant. Privacy-preserving data mining. In *Proc. ACM SIG-MOD Conference on Management of Data*, pages 439–450. ACM Press, May 2000.
3. M. Atallah and W. Du. Secure multi-party computational geometry. In *Proc. 7th International Workshop on Algorithms and Data Structures*, pages 165–179. Springer-Verlag, 2001.

4. M. Ben-Or, S. Goldwasser, and A. Wigderson. Completeness theorems for non-cryptographic fault-tolerant distributed computation. In *Proc. 20th ACM Symposium on the Theory of Computing (STOC)*, pages 1–10. ACM Press, 1988.

5. R. Canetti, Y. Ishai, R. Kumar, M. Reiter, R. Rubinfeld, and R. Wright. Selective private function evaluation with applications to private statistics. In *Proc. 20th Annual ACM Symposium on Principles of Distributed Computing*, pages 293–304. ACM Press, 2001.

6. R. Canetti, Y. Ishai, R. Kumar, M. Reiter, R. Rubinfeld, and R. Wright. Personal communication, 2003.

7. A. Evfimievski, J. Gehrke, and R. Srikant. Limiting privacy breaches in privacy preserving data mining. In *Proc. 22nd Symposium on Principles of Database Systems*, pages 211–222. ACM Press, 2003.

8. A. Evfimievski, R. Srikant, R. Agrawal, and J. Gehrke. Privacy preserving mining of association rules. In *Proc. 8th ACM SIGKDD International Conference on Knowledge Discovery and Data Mining*, pages 217–228. ACM Press, 2002.

9. J. Feigenbaum, Y. Ishai, T. Malkin, K. Nissim, M. Strauss, and R. Wright. Secure multiparty computation of approximations. In *Proc. 28th International Colloquium on Automata, Languages and Programming*, pages 927–938. Springer-Verlag, 2001.

10. M. Freedman, K. Nissim, and B. Pinkas. Efficient private matching and set intersection. In *Proc. Eurocrypt 2004*, LNCS 3027, pages 1–19. Springer-Verlag, 2004.

11. O. Goldreich, S. Micali, and A. Wigderson. How to play any mental game. In *Proc. 19th Annual ACM Conference on Theory of Computing*, pages 218–229. ACM Press, 1987.

12. M. Kantarcioglu and C. Clifton. Privacy-preserving distributed mining of association rules on horizontally partitioned data. In *Proc. ACM SIGMOD Workshop on Research Issues on Data Mining and Knowledge Discovery (DMKD'02)*, pages 24–31, June 2002.

13. Y. Lindell and B. Pinkas. Privacy preserving data mining. *J. Cryptology*, 15(3):177–206, 2002. An earlier version appeared in *Proc. Crypto 2000*.

14. D. Malkhi, N. Nisan, B. Pinkas, and Y. Sella. Fairplay – a secure two-party computation system. In *Proc. Usenix Security Symposium 2004*, 2004. To appear.

15. P. Paillier. Public-key cryptosystems based on composite degree residue classes. *In Advances in Cryptography - EUROCRYPT 99*, pages 223–238, 1999.

16. Y. Sella. Personal communication, 2004.

17. J. Vaidya and C. Clifton. Privacy preserving association rule mining in vertically partitioned data. In *Proc. 8th ACM SIGKDD International Conference on Knowledge Discovery and Data Mining*, pages 639–644. ACM Press, 2002.

18. J. Vaidya and C. Clifton. Privacy-preserving k-means clustering over vertically partitioned data. In *Proc. 9th ACM SIGKDD International Conference on Knowledge Discovery and Data Mining*, pages 206–215. ACM Press, 2003.

19. R. N. Wright and Z. Yang. Privacy-preserving Bayesian network structure computation on distributed heterogeneous data. In *Proc. 10th ACM SIGKDD International Conference on Knowledge Discovery and Data Mining*. ACM Press, 2004. To appear.

20. A. Yao. How to generate and exchange secrets. In *Proc. 27th IEEE Symposium on Foundations of Computer Science*, pages 162–167, 1986.

Achieving Privacy Preservation
when Sharing Data for Clustering

Stanley R.M. Oliveira[1,2] and Osmar R. Zaïane[1]

[1] Department of Computing Science
University of Alberta, Edmonton, Canada, T6G 2E8
{oliveira,zaiane}@cs.ualberta.ca
[2] Embrapa Informática Agropecuária
Av. André Tosello, 209   13083-886 Campinas, SP, Brasil

Abstract. In this paper, we address the problem of protecting the underlying attribute values when sharing data for clustering. The challenge is how to meet privacy requirements and guarantee valid clustering results as well. To achieve this dual goal, we propose a novel spatial data transformation method called Rotation-Based Transformation (RBT). The major features of our data transformation are: a) it is independent of any clustering algorithm, b) it has a sound mathematical foundation; c) it is efficient and accurate; and d) it does not rely on intractability hypotheses from algebra and does not require CPU-intensive operations. We show analytically that although the data are transformed to achieve privacy, we can also get accurate clustering results by the safeguard of the global distances between data points.

1   Introduction

Achieving privacy preservation when sharing data for clustering is a challenging problem. To address this problem, data owners must not only meet privacy requirements but also guarantee valid clustering results. The fundamental question addressed in this paper is: how can organizations protect personal data subjected to clustering and meet their needs to support decision making or to promote social benefits?

Clearly, sharing data for clustering poses new challenges for novel uses of data mining technology. Let us consider two real-life motivating examples where the sharing of data for clustering poses different constraints.

- Suppose that a hospital shares some data for research purposes (e.g. group patients who have a similar disease). The hospital's security administrator may suppress some identifiers (e.g. name, address, phone number, etc) from patient records to meet privacy requirements. However, the released data may not be fully protected. A patient record may contain other information that can be linked with other datasets to re-identify individuals or entities [11]. How can we identify groups of patients with a similar disease without revealing the values of the attributes associated with them?

W. Jonker and M. Petković (Eds.): SDM 2004, LNCS 3178, pp. 67–82, 2004.

– Two organizations, an Internet marketing company and an on-line retail company, have datasets with different attributes for a common set of individuals. These organizations decide to share their data for clustering to find the optimal customer targets so as to maximize return on investments. How can these organizations learn about their clusters using each other's data without learning anything about the attribute values of each other?

Note that the above scenarios describe two different problems of privacy-preserving clustering (PPC). We refer to the former as *PPC over centralized data*, and the latter as *PPC over vertically partitioned data*. The problem of PPC over vertically and horizontally partitioned data has been addressed in the literature [13, 7], while the problem of PPC over centralized data has not been significantly tackled. In this paper, we focus on PPC over centralized data.

There is very little literature regarding the problem of PPC over centralized data. A notable exception is the work presented in [10]. The key finding of this study was that adding noise to data would meet privacy requirements, but may compromise the clustering analysis. The main problem is that by distorting the data, many data points would move from one cluster to another jeopardizing the notion of similarity between points in the global space. Consequently, this introduces the problem of misclassification

One limitation with the above solution is the trade-off between privacy and accuracy of the clustering results. We claim that a challenging solution for PPC must do better than a trade-off, otherwise the transformed data will be useless. A desirable solution for PPC must consider not only privacy safeguards, but also accurate clustering results.

To support our claim, we propose a novel spatial data transformation method called Rotation-Based Transformation (RBT). The major features of our data transformation are: a) it is independent of any clustering algorithm, which represents a significant improvement over our previous work [10]; b) it has a sound mathematical foundation; c) it is efficient and accurate since the distances between data points are preserved; and d) it does not rely on intractability hypotheses from algebra and does not require CPU-intensive operations.

This paper is organized as follows. Related work is reviewed in Section 2. The basic concepts of data clustering and geometric data transformations are discussed in Section 3. In Section 4, we introduce our RBT method. In Section 5, we discuss and prove some important issues of security and accuracy pertained to our method. Finally, Section 6 presents our conclusions.

2   Related Work

Some effort has been made to address the problem of privacy preservation in data clustering. The class of solutions has been restricted basically to data partitioning [13, 7] and data distortion [10]. The work in [13] addresses clustering vertically partitioned data, whereas the work in [7] focuses on clustering horizontally partitioned data. In a horizontal partition, different objects are described with the same schema in all partitions, while in a vertical partition the attributes of the same objects are split across the partitions.

The work in [13] introduces a solution based on security multi-part computation. Specifically, the authors proposed a method for k-means clustering when different sites contain different attributes for a common set of entities. In this solution, each site learns the cluster of each entity, but learns nothing about the attributes at other sites. This work ensures reasonable privacy while limiting communication cost.

The feasibility of achieving PPC through geometric data transformation was studied in [10]. This investigation revealed that geometric data transformations, such as translation, scaling, and simple rotation are unfeasible for privacy-preserving clustering if we do not consider the normalization of the data before transformation. The reason is that the data transformed through these methods would change the similarity between data points. As a result, the data shared for clustering would be useless. This work also revealed that the distortion methods adopted to successfully balance privacy and security in statistical databases are limited when the perturbed attributes are considered as a vector in the n-dimensional space. Such methods would exacerbate the problem of misclassification. A promising direction of the work in [10] was that PPC through data transformation should be to some extent possible by isometric transformations, i.e., transformations that preserve distances of objects in the process of moving them in the Euclidean space.

More recently, a new method, based on generative models, was proposed to address privacy preserving distributed clustering [7]. In this approach, rather than sharing parts of the original data or perturbed data, the parameters of suitable generative models are built at each local site. Then such parameters are transmitted to a central location. The best representative of all data is a certain "mean" model. It was empirically shown that such a model can be approximated by generating artificial samples from the underlying distributions using Markov Chain Monte Carlo techniques. This approach achieves high quality distributed clustering with acceptable privacy loss and low communication cost.

The work presented here is orthogonal to that one presented in [13, 7] and differs in some aspects from the work in [10]. In particular, we build on our previous work. First, instead of distorting data for clustering using translations, scaling, rotations or even some combinations of these transformations, we distort attribute pairs using rotations only to avoid misclassification of data points. Second, our transformation presented here advocates the normalization of data before transformation. We show that successive rotations on normalized data will protect the underlying attribute values and get accurate clustering results. Third, we provide an analysis of the complexity of RBT and discuss a relevant feature of our method - the independence of clustering algorithm, which represents a significant improvement over the existing solutions in the literature. In addition, we show that the computational security of RBT does not rely on formal proof of security. Rather, it is based on the amount of computational work required to reverse the transformation process.

3 Basic Concepts

In this section, we review the basic concepts that are necessary to understand the issues addressed in this paper.

3.1 Isometric Transformations

An *isometry* (also called congruence) is a special class of geometric transformations [12,4]. The essential characteristic of an isometry is that distances between objects are preserved in the process of moving them in a n-dimensional Euclidean space. In other words, distance must be an invariant property. Formally, an isometric transformation can be defined as follows [4]:

Definition 1 (Isometric Transformation). *Let T be a transformation in the n-dimensional space, i.e., $T : \Re^n \rightarrow \Re^n$. T is said to be an isometric transformation if it preserves distances satisfying the following constraint: $|T(p) - T(q)| = |p - q|$ for all $p, q \in \Re^n$.*

Isometries also preserves angles and transform sets of points into *congruent* ones. Special cases of isometries include: (1) *translations*, which shift points a constant distance in parallel directions; (2) *Rotations*, which have a center a such that $|T(p) - a| = |p - a|$ for all p; and (3) *Reflections*, which map all points to their mirror images in a fixed $(d - 1)$-dimensional plane.

In this work, we focus primarily on rotations. For the sake of simplicity, we describe the basics of such a transformation in a 2D discrete space. In its simplest form, this transformation is for the rotation of a point about the coordinate axes. Rotation of a point in a 2D discrete space by an angle θ is achieved by using the transformation matrix in Equation (1). The rotation angle θ is measured clockwise and this transformation affects the values of X and Y coordinates. Thus, the rotation of a point in a 2D discrete space could be seen as a matrix representation $v' = Rv$, where R is a 2×2 rotation matrix, v is the vector column containing the original coordinates, and v' is a column vector whose coordinates are the rotated coordinates.

$$R = \begin{bmatrix} cos\ \theta & sin\ \theta \\ -sin\ \theta & cos\ \theta \end{bmatrix} \tag{1}$$

3.2 Data Matrix

Objects (e.g. individuals, patterns, events) are usually represented as points (vectors) in a multi-dimensional space. Each dimension represents a distinct attribute describing the object. Thus, an object is represented as an $m \times n$ matrix D, where there are m rows, one for each object, and n columns, one for each attribute. This matrix is referred to as a data matrix, represented as follows:

$$D = \begin{bmatrix} a_{11} & \dots & a_{1k} & \dots & a_{1n} \\ a_{21} & \dots & a_{2k} & \dots & a_{2n} \\ \vdots & & \vdots & \ddots & \vdots \\ a_{m1} & \dots & a_{mk} & \dots & a_{mn} \end{bmatrix} \tag{2}$$

The attributes in a data matrix are sometimes normalized before being used. The main reason is that different attributes may be measured on different scales (e.g. centimeters and kilograms). For this reason, it is common to standardize the data so that all attributes are on the same scale. There are many methods for data normalization [6]. We review only two of them in this section: *min-max normalization* and *z-score normalization*.

Min-max normalization performs a linear transformation on the original data. Each attribute is normalized by scaling its values so that they fall within a small specific range, such as 0.0 and 1.0. Min-max normalization maps a value v of an attribute A to v' as follows:

$$v' = \frac{v - min_A}{max_A - min_A} \times (new\_max_A - new\_min_A) + new\_min_A \qquad (3)$$

where min_A and max_A represent the minimum and maximum values of an attribute A, respectively, while new_min_A and new_max_A are the new range in which the normalized data will fall.

When the actual minimum and maximum of an attribute are unknown, or when there are outliers that dominate the min-max normalization, z-score normalization (also called zero-mean normalization) should be used. In z-score normalization, the values for an attribute A are normalized based on the mean and the standard deviation of A. A value v is mapped to v' as follows:

$$v' = \frac{v - \overline{A}}{\sigma_A} \qquad (4)$$

where $\overline{A}$ and σ_A are the mean and the standard deviation of the attribute A, respectively.

3.3   Dissimilarity Matrix

A dissimilarity matrix stores a collection of proximities that are available for all pairs of objects. This matrix is often represented by an $m \times m$ table. In (5), we can see the dissimilarity matrix D_M corresponding to the data matrix D in (2), where each element $d(i, j)$ represents the difference or dissimilarity between objects i and j.

$$D_M = \begin{bmatrix} 0 & & & \\ d(2,1) & 0 & & \\ d(3,1) & d(3,2) & 0 & \\ \vdots & \vdots & \vdots & \\ d(m,1) & d(m,2) & \ldots & \ldots & 0 \end{bmatrix} \qquad (5)$$

In general, $d(i, j)$ is a nonnegative number that is close to zero when the objects i and j are very similar to each other, and becomes larger the more they differ.

To calculate the dissimilarity between objects i and j one could use either the distance measure in Equation (6) or in Equation (7), or others, where $i = (x_{i1}, x_{i2}, ..., x_{in})$ and $j = (x_{j1}, x_{j2}, ..., x_{jn})$ are n-dimensional data objects.

$$d(i,j) = [\sum_{k=1}^{n} (x_{ik} - x_{jk})^2]^{1/2} \qquad (6)$$

$$d(i,j) = \sum_{k=1}^{n} |x_{ik} - x_{jk}| \qquad (7)$$

The metric in Equation (6) is the most popular distance measure called Euclidean distance, while the metric in Equation (7) is known as Manhattan or city block distance. Both Euclidean distance and Manhattan distance satisfy the following constraints:

- $d(i,j) \geq 0$: distance is a nonnegative number.
- $d(i,i) = 0$: the distance of an object to itself.
- $d(i,j) = d(j,i)$: distance is a symmetric function.
- $d(i,j) \leq d(i,k) + d(k,j)$: distance satisfies the triangular inequality.

4   The Rotation-Based Transformation Method

In this Section, we introduce our method Rotation-Based Transformation (RBT). This method is designed to protect the underlying attribute values subjected to clustering by rotating the values of two attributes at a time.

4.1   General Assumptions

Our approach to distort data points in the n-dimensional Euclidean space draws the following assumptions:

- The data matrix D, subjected to clustering, contains only confidential numerical attributes that must be transformed to protect individual data values before clustering.
- The existence of an object (e.g. ID) may be revealed but it could be also anonymized by suppression. However, the values of the attributes associated with an object are private and must be protected.
- The transformation RBT when applied to a database D must preserve the distances between the data points.

We also assume that the raw data is pre-processed as follows:

- *Suppressing Identifiers.* Attributes that are not subjected to clustering (e.g. address, phone, etc) are suppressed. Again, the existence of a particular object, say ID, could be revealed depending on the application (e.g. our first real-life example), but it could be suppressed when data is made public (e.g. census, social benefits).
- *Normalizing Numerical Attributes.* Normalization helps prevent attributes with large ranges (e.g. salary) from outweighing attributes with smaller ranges (e.g. age). The Equations (3) and (4) can be used for normalization.

Fig. 1. Major steps of the data transformation before clustering analysis.

The major steps of the data transformation, before clustering analysis, are depicted in Figure 1. In the first step, the raw data is normalized to give all the variables an equal weight. Then, the data are distorted by using our RBT method. In doing so, the underlying data values would be protected, and miners would be able to cluster the transformed data. There is no need for normalizing after the transformation process occurs.

4.2   General Approach

Now that we have described the assumptions associated with our method, we move on to defining a function that distorts the attribute values of a given data matrix to preserve privacy of individuals. We refer to such a function as rotation-based data perturbation function, defined as follows:

Definition 2 (Rotation-Based Data Perturbation Function). *Let $D_{m \times n}$ be a data matrix, where each of the m rows represents an object, and each object contains values for each of the n numerical attributes. We define a Rotation-Based Data Perturbation function f_r as a bijection of n-dimensional space into itself that transforms D into D' satisfying the following conditions:*

- *Pairwise-Attribute Distortion: $\forall i, j$, such that $1 \leq i, j \leq n$ and $i \neq j$, the vector $V = (A_i, A_j)$ is transformed into $V' = (A'_i, A'_j)$ using the matrix representation $V' = R \times V$, where $A_i, A_j \in D$, $A'_i, A'_j \in D'$, and R is the transformation matrix for rotation.*
- *Pairwise-Security Threshold: the transformation of V into V' is performed based on the Pairwise-Security Threshold $PST(\rho 1, \rho 2)$, such that the constraints must hold: $Variance(A_i - A'_i) \geq \rho_1$ and $Variance(A_j - A'_j) \geq \rho_2$, with $\rho_1 > 0$ and $\rho_2 > 0$.*

The first condition of Definition 2 states that the transformation applied to a data matrix D distorts a pair of attributes at a time. In case of an odd number of attributes in D, the last attribute can be distorted along with any other already distorted attribute, as long as the second condition is satisfied.

The second condition (Pairwise-Security Threshold) is the fundamental requirement of a data perturbation method. It quantifies the security of a method based on how closely the original values of a modified attribute can be estimated.

Traditionally, the security provided by a perturbation method has been measured as the variance between the actual and the perturbed values [1, 9]. This measure is given by $Var(X - Y)$ where X represents a single original attribute and Y the distorted attribute. This measure can be made scale invariant with respect to the variance of X by expressing security as $Sec = Var(X - Y)/Var(X)$.

In particular, RBT adopts the traditional way to verify the security of a perturbation method. However, the security offered by RBT is more challenging. We impose a pairwise-security threshold for every two distorted attributes. The challenge is how to strategically select an angle θ for a pair of attributes to be distorted so that the second condition is satisfied. In Section 4.3, we introduce the algorithm that strategically computes the value of θ.

Based on the definition of the rotation-based data perturbation function, now we define our RBT method as follows:

Definition 3 (RBT Method). *Let $D_{m \times n}$ be a data matrix, where each of the m rows represents an object, and each object contains values for each of the n numerical attributes. The Rotation-Based Data Perturbation method of dimension n is an ordered pair, defined as $RBT = (D, f_r)$, where:*

- $D \in \Re^{m \times n}$ *is a normalized data matrix of objects to be clustered.*
- f_r *is a rotation-based data transformation function, $f_r : \Re^n \to \Re^n$*

4.3   The Algorithm for the RBT Method

The procedure to distort the attributes of a data matrix has essentially 2 major steps, as follows:

Step 1. Selecting the attribute pairs: We select k pairs of attributes A_i and A_j in D, where $i \neq j$. If the number of attributes n in D is even, then $k = n/2$. Otherwise, $k = (n+1)/2$. The pairs are not selected sequentially. A security administrator could select the pairs of attributes in any order of his choice. If n is odd, the last attribute selected is distorted along with any other attribute already distorted. We could try all the possible combinations of attribute pairs to maximize the variance between the original and the distorted attributes. However, given that we ditort normalized attributes, the variance of any attribute pairs tends to lie in the same range. We illustrate this idea in our example presented in Section 5.1.

Step 2. Distorting the attribute pairs: The pairs of attributes selected previously are distorted as follows:

- *(a) Computing the distorted attribute pairs as a function of θ:* We compute $V(A_i', A_j') = R \times V(A_i, A_j)$ as a function of θ, where R is the rotation matrix, defined in Equation (1).
- *(b) Meeting the pairwise-security threshold:* We derive two inequations for each attribute pair based on the constraints: $Variance(A_i - A_i') \geq \rho_1$ and $Variance(A_j - A_j') \geq \rho_2$, with $\rho_1 > 0$ and $\rho_2 > 0$.
- *(c) Choosing the proper value for θ:* Based on the inequations found previously, we identify a range for θ that satisfies the pairwise-security threshold $PST(\rho_1, \rho_2)$. We refer to such a range as *security range*. Then, we randomly select a real number in this range and assign it to θ.
- *(d) Outputting the distorted attribute pairs:* Given that θ is already determined, we now recompute the substep (a), i.e., $V(A_i', A_j') = R \times V(A_i, A_j)$, and output the distorted attribute pairs.

Each inequation in substep (b) is solved by computing the variance of the matrix subtraction $[A_i - A'_i]$. In [5], it is shown that the sample variance of N values $x_1, x_2, ..., x_N$ is calculated by:

$$Var(x_1, x_2, ..., x_N) = \frac{1}{N} \times \sum_{i=1}^{N} (x_i - \overline{x})^2 \qquad (8)$$

where $\overline{x}$ is the arithmetic mean of the values $x_1, x_2, ..., x_N$.

The inputs for the RBT algorithm are a normalized data matrix D and a set of k pairwise-security thresholds T_k. We assume that there are k pairs of attributes to be distorted. The output is the transformed data matrix D' which is shared for clustering analysis. The sketch of the RBT algorithm is given as follows:

RBT_Algorithm
Input: $D_{m \times n}, T_k$
Output: $D'_{m \times n}$
1. $k \leftarrow \lceil n/2 \rceil$
2. $P_k \leftarrow k$ Pairs(A_i, A_j) in D such that $1 \leq i, j \leq n$ and $i \neq j$
3. **For each** selected pair P_k in $Pairs(D)$ **do**
    3.1 $V(A'_i, A'_j) \leftarrow R_\theta \times V(A_i, A_j)$ //V is computed as a function of θ
    3.2 Compute$(Var(A_i - A'_i) \geq \rho_1, Var(A_j - A'_j) \geq \rho_2)$
    3.3 $\theta_k \leftarrow SecurityRange(Var(A_i - A'_i) \geq \rho_1, Var(A_j - A'_j) \geq \rho_2)$
    3.4 $V(A'_i, A'_j) \leftarrow R_{\theta_k} \times V(A_i, A_j)$ //Output the distorted attributes of D'
End_for
End_Algorithm

Theorem 1. *The running time of the RBT_Algorithm is $O(m \times n)$, where m is the number of objects and n is the number of attributes in a data matrix D.*

Proof. Let D be a data matrix composed of m rows (objects) and n numerical attributes, and k the number of attribute pairs in D to be distorted.

Line 1 is a straightforward computation that takes $O(1)$. In line 2, the algorithm does not select all the possible combinations of pairs. The selection of the attribute pairs is performed by simply grouping the attributes in pairs but not sequentially. In general, this computation takes $n/2$ when n is even and $(n+1)/2$ when n is odd. Thus, the running time for Step 1 (lines 1 and 2) is $O(n)$.

The matrix product in line 3.1 takes $2 \times 2 \times m$. When m is large, line 3.1 takes $O(m)$. Line 3.2 encompasses two vector subtractions, each one taking $m \times 1$, resulting in $2 \times m$ iterations. After computing the vector subtractions, we compute the variance of these vectors. We scan both vectors once to compute their mean since they have the same order. Then we scan these vectors again to compute their variance. Each scan takes $m \times 1$. Thus, line 3.2 takes $2 \times m + 2 \times m$. Therefore, the running time of line 3.2 is $O(m)$. Line 3.3 is a straightforward computation that takes $O(1)$ since one value for θ is selected randomly. Line 3.4

is similar to line 3.1 and takes $O(m)$. Recall that the whole loop is performed at most n times. Thus, the running time for line 3 is $O(n \times (m + m + 1 + m))$, which can be simplified to $O(n \times m)$.

The running time of the RBT_algorithm is the sum of running times for each step, i.e, $O(n + n \times m)$. When m is large, $n \times m$ grows faster than n. Thus, the running time of the RBT_algorithm takes $O(m \times n)$.   □

5   RBT Method: Accuracy Versus Security

In this Section, we analyze some issues of accuracy, security, and privacy pertained to the RBT method.

5.1   RBT Method: Accuracy

We illustrate the accuracy of the RBT method through one example. Then we show analytically that the accuracy of our method is independent of the database size.

Let us consider the sample relational database in Table 1 and the corresponding normalized database in Table 2, using Equation (4). This sample contains real data of the Cardiac Arrhythmia Database available at the UCI Repository of Machine Learning Databases [2]. We purposely selected only three numerical attributes of this database: age, weight, and heart_rate (number of heart beats per minute).

Table 1. A sample of the cardiac arrhythmia database.

ID	age	weight	heart_rate
1237	75	80	63
3420	56	64	53
2543	40	52	70
4461	28	58	76
2863	44	90	68

Table 2. The corresponding normalized database.

ID	age	weight	heart_rate
1237	1.4809	0.7095	-0.3476
3420	0.4151	-0.3041	-1.5061
2543	-0.4824	-1.0642	0.4634
4461	-1.1556	-0.6841	1.1586
2863	-0.2580	1.3430	0.2317

First, we select the pairs of attributes to distort. Let us assume that the pairs selected are: pair1 = [age; heart_rate], and pair2 = [weight, age]. Then, we set a pairwise-security threshold for each pair of attributes selected: $PST_1 = (0.30, 0.55)$ and $PST_2 = (2.30, 2.30)$.

After setting the pairwise-security thresholds, we start the transformation process for the first attribute pair by computing $V'(age', heart\_rate') = R \times V(age, heart\_rate)$:

$$V' = \begin{bmatrix} \cos\theta & \sin\theta \\ -\sin\theta & \cos\theta \end{bmatrix} \times \begin{bmatrix} 1.4809 & 0.4151 & -0.4824 & -1.1556 & -0.2580 \\ -0.3476 & -1.5061 & 0.4634 & 1.1586 & 0.2317 \end{bmatrix} \quad (9)$$

Note that the vector $V'(age', heart\_rate')$ is computed as a function of θ. Therefore, the following constraints are function of θ as well.

– $Variance(age - age') \geq 0.30$
– $Variance(heart\_rate - heart\_rate') \geq 0.55$

Recall that the values for *age* and *heart_rate* are available in the normalized data matrix in Table 2. Our goal is to find the proper angle θ to rotate the attributes *age* and *heart_rate* satisfying the above constraints. The rotated attributes are *age'* and *heart_rate'*. To accomplish that, we plot the above inequations and identify the security range, as can be seen in Figure 2. In this Figure, there are two lines representing the pairwise-security threshold $PST_1 = (0.30, 0.55)$. We identify the security range for θ that satisfies both thresholds at the same time. As can be seen, this interval ranges from 48.03 to 314.97 degrees. Then we randomly choose one angle θ in this interval, say $\theta = 312.47$. For this choice, the values of $Variance(age - age') = 0.318$ and $Variance(heart\_rate - heart\_rate') = 0.9805$, which satisfies the pairwise-security threshold $PST_1 = (0.30, 0.55)$.

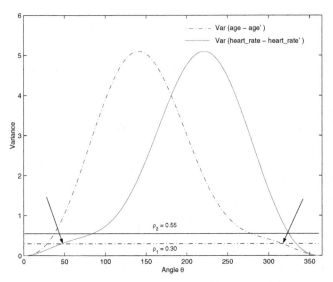

Fig. 2. The security range for $Var(age - age')$ and $Var(heart\_rate - heart\_rate')$.

After distorting the attributes *age* and *heart_rate*, we now repeat the steps performed previously to distort the attributes *weight* and *age*. We combine *weight* with *age* because we need exactly two attributes to be distorted at a time. We could combine *weight* with *heart_rate* as well. The values of the attribute *age* have been distorted in the previous steps.

We plot the inequations and identify the security range, as can be seen in Figure 3. This interval ranges from 118.74 to 258.70 degrees. Then we randomly choose one angle θ in this interval, say $\theta = 147.29$. For this choice, the values of $Variance(weight - weight') = 2.9714$ and $Variance(age - age') = 6.9274$, which satisfies the pairwise-security threshold $PST_2 = (2.30, 2.30)$.

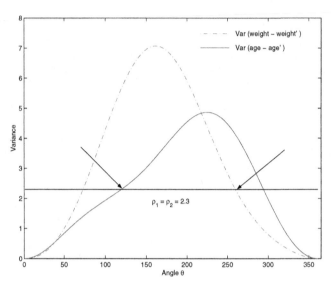

Fig. 3. The security range for $Var(weight - weight')$ and $Var(age - age')$.

The cardiac arrhythmia database after transformation is showed in Table 3, while Table 4 shows the dissimilarity matrix corresponding to Table 3.

Table 3. The cardiac arrhythmia database after transformation.

ID	age	weight	heart_rate
1237	-1.4405	0.0819	0.8577
3420	-1.0063	1.0077	-0.7108
2543	1.1368	0.5347	-0.0429
4461	1.7453	-0.3078	-0.0701
2863	-0.4353	-1.3165	-0.0339

Table 4. The dissimilarity matrix corresponding to Table 3.

$$
\begin{bmatrix}
0 & & & & \\
1.8723 & 0 & & & \\
2.7674 & 2.2940 & 0 & & \\
3.3409 & 3.1164 & 1.0396 & 0 & \\
1.9393 & 2.4872 & 2.4287 & 2.4029 & 0
\end{bmatrix}
$$

Here we highlight an interesting outcome yielded by our method: the dissimilarity matrix corresponding to the normalized database in Table 2 is exactly the dissimilarity matrix in Table 4. This result suggests that RBT method is one isometry in the n-dimensional space, independent of the database size to be transformed:

Theorem 2. *The RBT method is one isometric transformation in the n-dimensional space.*

Proof. By using the concept of distance between objects.

Let $D_{m \times n}$ be a data matrix where m is the number of objects and n is the number of attributes. Without loss of generality, the rotation of any two attributes A_i and A_j in D, where $i \neq j$, will maintain the distance between the m objects invariant. The preservation of such distances is assured because rotations are isometric transformations [4, 8]. Applying the RBT method to D will result in a transformed data matrix D' where all the attributes in D' are transformed by successive rotations of an attribute pair at a time. Hence, the RBT method is one isometric transformation in the n-dimensional space.   □

A natural consequence of Theorem 2 is that our transformation method is independent of the clustering algorithm. After applying the RBT method to a data matrix D, the clusters mined from the released data matrix D' will be exactly the same as those mined in D, given the same clustering algorithm:

Corollary 1. *Given a data matrix D and a transformed data matrix D' by using the RBT method, the clusters mined from D and D' are exactly the same for any clustering algorithm.*

Proof. By using the concept of dissimilarity matrix.

From Theorem 2 we know that the distances between the objects in a data matrix D is exactly the same as the distances between the corresponding objects in the transformed data matrix D'. Hence, applying any distance-based clustering algorithm to D and D' will result in the same clusters.   □

5.2   RBT Method: Computational Security

Unlike methods in cryptography that requires formal proof of security, the computational security of RBT is based on the amount of computational work required to reverse the transformation process. A brute force attack would require a great deal of computational power to get the original data.

In general, the computational security of RBT is a function which depends on the following factors:

- *The selection of attribute pairs*: the combination of the attribute pairs is extremely important since each attribute pair will lead to a particular security range.
- *The order of attribute pairs*: the order of an attribute in a pair gives the direction of the vectors representing data objects in the n-dimensional space.
- *The selection of pairwise-security thresholds*: the lower the pairwise-security threshold selected by a security administrator the broader the security range.
- *The selection of the angle θ*: the angle θ for each attribute pair is selected randomly in a continuous interval (the security range).

In our previous example, the security range for the attribute pairs would be completely different if we had selected the pairs as follows: pair1 = [weight; heart_rate], and pair2 = [heart_rate, age]. In addition, the order of the attributes in an attribute pair will indicate the direction of the rotation in the space. Clearly, the computational difficulty becomes progressively harder as the number

Table 5. The dissimilarity matrix corresponding to Table 3 after normalization.

Table 6. A copy of the dissimilarity matrix corresponding to Table 3 without normalization.

$$\begin{bmatrix} 0 & & & & \\ 3.0121 & 0 & & & \\ 2.5196 & 2.0314 & 0 & & \\ 2.8778 & 2.7384 & 1.0499 & 0 & \\ 2.3604 & 2.9205 & 2.3811 & 1.9492 & 0 \end{bmatrix}$$

$$\begin{bmatrix} 0 & & & & \\ 1.8723 & 0 & & & \\ 2.7674 & 2.2940 & 0 & & \\ 3.3409 & 3.1164 & 1.0396 & 0 & \\ 1.9393 & 2.4872 & 2.4287 & 2.4029 & 0 \end{bmatrix}$$

of attributes in a database increases. Apart from that, it is not trivial for an attacker to guess the angle θ for a particular attribute pair since the security range is a continuous interval. Note that the angles selected in our previous example are real numbers.

Based on the four factors above, RBT can be seen as a technique on the border with obfuscation. Obfuscation techniques aim at making information highly illegible without actually changing its inner meaning [3]. In other words, using RBT the original data is transformed so that the transformed data captures all the information for clustering analysis while protecting the underlying data values.

Now we show the security of our method against attacks. We know that the variances of the attributes in a database are equal to 1 after normalization, using Equation (4). For instance, the variances of the attributes in Table 2 are [1.000; 1.000; 1.000]. On the contrary, the variances of the distorted database in Table 3 are [1.9039; 0.7840; 0.3122]. Note that although the variances of the attributes in Table 2 and Table 3 are different, we know that their dissimilarity matrices are exactly the same, as showed in Section 5.1. Even that an attacker who has access to the perturbed data also has access to the variances of the original data (normalized), this attacker cannot reverse the transformation process. The reason is that the variances of the original data (normalized) and the variances of the distorted data are completely different. On the other hand, if this attacker tries to normalize the data in Table 3 trying to reverse the transformation process, the distances between the objects will be changed as can be seen in the dissimilarity matrix in Table 5. In this case, the data normalized after the distortion process would be useless and the attempt to reverse the transformation process would be frustrated.

5.3   RBT Method: The Privacy Preservation Process

The process of protecting privacy of objects through the RBT method is accomplished in three major steps as follows:

Step 1: Data Obscuring. First, we try to obscure the raw data by normalization. Clearly, normalization is not secure at all, even though it is one way to obfuscate attribute values subjected to clustering. On the other hand, data normalization brings two important benefits to PPC: a) it gives an equal weight to all attributes; and most importantly b) it makes difficult the re-identification of objects with other datasets since in general public data are not normalized.

Step 2: Data Anonymization. We could also anonymize the released database by removing identifiers from the distorted data. For example, the attribute ID in Table 3 could be suppressed from the data. In doing so, the privacy of individuals would be enhanced.

Step 3: Data Distortion. Disguising the data by normalization and by anonymization is not enough. So we distort attribute values by rotating two attributes at a time. Note that RBT follows the security requirements of traditional methods for data distortion. The fundamental basis of such methods is that the security provided after data perturbation is measured as the variance between the actual and the perturbed values. RBT is more flexible than the traditional methods in the sense that a security administrator can impose a security threshold for each attribute pair before the distortion process.

6 Conclusions

In this paper, we have introduced a novel spatial data transformation method for Privacy-Preserving Clustering, called Rotation-Based Transformation (RBT). Our method was designed to protect the underlying attribute values subjected to clustering without jeopardizing the similarity between data objects under analysis. Releasing a database transformed by RBT, a database owner meets privacy requirements and guarantees valid clustering results. The data shared after the transformation to preserve privacy do not need to be normalized again.

RBT can be seen as a technique on the border with obfuscation since the transformation process makes the original data difficult to perceive or understand, and preserves all the information for clustering analysis.

The highlights of our method are as follows: a) it is independent of any clustering algorithm, which represents a significant improvement over the existing methods in the literature; b) it has a sound mathematical foundation; c) it is efficient, accurate and provides security safeguard to protect privacy of individuals; and d) it does not rely on intractability hypotheses from algebra and does not require CPU-intensive operations.

Acknowledgments

Stanley Oliveira was partially supported by CNPq, Brazil, under grant No. 200077/00-7. Osmar Zaïane was partially supported by a research grant from NSERC, Canada. The authors would like to acknowledge the helpful comments made by the anonymous reviewers of this paper.

References

1. N. R. Adam and J. C. Worthmann. Security-Control Methods for Statistical Databases: A Comparative Study. *ACM Computing Surveys*, 21(4):515–556, December 1989.
2. C.L. Blake and C.J. Merz. UCI Repository of Machine Learning Databases, University of California, Irvine, Dept. of Information and Computer Sciences, 1998.
3. C. Collberg, C. Thomborson, and D. Low. A Taxonomy of Obfuscating Transformations. Technical report, TR–148, Department of Computer Science, University of Auckland, New Zealand, July 1997.
4. H. T. Croft, K. J. Falconer, and R. K. Guy. *Unsolved Problems in Geometry: v.2.* New York: Springer-Verlag, 1991.
5. M. H. DeGroot and M. J. Schervish. *Probability and Statistics, 3rd ed.* Addison-Wesley, 2002.
6. J. Han and M. Kamber. *Data Mining: Concepts and Techniques.* Morgan Kaufmann Publishers, San Francisco, CA, 2001.
7. S. Meregu and J. Ghosh. Privacy-Preserving Distributed Clustering Using Generative Models. In *Proc. of the 3rd IEEE International Conference on Data Mining (ICDM'03)*, pages 211–218, Melbourne, Florida, USA, November 2003.
8. M. E. Mortenson. *Geometric Transformations.* New York: Industrial Press Inc., 1995.
9. K. Muralidhar, R. Parsa, and R. Sarathy. A General Additive Data Perturbation Method for Database Security. *Management Science*, 45(10):1399–1415, October 1999.
10. S. R. M. Oliveira and O. R. Zaïane. Privacy Preserving Clustering By Data Transformation. In *Proc. of the 18th Brazilian Symposium on Databases*, pages 304–318, Manaus, Brazil, October 2003.
11. P. Samarati. Protecting Respondents' Identities in Microdata Release. *IEEE Transactions on Knowledge and Data Engineering*, 13(6):1010–1027, 2001.
12. J. R. Smart. *Modern Geometries.* 3rd ed., Pacific Grove, Calif.: Brooks/Cole Publishing Company, 1988.
13. J. Vaidya and C. Clifton. Privacy-Preserving K-Means Clustering Over Vertically Partitioned Data. In *Proc. of the 9th ACM SIGKDD Intl. Conf. on Knowlegde Discovery and Data Mining*, pages 206–215, Washington, DC, USA, August 2003.

Privacy-Preserving Digital Rights Management

Claudine Conrado, Milan Petković, and Willem Jonker

Information and System Security Department
Philips Research
Prof. Holstlaan 4, WY71
5656AA Eindhoven, The Netherlands
{Claudine.Conrado,Milan.Petkovic,Willem.Jonker}@philips.com

Abstract. DRM systems provide a means for protecting digital content, but at
the same time they violate the privacy of users in a number of ways. This paper
addresses privacy issues in DRM systems. The main challenge is how to allow a
user to interact with the system in an anonymous/pseudonymous way, while
preserving all security requirements of usual DRM systems. To achieve this
goal, the paper proposes a set of protocols and methods for managing user identities and interactions with the system during the process of acquiring and consuming digital content. Furthermore, a method that supports anonymous transfer
of licenses is discussed. It allows a user to transfer a piece of content to another
user without the content provider being able to link the two users. Finally, the
paper demonstrates how to extend the rights of a given user to a group of users
in a privacy preserving way. The extension hides the group structure from the
content provider and at the same time provides privacy among the members of
the group.

1 Introduction

Recent developments in digital technologies, along with increasingly interconnected
high-speed networks and the decrease in prices for high-performance digital devices,
have established digital content distribution as one of the most quickly emerging activities nowadays and made possible new ways for consumers to access, use, enjoy,
and pay for digital content. As a consequence of this trend and big success of one of
the first online music shops - Apple's iTunes, which sold more than 70 million songs
in its first year [1], a number of shops have been opened and both consumers and content providers have clearly shown high interest in electronic distribution of audio/video
content.

However, digital content can be very easy illegally copied, exchanged, and distributed, which is seen by the content industry as a big threat. Therefore, content providers
need a technology, which can protect digital content from illegal use. Digital Rights
Management (DRM) is a technology that provides content protection by enforcing the
use of digital content according to granted rights. It enables content providers to protect their copyrights and maintain control over distribution of and access to content. To
fulfill the needs of content providers, a number of DRM systems have quickly ap-

W. Jonker and M. Petković (Eds.): SDM 2004, LNCS 3178, pp. 83–99, 2004.

peared such as Microsoft Windows Media DRM [2], IBM's Electronic Music Management System (EMMS) [3], Sony's Open MagicGate [4], and Thomson's SmartRight [5]. Early DRM systems have been device-based, which means that they bound content and rights to devices so that content can be only accessible at a specific device. However, in order to allow a consumer to access his content anytime, anywhere, at any device, the idea of person-based DRM has emerged. Furthermore, some DRM systems, such as Authorized Domain Digital Rights Management (ADDRM) system from Philips [6][7], take into account along with the requirements of content owners also the requirements of content consumers. Philips' ADDRM allows content to freely flow inside a domain (typically a household), so that it can be freely copied inside that domain and exchanged among the domain devices, while transactions between different domains are controlled.

A typical DRM system normally provides means for protecting content, creating and enforcing rights, identification of users, monitoring of the usage of content, and so on. Therefore, these systems are very privacy-invasive. They violate users' privacy in a number of ways. Firstly, they do not support anonymous and un-linkable buying or transfer of content as in the traditional business model where a user anonymously buys a CD using cash. Furthermore, they generally involve tracking of the usage of content in order to keep control over the content [8]. For example, in person-based DRM systems a user has to authenticate himself each time he accesses a piece of content. Therefore, information such as user identification, content identification, time, place, etc. might be collected. The same holds for device-based DRM system, except that user identification might not be revealed in such a straightforward way, although this information can be derived from other data that perhaps link unique device identification or content identification with user identification.

In an increasingly privacy-aware world, such possibilities of creating user profiles or tracking users create numerous privacy concerns. In order to overcome the aforementioned privacy problems with DRM systems, this paper proposes a Privacy-Preserving DRM system (P2DRM). The main idea is to allow a user to interact with the system in an anonymous/pseudonymous way during the whole process of buying and consuming digital content. This has to be done in a way that all security requirements of the usual DRM systems are satisfied, and that content providers are assured that content will be used according to issued licenses and cannot be illegally copied. Furthermore, the paper discusses an approach to an anonymous transfer of licenses, so that a piece of content can be sold or gifted to another user without the content provider being able to link the two users. Finally, the paper demonstrates how the basic system can be extended to achieve authorized domain functionality in a privacy preserving way. This extension hides the domain structure from the content provider and at the same time provides privacy among the members of the domain.

The remainder of the paper is organized as follows. In Section 2, the basic system is introduced. Section 3 discusses a solution that extends the basic system to support an anonymous transfer of licenses. In Section 4, a description of an additional extension of the system that allows privacy preserving creation of a domain and its functioning is given. Finally, Section 5 draws conclusions.

2 Basic System

In the basic privacy-preserving DRM system, the real identity of the user is decoupled from identifiers which the user possesses in the system. These identifiers, i.e. user pseudonyms, in the P2DRM system are used to link a user (or his ID device, e.g. a smart card) to content, thus allowing a user to access the content for which he bought the rights. Moreover, the identifiers may be also used to keep track of the behaviour of that user ID device, thus preventing that known hacked user ID devices continue to be used in the system.

There are a number of entities which are present in the P2DRM system. They comprise:

- User,
- Smart card (SC), the user ID device,
- Smart card issuer (SCI),
- Compliance certificate issuer for smart cards (CA-SC),
- Content provider (CP),
- Compliant device (CoD), a device that behaves according to the DRM rules,
- Compliance certificate issuer for compliant devices (CA-CoD).

There are also a number of threats, which are mentioned below, relating to the security of the system and the privacy of the users of this system. These threats are handled by the P2DRM system by means of schemes which are discussed in the sections below.

The basic privacy threat that P2DRM circumvents is the association of a user's real identity and content that the user owns, association which may happen with the use of personal licenses for content access. This also prevents that users are tracked while accessing the content.

General security threats for the DRM system include the possibility of hacking smart cards as well as the devices on which content is accessed. These threats are avoided in the P2DRM system by means of compulsory mutual compliance checks between smart cards and devices. These checks, on their turn, may violate users' privacy which is circumvented with the use of temporary users' pseudonyms.

When the transfer of licenses amongst users is made possible, security and privacy threats are also present. Security threats relate to the fact that users may be able to continue using their licenses after they have transferred those licenses to other users. Privacy threats relate to the possible disclosure of the association between the user who transfers and the user who receives a given license. These threats are avoided in the P2DRM system by means of revocation lists and generic (or anonymous) licenses issued by the CP.

Finally, concerning the composition of a group (or domain) of users who are allowed to share licenses (e.g., users in a household), the basic privacy threat is the disclosure of the domain structure. P2DRM avoids this threat by means of a trusted domain manager device.

Within the P2DRM system, a number of different transactions, schematically depicted in Figure 1, are performed by/with the entities listed above. These transactions are described in the sections below, where references to the numbered links in Figure 1 are made at the appropriate points. Moreover, several security assumptions are made, which are indicated for each phase of usage of the DRM system.

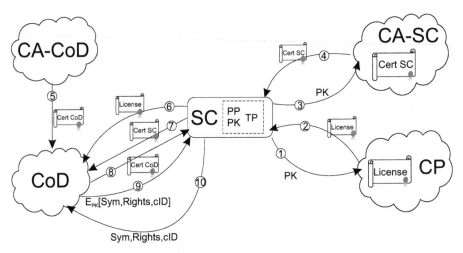

Fig. 1. Representation of the various interactions between parties in the P2DRM system.

2.1 Acquisition of a Smart Card by the User

The user buys a smart card from a retailer which is taken from a pool of identically "looking" smart cards pre-issued by the SCI. Each smart card has a different secret public/private key pair PK/SK in it and an un-set PIN (say, all PINs are set initially to 0000). The SCI guarantees that until anyone interacts with the card for the first time, the public key of that specific card is not revealed to any party, nor is a PIN (used to activate the card) set. So, in this way, the user (as the first interacting party) is the only entity which can learn the public key (and therefore know the association between the real user identity and PK) and which can set the PIN used to activate the card. Note that the private key SK is securely stored on the smart card and it is not accessible to the user.

Security assumptions in this context are:

- Only after the first transaction, is the public key PK of a SC revealed and the PIN number set.
- The private key corresponding to public key PK is stored secretly and only known to the SC.

2.2 Acquisition of the Content and the Rights by the User

When the user wants to buy the rights to access some content, he contacts the CP by means of an anonymous channel requesting the rights to a given content. After an anonymous payment scheme is conducted (such as the pre-payment scheme described in [9]), the user sends his public key PK to the CP (link 1 in Figure 1), which can then create the right or license for that content. The content itself is encrypted by the CP with a symmetric key Sym and sent to the user together with the license (link 2 in Figure 1), whose format is given in (1). The channel must be also secret to prevent that an eavesdropper associates the public key PK to the sent license.

$$\{ PK[Sym//Rights//contentID] \}_{signCP} . \tag{1}$$

In the license above, PK encrypts the concatenated values [Sym//Rights//contentID], Rights describe the rights bought by the user, contentID identifies the content and signCP is the signature of the CP on the certificate.

Given that PK encrypts the value [Sym//Rights//contentID], the SC is the only entity which is capable of obtaining the key Sym from the license by using the private key SK (only known to the SC). Moreover, a compliant SC (as attested by the compliance certificate discussed in the next section) will reveal the key Sym only to the CoD during the action of content access discussed in section 2.4. The license in (1), when inspected, does not reveal the public key PK nor the rights, nor content identifier, so it preserves the user's privacy with respect to content and rights ownership. Therefore, if found in a user's storage device, it does not compromise the user's privacy.

Note that during the buying procedure the CP learns the association $(PK \leftrightarrow (contentID, Rights, Sym))$, but not the real user's identity due to the anonymous channel.

Security assumptions in this context are:
- The user contacts the CP by means of an anonymous channel.
- There is in place a mechanism which allows the user to pay anonymously for the license it requests.
- A secret channel is used for the communication between the user's SC and the CP.

2.3 Acquisition of SC Compliance Certificate by the User

In order for a user to securely access content on a CoD, a compliance certificate for his SC must be shown to the CoD. This compliance certificate does not contain, however, the public key PK, but it is issued by the CA-SC with a changeable SC's pseudonym. To obtain the compliance certificate for the SC, the user/SC contacts the CA-SC anonymously, sends its public key PK (link 3 in Figure 1) and asks for the certificate. Again, a secret channel is used between the SC and the CA-SC to prevent eavesdropping. Assuming that the SCI keeps track of smart cards' behaviour by means of a revocation list with the PKs of hacked SCs, the CA-SC checks with the SCI whether PK belongs to the black revocation list or not[1]. If it does not, the CA-SC then generates a pseudonym for the SC, say a random number RAN, and issues the following compliance certificate, which is sent to the SC (link 4 in Figure 1):

---

[1] This check of the revocation list for SCs may be performed by the CP as well when the anonymous user sends his PK and asks for a license for a given content. If the SC has been revoked by the SCI, the CP can refuse the issuance of the license for that SC/user.

$$\{H(RAN) , PK[RAN]\}_{signCA\text{-}SC} , \tag{2}$$

where H( ) is a one-way hash function, PK encrypts RAN and signCA-SC is the signature of the CA-SC on the certificate.

The certificate in (2), when inspected, does not reveal the public key PK nor the SC's pseudonym RAN. Moreover, the only entity which can obtain RAN from the certificate is the SC (via decryption with the private key SK). The value RAN may then be checked by a verifier via the hash value in the certificate. The use of a pseudonym RAN allows the verifier to check the compliance of the SC without learning its public key PK. Moreover, linkability of different shows of a given SC's compliance certificate can be minimised. This is due to the fact that frequent renewal of compliance certificates is a requirement of the DRM system, since it implies that the compliance of the SC is frequently checked and certified by the CA-SC. Frequent renewal can be achieved by including a validity date in the compliance certificate, and when this date has passed, the SC is obliged to obtain a new compliance certificate to show to the CoD. By renewing the value RAN every time a new certificate is obtained, linkability of different certificate shows towards the CoD is minimised.

In order to prevent linkability of pseudonyms, there are methods such as the convertible credentials of [10], which allow a user to obtain a credential from a given organization under a given pseudonym, and show that credential to another organization under another pseudonym. This type of approach involves protocols which are significantly more complex than the simple protocols described in this paper, which involve only simple hash operations.

Note that during the procedure above the CA-SC learns the association (PK↔RAN), but not the real user's identity due to the anonymous channel.

Security assumptions in this context are:

- The user contacts the CA-SC by means of an anonymous channel.
- A secret channel is used for all communication between the user's SC and the CA-SC.
- The SCI is responsible for keeping track of SC's behaviours.

2.4 Access to Content by the User

Now the user can access the content for which he has the license, which can only be performed on a CoD (a device that behaves according to the DRM rules). To do so, he must either carry the content and license with him (e.g. in an optical disk) or have them stored in some location over the network. In either case, the encrypted content and the license (link 6 in Figure 1) must be first transferred to the CoD. Moreover, since the user is now physically present in front of the CoD, his real identity may be "disclosed" to the CoD (e.g., the CoD may have a camera) or to any observer that may also be physically present near the CoD. Therefore, in order to prevent the disclosure of the association between the user's real identity and PK to any party, the public key PK of the user should not be revealed to the CoD at the time of content access. That is the reason why the compliance certificate for the SC is issued with the changeable pseudonym RAN. Upon check of that certificate, the CoD learns RAN but does not learn PK. The full content access procedure is described below.

Before the SC and the CoD interact with one another, they do a mutual compliance check:

- Compliance of the CoD is proved by means of a CoD compliance certificate. This certificate is issued by the CA-CoD, which certifies the public key of the CoD, and sent to the CoD (link 5 in Figure 1) beforehand. Upon mutual compliance check, the certificate is shown to the SC (link 8 in Figure 1). The SC must therefore store the public key of the CA-CoD. This key may be changed periodically, which obliges the CoD to periodically renew its compliance certificate. This also implies that the SC must renew that key periodically, what can be done at the time that the SC obtains its own compliance certificates with the CA-SC.

- Compliance of the SC is proved by means of the pseudonymous compliance certificate in (2) which is shown to the CoD (link 7 in Figure 1). As mentioned above, the SC obtains the value RAN via decryption with the private key SK and sends it to the CoD which checks the value via the term H(RAN). Since the CoD can have a clock, the SC compliance certificate may have its time of issuance added to it, which obliges the SC to periodically renew the certificate when it gets too old. Note that it is also in the interest of the SC to renew its compliance certificate often enough so as to minimise the linkability mentioned above.

After the mutual compliance check, the CoD sends the term PK[Sym//Rights//contentID] from the license to the SC (link 9 in Figure 1) which decrypts it and sends the values Sym, Rights and contentID back to the CoD (link 10 in Figure 1). The CoD can then use Sym to decrypt the content and give the user access to it, according to Rights.

Note that during the procedure above the CoD learns the association (RAN↔(contentID, Rights, Sym)), and may learn the real user's identity. Therefore, an attacker in control of the CoD may be able to obtain the real user's identity (e.g., a picture of the user), his SC's pseudonym RAN as well as the ID of the content which was accessed by the user during that transaction and the accompanying rights[2]. This fact, however, compromises the user's privacy only concerning the specific content and rights involved in that transaction. This type of attack cannot be really avoided. However, the attacker cannot learn PK, but only the value RAN. As this value changes often, the user may be tracked but only for a limited number of transactions.

Security assumptions in this context are:

- The CA-CoD is responsible for keeping track of CoD's behaviours as well as for issuing compliance certificates for those devices.
- A compliant SC will only reveal the decryption key Sym to a compliant device (CoD).
- The CoD will not reveal the key Sym to any party, except for perhaps another (proven) compliant device.

---

[2] Note, however, that Sym is not revealed to the attacker since the CoD is assumed to be DRM-compliant.

3   Anonymous Transfer of Licenses

In order for a user (from now on referred to as *first user*), whose public key is PK, to transfer his license to a second user, whose public key is PK', in a secure (i.e., in a way that prevents the former user from still being able to access the content) and anonymous way, solutions must be found which deal with license revocation and anonymity. These are discussed below.

3.1   License Revocation

When the first user wants to transfer his license, he contacts the CP via an anonymous channel, authenticates himself as user PK, presents the license to be transferred to the second user and provides the public key PK' of the second user. Note that here the transfer is not anonymous. The CP marks that license of PK as "revoked", but before the CP creates a new license with PK', revocation of the old license must be dealt with.

The revocation problem above can be solved by including in the compliance certificate of the first user's SC a list with all the licenses of that user that have been marked as "revoked" by the CP (i.e., a black revocation list). This can be done during the protocol between the SC and the CA-SC, in which the SC obtains his compliance certificate as given in (2). During this protocol, the CA-SC contacts the CP, sends PK and asks for the list of *all* revoked licenses corresponding to that PK. Since the symmetric key Sym that encrypts the content is unique per license, the CP can use this value to identify each revoked license associated with PK. The CP then creates a list with the values:

$$H(Sym\_1 \; // \; Time),$$
$$H(Sym\_2 \; // \; Time),$$
$$...$$
$$H(Sym\_n \; // \; Time),\cdot$$

(3)

where each value is the hash of the key Sym_i of a revoked license concatenated with the current time. The one-way hash function H( ) is used to reduce the size of each term in the revocation list in (3) but also to hide the values of Sym_i from any party which does not need to learn those values. The current time is concatenated with each Sym_i in order to prevent the linkability via the revocation list of compliance certificates issued for PK in different occasions.

Once the values for all revoked licenses of PK are included in the list, this list is sent by the CP to the CA-SC together with the value Time. At this point, the CP can consider as "dealt with" the revocation of the licenses of PK which had been previously marked as "revoked". In this case the CP can create, for instance, the new license for the second user with his public key PK'.

The CA-SC on the other hand can now include the revocation list as well as the time in which this list was created in the SC's compliance certificate as

$$\{H(RAN), PK[RAN], Time, H(Sym\_1//Time), H(Sym\_2//Time),...\}_{signCA-SC} , \qquad (4)$$

where the terms H(Sym_1//Time), H(Sym_2//Time),… refer to all revoked licenses of PK at time 'Time'.

The certificate above is then sent to the SC, which may keep it stored in the SC itself. At the present time, a typical SC (with public key PK) may store a compliance certificate whose revocation list has up to around five hundred revoked licenses of that PK. When/if the revocation list becomes too big that storage in the SC is no longer possible, the certificate can be stored, for instance, on a server in the network or on an optical storage medium, pretty much like the storage of the content and the license mentioned previously.

As discussed in the Section 2.4, when a user requests access to content on a CoD, the content plus license must be first transferred to the CoD. And since the SC must *always* prove its compliance to the CoD upon a user's request to content, it must present the compliance certificate as given in (4). So, after the mutual compliance check, the CoD sends the term PK[Sym//Rights//contentID] from the license to the SC which decrypts it and sends the values Sym, Rights and contentID back to the CoD. But before the CoD uses Sym to decrypt the content and give the user access to it (according to Rights), it calculates H(Sym//Time) and checks whether this value is in the revocation list or not. If it is not, the CoD then proceeds with the handling of the access request.

3.2 Anonymous Licenses

When the license is transferred from the first to the second user, the CP learns the association between those users, i.e., the association between the public keys PK and PK'. The knowledge of this association may be unwanted by the users. A solution to this problem is the use of generic licenses, from now on referred to as "anonymous licenses", in which a user identity is not specified.

An anonymous license is a license for a specified content with specified rights (as the license given in (1)), but which is not associated with a user (i.e., with a public key). Such a license can be issued by the CP for any anonymous user who pays for a given content with given rights. It can also be issued for the first user who requested the revocation of his license in order for it to be transferred to the second user (as described in Section 3.1). Since the license is not associated with a given person, it can be transferred (given, sold, etc) to any other person. This person can later present the license to the same CP to be exchanged for a personalised license as given in (1), which can then be used for content access. The procedure is shown schematically below.

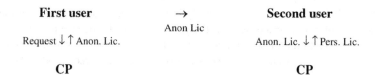

Fig. 2. Schematic representation of the anonymous license transactions between the users and the CP.

For security reasons, however, before the CP issues the anonymous license, a unique identifier must be assigned to it. This is done in order to prevent that, once the anonymous license has been already redeemed, any copy of it (which can be easily made by the user) can be also redeemed. If this identifier is chosen by the CP, however, it will be able to link the public keys of both users (the one who transfers and the one who later redeems the anonymous license). In order to prevent that, blind signatures [11] can be used as described below.

The first user creates a secret random identifier ID, blinds this value (by, e.g., multiplying the value ID by another randomly chosen value) and sends it to the CP. Together with this blinded value, the user may also send a specification of the new rights NewRights which are to be associated with the anonymous license (in case the license is being transferred between users), provided that the specified rights allow less than the original rights. This possibility allows a user to give one of his licenses to another user but with more restrictive rights than the original rights he had, if he so wishes.

The CP, on the other hand, must have a unique pair of public/private keys for each combination of right and content {Rights, contentID}. It is assumed here that the set of all rights is pre-specified comprising, say, R rights and the set of all content has C items. This means that the CP must have $R \times C$ different public/private key pairs. Given this setting, once the CP receives the data { Blind[ID] , NewRights } from the first user, it can sign the blind identifier, Blind[ID], with the private key for the combination {NewRights, contentID} and return to the user the value $\{Blind[ID]\}_{signed-NewRights-contentID}$. The user then un-blinds the signed identifier to obtain $\{ID\}_{signed-NewRights-contentID}$ and can give this value, together with the license specification {NewRights, contentID}, to the second user.

In order to later obtain a personalised license, the second user contacts the CP anonymously, authenticates himself with his public key PK' and sends to the CP the signed identifier $\{ID\}_{signed-NewRights-contentID}$ together with {NewRights, contentID}. The CP can then find the correct key pair, check its own signature in the value ID, and if correct it can finally issue a personalised license to the second user (which is sent to him together with the content encrypted with a personalised key Sym):

$$\{ PK'[Sym' \mathbin{/\mkern-3mu/} NewRights \mathbin{/\mkern-3mu/} contentID] \}_{signCP} . \tag{5}$$

After the issuance of the license above, the value ID is entered by the CP into a list of used IDs. This prevents the personalised license request for an already redeemed anonymous license.

As mentioned previously, one application of anonymous licenses is the unlinkable transfer of licenses between users. In this case, when the revocation of the old license of the first user is dealt with, the CP simply issues an anonymous license for that user, rather than issuing a new license with the public key of the license receiver. Another application relates to the business model of giving an incentive for users to buy a certain content, for instance, the "buy one, get a second one for free" model. The second license can be issued as an anonymous license which can be transferred to any person.

3.3 Identity-Based Cryptography for Key Management by the CP

In the solution described above, the CP has to maintain a huge list with R×C different public/private key pairs and the corresponding "Rights" and "contentID" values. This solution can be simplified with techniques from identity-based cryptography, in particular the identity-based blind signature method described in [12]. This method can be applied in the present context, but instead of using the identity of people or different parties to generate the keys (as proposed in [12]), the concatenation of the content identifier, the rights and the CP's name can be used for key generation. In this way, a public key can simply be defined as the string [ContentID//Rights//CPname] and the corresponding private key is generated based on that string and on a master key generated by the CP.

4 Privacy-Preserving Domain Creation

According to the basic idea of Authorized Domains [6][7], when a user of the P2DRM system buys a piece of content, other users in his home may be allowed to access that content as well. However, while supporting the authorized domain idea, the system should preserve the user's privacy. Ideally, the system should support that within a domain different users have different rights for the same piece of content. Furthermore, the structure of the domain should remain private. This means that no parties in the system, except maybe the one that is responsible for the creation of domains, should be able to link the domain members (or their identifiers) together, as well as with a domain identifier. Therefore, the first problem addressed in this section is to preserve privacy of the domain structure and allow differentiations of the rights inside a domain.

The second problem addressed is the management of countable rights in the P2DRM system. The countable rights are rights that the user can spend (as play n times, or copy once). These rights are dynamic, because they change over time. This causes a problem in the P2DRM system, as the licenses are in the form of certificates signed by a content provider (CP). Therefore, the usage of countable rights requires that the license, which the user gets from the CP, be changed and signed again every time the user spend the rights. Furthermore, the system has to support revocation of the old licenses, because the user can easily copy the license before spending the rights, spend the rights, then delete the changed license, and finally use the copy of the old license to spend the rights again. However the privacy problem remains, and this is how to prevent the CP from learning the time, content, device, and user's PK for each user action that involves countable rights.

In this section, we address these two problems: (1) privacy preserving domain formation, and (2) privacy preserving management of countable rights.

The solution to the aforementioned problems is presented step by step. In the following two sections we first provide two simple straightforward approaches to the solution of the problems. By describing their drawbacks, we emphasize the privacy problems. Then in the third section, we explain a privacy-enhanced solution that overcomes the privacy problems found with the previous solutions.

4.1 Domain with PK$_D$

In this section, we describe a solution for the domain construction in the P2DRM system based on a shared domain key PK$_D$. The domain has to be registered with a domain authority (e.g. the municipality), which can check that indeed the members form a group, e.g. family. The same domain authority can assign a PK$_D$ to that group of users and add SK$_D$ to their smartcards[3]. Having done that, a user can buy content for his personal use (using his personal PK) or for the whole domain using the domain key PK$_D$. In the case of buying content for the whole domain, the user distributes the content and the license to the other users of the domain. They will use it in the same way in which they use their personal content (as they can choose between two keys in their smartcards, one for personal content and another one for the shared content)[4]. However, when buying content with PK$_D$, there is no possibility to assigned different rights to different members of the domain, as they use the same license.

With respect to countable rights, a device (which the user operates) can contact the CP online when the spending of the rights occurs. The CP can issue a new license and revoke the old license when the spending of countable rights occurs. Revocation can be done as described in Section 3. However, inserting old licenses into a black revocation list only when user goes to the Certificate Authority which certifies compliance of smart cards (CA-SC) might not be an effective measure, because this does not happen immediately after spending countable rights, but periodically. Therefore the user will be able to use old licenses until he is not forced to obtain a new smart card compliance certificate. Even if this problem is solved, the following privacy problem remains. As the CP must change and revoke a license at the time the user spends rights, the CP will learn when, which user (PK), what content, and on which device was used.

With the solution described above, we have achieved privacy towards the CP for the domain structure, because the CP does not learn the structure of the domain. However, there are no rights differentiations within the domain, which means that all members have the same rights as the user who has bought the content, or all others have no rights. Furthermore, the CP knows the time, content, device, and user's PK for each user action that involves changing of countable rights. Finally, the solution for countable rights revocation is not appropriate, because it will be too late to include the revocation list when the user go to CA-SC for a new RAN (until that he can copy content n times instead of only once).

---

[3] To do that, the domain authority has to contact the smart card issuer for the secret keys, which will allow insertion of the domain keys into the secure storage of the smartcards. Note that in this process the smartcard issuer will not learn the structure of the domain (e.g. the domain authority will not send a separate request to the smartcard issuer for each domain, but can do for several domains in a bulk). Note also that there is no need for the domain authority to learn the user personal public keys. Therefore the unlinkability between personal PKs and user identities will remain.

[4] To facilitate the management of licenses, a license can be accompanied by an identifier, which defines if the license is personal or shared in the domain. The smartcard can use this information to choose the right key (SK$_D$ or the personal SK) when decrypting a license.

4.2 Domain with Different Rights

The user who is buying the content may want to assign different rights to different members of his domain. For that, the user may create a data structure,

$$PK_1 \text{ Rights}_1 ,$$
$$PK_2 \text{ Rights}_2 ,$$
$$\cdot$$
$$PK_n \text{ Rights}_n , \tag{6}$$

where PK_1, PK_2, ..., PK_n, are the public keys of the domain members (possible including the user who buys), while Rights_1, Rights_2 Rights_n are different rights expressions.

The list above is sent to the CP in the process of content buying. The process is similar to the one described in Section 2. The difference here is that the CP checks with the domain authority if the group of keys from the list really forms a domain. The CP can do that interactively with a domain authority. On the other hand, the user can also obtain a certificate from the domain authority, certifying that $\{PK_1, PK_2, ... PK_n\}$ are in the same domain. In both cases if the CP is assured, he can (using the list (6)) directly create for each domain member i a personal certificate:

$$\{ PK_i[\text{ Sym} // \text{Rights}_i // \text{contentID}] \}_{\text{signCP}} . \tag{7}$$

Note that the key Sym is the same for all users in the domain for a given content, therefore only one copy of Sym[content] needs to be kept for the whole domain. Each user in the domain gets only a personalised rights package. Note also that the provider will create the certificates as in (7) only if the condition (Rights i ≤ Rights) holds, where Rights are the rights that have been bought.

The assignment of rights to domain users may happen at a later stage as well. In this case, the data structure as in (6) is sent to the provider along with PK and contentID of the content to be shared in the domain. The CP can check that indeed PK bought contentID, and can check with the domain authority the keys of the domain members. The CP may then create and send back to the purchaser the certificates as given in (7).

With this solution, we have achieved rights differentiations within the domain without using an extra key (the domain key PK_D). However, consumers lose their privacy towards the CP regarding the domain structure, because the CP learns the structure of the domain (not the real user identities, but the PKs which form the domain). This can be used for advertisement, spam, etc. Problems regarding behavioral privacy and revocation of countable rights remain as described in the previous subsection.

4.3 Domain with PK_D and Different Rights

Let us assume that the users who form a domain have been registered by a domain authority and obtained PK_D/SK_D as described in Section 4.1. When buying a piece of content, the user with public key PK obtains the following master certificate:

$$\{\{PK_D[Sym//Rights//contentID\},1\}_{signCP},MR\}_{signCP}. \tag{8}$$

The master license consists of the domain license shown in (9) and the master rights tag (MR), signed all together by the CP. The domain license consists of symmetric key, master rights, and content ID encrypted by the domain key PK_D as well as the delegation tag (set to 1), signed all together by the CP.

$$\{PK_D[Sym//Rights//contentID\},1\}_{signCP}. \tag{9}$$

At the end of the process of obtaining this certificate from the CP, the user can encrypt the master certificate (as in (10)) in order to preserve his privacy towards the domain members who share the PK_D. So, no user in the domain will be able to see the license and rights of the user who has bought the content.

$$PK[\{\{PK_D[Sym//Rights//contented\},1\}_{signCP},MR\}_{signCP}]. \tag{10}$$

To create license(s) for domain member(s), the master license has to be supplemented with licenses for particular domain members. The creation of personalized user rights (for particular domain members) is done by a Domain Manager device (DM). The user who has bought the content prepares the rights for other domain users (structure (6) in Section 4.2) and sends it together with the master license to the DM. In the interaction with the DM, the user decrypts the encrypted certificate (10) and consequently the term $PK_D[Sym//Rights//contentID]$. The user has to show to the DM also certificates that attest that all PK_i that are mentioned in the structure (6) (for which he wants to prepare licenses) actually belong to his domain[5]. Then, the DM creates an extra license (second license in (11)).

$$\{PK_D[Sym//Rights//contentid\},1\}_{signCP},$$
$$\{PK_i[Sym//Rights_i//contentid], PK_{DM}\}_{signDM}. \tag{11}$$

Finally, the user distributes these rights to the domain members. When accessing the content, a domain member must present to the device both licenses in (11) and the compliance certificate for the DM[6]. The reason to present both licenses is to allow the device to check if the user belongs to the domain (if he knows both PKi and PK_D) but also to check that the rights $Rights_i \le Rights$ (as an extra insurance for the CP because at the end the licence issued by the CP is checked).

The procedure described above makes sure that only the user who has bought the content and has the master certificate (8) can create licenses for the domain members[7].

The introduction of the DM as a party who takes care of the user rights within the domain is also beneficial for the management of the countable rights. Now, the DM

---

[5] The certificate links the domain key PK_D with member's keys $\{PK_1, PK_2, ... PK_n\}$. Alternatively, the DM can store this certificate.

[6] The compliance certificate for the DM might be issued by an authority, which certifies compliance of devices.

[7] If we do not use the double certificate as a master license, any domain member could use the master right to create the maximum rights for himself (as he will obtain exactly the master right as the delegation right in (11).

can issue new licenses and revoke old licenses when the spending of a countable right occurs. In that way the user privacy towards the CP is protected, because the CP is not contacted every time the user spends rights. Therefore the CP cannot create logs that link user's PK, content identifiers, device identifiers and time when spending of countable rights occurs. Moreover, this solution is also beneficial for the CP, because the revocation of the old license is managed[8] by the DM and therefore it is instant (which resolves the problem of late revocation with the CA-SC).

The presented approach achieves both rights differentiations within the domain and privacy towards CP for the domain structure (because the CP does not learn the structure of the domain). Furthermore, the problem of behavioral privacy towards the CP is solved, because the CP cannot learn the time, content, device, and user's PK for each user action that involves changing of countable rights. Finally, the solution for countable rights revocation is appropriate as licenses are revoked instantly. However, the solution brings some complexity in the form of the introduction of the DM and one more license and certificate, but the CP has much less work (domain rights are issued by the DM, revocation is also done by the DM).

5 Discussion

In this paper, a DRM system is described which protects users' privacy while preserving the system's security. The privacy and security aspects of the system are discussed below.

In the basic system, user privacy is achieved by decoupling the real user identity from his identifiers, namely PK and RAN, in the DRM system. Concerning the relevant entities in the system:

- the SCI does not know any association of user's identities and content/rights,
- the CP knows the association   (PK $\leftrightarrow$ (content, Rights, Sym)),
- the CA-SC knows the association   (PK $\leftrightarrow$ RAN),
- the CoD knows the association   (RAN $\leftrightarrow$ (content, Rights, Sym)).

Therefore, even by a collusion of the CP, the CA-SC and the CoD, the real identity of the user cannot be revealed since only the user knows the association (real user identity $\leftrightarrow$ PK).

Furthermore, if an attacker is able to obtain user-related information from the CoD after a content access transaction happens, the associations

- (real user identity $\leftrightarrow$ RAN),
- (real user identity $\leftrightarrow$ (content, Rights, Sym))

become known to him. But since RAN changes periodically and only one piece of content is associated with the user's real identity, the privacy damage is minimal. As the attacker cannot learn the user's public key PK from the CoD, he cannot create a full log of the user's ownership of content and pattern of content usage.

---

[8] Domain Manager can store a black revocation list of revoked licenses and request that each time before content is accessed on a device, the device checks that list. If the license used to access the content is in the list, device refuses the license and blocks access.

As for security requirements of the basic DRM system, the solution proposes a compulsory mutual compliance check upon a content access transaction. That is, the SC must always check if the CoD is compliant by means of a compliance certificate issued by the CA-CoD, and the CoD, in its turn, must also always check the SC for compliance, also by means of a compliance certificate. These certificates are such that they must be renewed often. The privacy of the user is preserved with the use of temporary pseudonyms for the SC.

Concerning the transfer of licenses between users, the solution proposed also guarantees the security of the DRM system and the privacy of the user.

Security is dealt with via revocation of transferred licenses. This is achieved by means of the compliance certificate in (4), which includes the revocation list with all revoked licenses of a given SC. A requirement is that the compliance certificate in (4) be frequently renewed by the SC. This is done in the interest of both, the user and the DRM system, for the following reasons:

- in the interest of the user, it is done in order to minimise linkability via the pseudonym RAN of the user's content access requests to different content[9], and
- in the interest of the DRM system, it is done as a requirement of the CoD which checks if the certificate (and therefore the license revocation list) is too old via the value Time.

In case the user does not care much about the linkability problem (which would cause infrequent renewal actions on the part of the user), the renewal can be forced as a requirement of the CoD. As a consequence of this frequent renewal of compliance certificates, renewed values of revoked licenses of PK are also frequently available to the CoD.

User privacy in the license transfer process is achieved by means of anonymous licenses. These are licenses which can be redeemed at the CP for real usable licenses. They are anonymous since they do not include any identifier of the user who bought or exchanged his old license for the anonymous license. For security reasons, however, they must include a unique identifier that can be checked by the CP to prevent that an anonymous license is copied and redeemed multiple times. While guaranteeing security for the DRM system, this unique license identifier may be used by the CP to link the first user (who revoked his license) and the second user (who later redeems the anonymous license). Users' privacy in this case is preserved with the use of blind signatures.

The use of identity-based cryptography to generate the signing key pairs for the CP also enhances the system's security. In addition to greatly facilitating key management by the CP[10], the solution allows anyone to check the CP's signature on the anonymous license if they know the content identifier, the rights and the provider's name (since

---

[9] Note that, even if RAN changes, a given user's content access requests *to the same content and in the same CoD* allows that CoD to link the two actions via the license, but this only if the CoD keeps a record of each and every license shown to it.

[10] In this case, the CP does not need to store the list of all R×C key pairs anymore (a private key can be generated each time it is needed). And even in case storage is preferred over computation, only the private keys need to be stored.

these values make up the public key). The check of the CP's signature is essential in case the second user buys the license from the first user. The second user needs to be sure that the anonymous license he receives from the first user indeed refers to a given content with given rights, and that the license can be redeemed with a given CP.

Finally, regarding the distribution of licenses to domain members, the solution proposed also guarantees the privacy of users while preserving the security of the DRM system. This is achieved by means of an approach for private creation and functioning of an authorized domain.

The approach provides privacy concerning the domain structure by preventing the CP from learning which domain members compose a domain. A Domain Manager device is introduced to solve privacy problems within the domain. It is used for issuing rights to domain members, which in turn allows differentiations of rights among them without the involvement of the CP. This device is a compliant device, which is trusted by the CP, thus guaranteeing the DRM system's security. Furthermore, the Domain Manager device decreases the workload of the CP, taking over the management of countable rights. While solving the problem of late revocation of those rights, this further provides behavioral privacy for users in the domain.

References

1. Apple iTunes, http://www.apple.com/itunes/
2. Windows Media 9 Series: Digital Rights Management (DRM) http://www.microsoft.com/windows/windowsmedia/drm/default.aspx
3. IBM's Electronic Music Management System (EMMS), http://www-306.ibm.com/software/data/emms/
4. Open MagicGate, http://www.sony.net/Products/homeaudio/net_md/faq02.html
5. SmartRight, http://www.smartright.org/
6. W. Jonker, J.-P. Linnartz, Digital rights management in consumer electronics products, IEEE Signal Processing Magazine, Volume: 21 , Issue: 2 , March 2004 Pages:82 – 91
7. S.A.F.A. van den Heuvel, W. Jonker, F.L.A.J. Kamperman, P.J. Lenoir, "Secure Content Management in Authorised Domains", In Proceedings of the International Broadcasting Convention (IBC), 2002.
8. J. Feigenbaum, M. J. Freedman, T. Sander and A. Shostack, *Privacy Engineering for Digital Rights Management Systems*, In Proceedings of the ACM Workshop on Security and Privacy in Digital Rights Management, 2001.
9. C. Conrado, F. Kamperman, G.J. Schrijen and W. Jonker, *Privacy in an Identity-based DRM System*, Proceedings of the 14th International Workshop on Databases and Expert Systems Applications, Prague, Czech Republic, 2003.
10. A. Lysyanskaya, *Pseudonymous Systems*, Master's Thesis at the Massachusetts Institute of Technology, June 1999.
11. D. Chaum, *Blind signatures for untraceable payments*, Advances in Cryptology: Proceedings of Crypto'82, Springer-Verlag, 1982.
12. F. Zhang and K. Kim, *ID-Based Blind Signature and Ring Signature from Pairings*, Proc. of Asiacrypt 2002, LNCS, Springer-Verlag, vol. 2501, pp. 533-47, 2002.

Management of Private Data: Addressing User Privacy and Economic, Social, and Ethical Concerns*

Dawn Jutla[1], Peter Bodorik[2], and Deyun Gao[2]

[1] Sobey School of Business, Saint Mary's University
Halifax, Nova Scotia, Canada
Dawn.Jutla@smu.ca
[2] Faculty of Computer Science, Dalhousie University
Halifax, Nova Scotia, Canada
bodorik@cs.dal.ca

Abstract. Coordinated Web services can help alleviate user's privacy and economic, social, and ethical concerns that arise from third parties' access and use of user private data. This paper focuses on the requirements and design of such services in support of a client-side private data management system. Appropriate management of private data on the client side can both educate and assure users that their privacy is well guarded, and that their private data is being used by entities which satisfy economic and/or ethical user concerns. Our solutions describe novel Web services, interaction with P3P agents, and a client-side privacy architecture. A preliminary prototype implementation of our Web services using standard UDDI, SOAP, and WSDL technologies and rudimentary delay estimates are briefly discussed.

Keywords: P3P, Privacy Web Services, Private Data Management

1 Introduction

Industry watchdog Gartner Group has predicted that, by 2006, the number one barrier to electronic business and commerce will be user concerns over information privacy (Gartner, 2003). Empirical evidence shows users' trust in electronic business can be heightened by pragmatic means such as the use of privacy enhancing tools at the client-side, and simple support mechanisms at the business side (Jutla et al. 2004). Thus users' influence on business' fair information practices will increase as we become empowered with more powerful online privacy tools. Businesses, in future, could use their handling of online privacy as a competitive advantage as opposed to a cost or barrier to business opportunities. An example is the business that appears as a hit on search results pages as search engines become enabled with adding user privacy preferences to search criteria. AT&T scientists are currently building such a prototype search engine incorporating agents based on the Platform for Privacy Preferences (P3P) specification (Byers et al. 2004).

---

* This work was supported in part by the Canadian National Science and Engineering Research Council (NSERC) Grant #203111.

W. Jonker and M. Petković (Eds.): SDM 2004, LNCS 3178, pp. 100–117, 2004.

Although privacy is a major concern, it is not the only concern when considering handling of private data. Users would also like to be assured that their data is being shared with entities or businesses that they consider to use ethical labor and work practices, or who are environmentally friendly. They may also be concerned about market dislocation in a global economy. Many citizens, especially small business owners support local or national economies, and may express this by a preference to buy Canadian, for example.

Important technical projects, such as P3P, address privacy. At heart, P3P provides an XML vocabulary and a data model for supporting user's online privacy. The P3P protocol and agents are designed for the automatic machine reading of Web sites' privacy policies and their comparison with user privacy preferences specified at the client-side. P3P-enabling of a Web site refers to the business' storage of its privacy policy in XML-based P3P format on its Web site. Currently support of P3P from business stands at 30 percent of top 100 Web sites and 23% of top 500 Web sites are P3P-enabled (Cranor 2003). Top 100 refers to the top 100 most visited Web sites. Adoption figures are not yet available for AT&T Bird. Judging from one author's observation of 150 university students' enthusiastic reaction to Bird, adoption figures will be favorable for the 18-24 year old demographic. While P3P agents and the P3P platform are significant steps for Web users' privacy protection, in this paper we will motivate complementary Web services, extensions to P3P agents, and other private client-side data management components to increase the user's control or management of his/her private data. As noted before, we want to allow the user to have control and manage his/her private data for purposes beyond privacy – purposes that include users' concerns over relationships with sites that have social and ethical values, and economic interests that are in conflict with those of the user.

The paper organization is as follows. Section 2 provides an example scenario to motivate and clearly position where our private data management solutions, including Web services, fit in the world of user concerns over private data. Section 3 presents the client-side private data management architecture and its agent objects that invoke Web services for further management support. Section 4 presents the design of Web services in UML. In section 5, implementation of the Web services, including access to a prototype privacy ontology that we created for the *Canadian Personal Information Protection and Electronic Documents Act (PIPEDA)*, and a generic user regulatory agent illustrate the implementation and execution feasibility of our Web-services design for electronic private data management. Related work is summarized in section 6. The final section offers summary and conclusions.

2 Example User Scenario and Requirements

Consider a busy professional living in the US who is seeking an online pharmacy to fill a prescription. She invokes the Google search engine and searches on "online pharmacy" keyword string. She sifts through the results and finds several Canadian pharmacies that have considerably lower prices for the medication. (We acknowledge that some large drug companies are introducing governance policies to suppress this practice, however the example is still applicable and analogies can be drawn across industries.) She normally buys from Walblue's with which she enjoys a trusted relationship. Switching to a Canadian supplier (CanPharma.ca) for this medication has uncertainty overhead associated with it.

Areas of uncertainty involve mainly privacy concerns, but also security, ethical, economic, and social concerns. The economic concern here is for herself as opposed to a local economy. Various issues that she may be concerned about are:

(1) She wants to know all the intended purposes/uses and possible dissemination of her medical information.
(2) She wants to do business only with firms that post a privacy policy.
(3) She wants to know that the business' privacy practices match her privacy preferences and be alerted if they do not.
(4) She wants a store that will not only encrypt her credit card information but also the prescription contents of her shopping basket.
(5) She wants to know whether her privacy preferences match the privacy practices of each of the pharmacy's third party business partners.
(6) She wants to know whether privacy laws and authorities exist in Canada to enforce the intentions stated within the privacy policies on the pharmacies' web sites.
(7) She also does not want to do business with a company that has CheatersInc or UnGreenCompany as a third party business partner because she considers these to be unethical or environmentally-unfriendly.
(8) She does not want to have her information shared with a third party business partner that is in a country with poor privacy laws.
(9) She does not want to deal with a company that shares customer data with a third party partner originating from a country with human rights abuses.
(10) She wants to know which laws/regulations on privacy and data protection are applicable to the context of her transaction.
(11) She wants to know which law/regulation on privacy and data protection has precedence for her transaction.
(12) She wants to know that she does not inadvertently provide information on a Web form at this site that goes against her stated privacy preferences. For instance, she has a preference not to give out her age, but she provides a site with her birth-date and weight in the context of buying prescription medication.
(13) She would like to negotiate a quick electronic contract with CanPharma.ca, in which the company becomes obligated to destroy her data if it and its assets are sold to another company.
(14) When she returns to CanPharma.ca, she would like to review her information and contracts.
(15) She wants to review her privacy beliefs for this site when she returns to CanPharma.ca.
(16) She wants to maintain online privacy beliefs for particular sectors.

Analyzing these requirements, we see that current P3P agents will support only the first three requirements on this list. The rest of these requirements can be supported by our private data management architecture. Requirement 4 can be satisfied by an extension to P3P with a <SAFEGUARDS> tag and accompanying extension of the P3P agent's matching algorithm to do a SAFEGUARDS comparison. Satisfying requirements 5-9 are the focus of the cooperating Web services introduced in this paper. Data support in a Web privacy ontology combined with client-side data support is envisaged to support requirements 10-11. Data support on the client-side to satisfy requirements 12-16 are provided in the client-side architecture briefly described in the next section. However, agents to implement negotiation, contracts, and client-side monitors for privacy are the subject of another report (He 2004). To be clear, we focus solely on motivating, designing, and implementing Web services to support private data management and which satisfy requirements 5-9 in this paper.

2.1 User Interface for Input of Preferences

Interface design is not a central issue for this paper. Yet it will be extremely important to the viability of any e-privacy or private data management application. Unless we have a breakthrough in UI design that is widely adopted in the coming year, it appears that form-based user interfaces and Y/N controls such as checkboxes or radio buttons are the most familiar, convenient, and user-friendly means to receive input into a system. Thus for the purposes of this paper, where we would like the reader to visualize a user setting preferences, we opt to suggest useful extensions to a form with similar content to the Privacy Preference Settings form that AT&T Bird uses (see www.privacybird.com/tour/1_2_beta/ privacypreferences.html):

We would add the following items to that form or to a subform that deals with third party-recipients:

- Warn me about companies that share customer information with other companies that do not have privacy statements
- Warn me about companies that share with other companies whose practices violate my privacy, ethical, and/or social preferences
- Warn me about a company that has a third party partner that is on my blocked list
- Warn me about businesses, 3rd party, or otherwise, that are in jurisdictions with no enforcement of the fair information practices

We acknowledge that input forms need to be short and P3P and P3P agents such as Bird kept functionality to an important core in order to improve chances of widespread adoption. Nonetheless, completeness around user privacy and private data handling concerns should be explored.

3 Architecture and Web-Services for Privacy

Empirical results obtained from structural equation modeling analysis of user data (Jutla et al. 2004) show that the adoption of *user intervention (UIV)* tools such as P3P-based agents, encryption, cookie cutters, pseudonymizers, and anonymizers increase users trusting beliefs in e-business and in Internet-based trust. These and other research results motivate the creation of client-side private data management architectures that are based on the industry recommended P3P protocol, and that are open to other user intervention tool add-ons. In (Bodorik and Jutla 2003, Jutla and Bodorik 2004a), a client-side privacy architecture based on the P3P platform is proposed and elaborated. The architecture fosters user's perception of control and thus increases user's trusting intentions to conduct e-business.

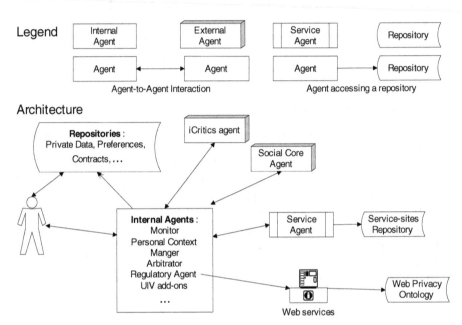

Fig. 3.1. Private Data Management Architecture.

We extend the original e-privacy architecture with the Web services proposed in this paper, thereby moving the architecture to the realm of private data management. A much simplified diagram depicting the resulting architecture is shown in Figure 3.1. The figure shows two key architectural components: a client-side component and a Web-side component (the regulatory web privacy ontology). The architecture includes internal and external agents and their interaction and access to repositories containing private data and privacy control information. For simplicity, the figure represents a number of internal agents by one agent icon and, similarly, a number of repositories by one repository icon. The repositories icon generically represents a number of repositories to store *private data, preferences, profile, contracts, service-site data, history, specific regulations,* and *audit trails*. The internal agent icon represents the following agents and services:

- *Monitor* agent that observes the user's actions and reports this to the user's *personal context* manager. Motivation for this agent is that users are known to take actions in contradiction to stated, static privacy preferences (Spiekermann et al. 2001). The architecture supports dynamic induction of a user's privacy preferences from multiple inputs including the monitor feed.

- *Arbitrator* agent that negotiates, with a human-in-the-loop escalation approach, privacy contract(s) with web sites.
- *Personal context* agent that maintains the context within which the user operates, provides the user with information on the context and her action, particularly when her preferences and actions conflict, and seeks her guidance/instructions related to preferences in context. The personal context agent has a preference induction engine that maintains the user's dynamically changing preferences within contexts. We elaborate on contexts and context agent in (Jutla and Bodorik 2004b).
- *Regulatory* agent maintains user privacy preferences and information about privacy regulations, guidelines, rules, and any user-pertinent privacy governance information that guide the user privacy agents during user transactions with service-sites. This agent invokes the Web private data management services described in this paper.
- Web services, shown in the figure, provide information about regulations that apply in different privacy regions/countries, information to be used by user agent(s) to adjust privacy preferences accordingly and by the user to take appropriate actions in terms of managing her private data collected by service sites.
- The Web privacy ontology structure(s) (ideally there should be a number of these ontologies – at least one per country, and possibly one per legal domain that deals with private data) shown in Figure 3.3, and presented in section 3.3, support the needs, for regulatory information over private data, of the client-side internal regulatory agent.

3.1 Data Model for Client-Side Private Data Management System

The data model for the private data management architecture, including data repositories for the *regulatory* agent (which invokes cooperating Web services to maintain a coherent regulatory knowledge base for the user), is shown in Figure 3.2. The diagram shows relationships among interacting objects, and significant attributes of these key objects. We use this diagram merely to show what types of information the client-side architecture stores. Specifically, the Web services populate the Regulation and Regulatory Belief stores. Information may be stored in RDF or OWL format in an ontology structure to promote storage of richer knowledge around user beliefs. The intent is to have semantic information kept on subjects such as jurisdiction, regulation, users' regulatory beliefs, business, users' trusting beliefs about a business, transaction context, user information, user role information, and user preferences per role information.

Jurisdiction covers information on geographical jurisdiction, legal, international, as well as community, and association guidelines. Regulation-related information includes applicable laws and other type regulations related to privacy per jurisdiction. A user context is made up of a set of beliefs about the current situation including user preference beliefs about release of certain data, trusting beliefs in business (substitute government, community, individual or other stakeholder instead of business), regulatory beliefs, and beliefs around transactions. Transaction refers to e-commerce related transactions such as browse, buy, register, and collaborate. The intent is for the user context to be also composed of beliefs around each type of transaction. For example, users may have a belief that a surf transaction implies potential for his/her clickstream data to be collected.

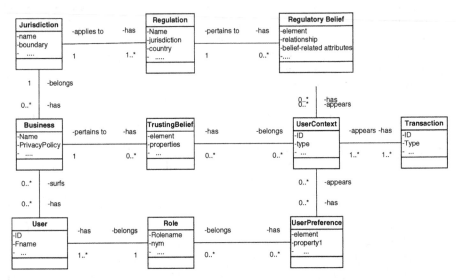

Fig. 3.2. A Data Model for private data management architecture.

3.2 Regulatory Privacy Ontology and Services

We have proposed a model for high level Web privacy ontology reported in (Jutla and Bodorik 2004a). We have also implemented one layer of this privacy ontology (Jutla et al. 2004b). In this paper, by adding P3P tags to the concepts and their definitions in the regulatory privacy ontology, we facilitate a Web service to perform a *three-way comparison among user preferences, business practices, and government regulations.* This comparison could be useful to an Internet user in several ways. A comparison between the contents of P3P elements representing business privacy practices and those representing privacy law may result in highlighting to the user (1) omissions in the business' P3P policy statements, or (2) concerns of mismatch of interpretation of privacy legislation. The P3P specification is not yet mature enough in terms of element definitions to cleanly handle many legal subtleties – hence a Web service can be useful to the user in flagging absence/presence, or ambiguity, of fair information principles regarding privacy as defined in law in the business' practices expressed in P3P policies.

Accessing privacy ontologies containing information expressed using P3P tags, can facilitate the user in populating their user preferences in an informed way. A P3P-agent comparison of user privacy preferences and the corresponding concepts in a regulatory Web privacy ontology can flag user inattention to details in their user preferences ruleset. For instance, the user's preference rule may state that a data element may be retained by a web-site company indefinitely while an applicable law may limit the retention of private data to six years.

In this paper we use WSDL (W3C WSDL 2003) to describe the functionality of each Web privacy ontology service, the sequence and cardinality of messages sent/received by a service operation, and binding specifications to multiple protocols (e.g. SOAP, HTTP, and MIME). WSDL files are defined for (a) GetPrivateDataConcerns(context), (b) GetPrivacyLaws(country), (c) GetFIPsInfo (principlename, country, privacylaw) where FIPS is the acronym for fair information practices, (d) MatchPolicyAndLaws(SitePolicy, jurisdiction), PrivateDataSearchService(SearchCriteria), and so on.

3.3 Web-Side Architectural Components and Services

The client-side *Private Data Management (PDM)* system includes Web-services that must exist to provide the users with requisite and useful privacy knowledge in support of the user's activities on the Web. Figure 3.3 illustrates our Web-services architectural model. Service providers first register their services with the *Universal Discovery, Description, and Integration (UDDI)* service – shown in the figure as step 1. The regulatory agent finds/discovers a service through UDDI directory lookup, shown as step 2, and binds/invokes a service (step 3) that may provide for composition of private data management services to answer deceptively simple, but yet complex, user queries on private data handling, and receives summary results (step 8).

Furthermore, these Web-services require a privacy knowledge base supported by an ontology. More specifically, a number of ontologies, spanning various countries and regulations regarding handling of private data, will be required. We utilize a standard, generic UDDI directory to get access to these ontological resources. We assume the extension of domain-specific classification for UDDI, in this case domain-specific classification for private data handling. The regulatory agent accesses the functionality of the UDDI registry through invoking a set of public Web services interface methods. The additional interface Web methods to the UDDI registry may be (recall PDM is an acronym for private data management):

a. GetProviderWSDL(providerID, aPDMService, nJurisdiction) where providerID is an output parameter that contains a list of providers that can perform aPDMService. The aPDMService input parameter represents a generic name for a particular private data management service, and the nJurisdiction input parameter refers to one or more jurisdictions. An example of aPDMService is "GetViolationPenalties" where the latter refers to retrieving providers that can identify legal penalties for handling private data violations in the specified jurisdiction(s). In February 2004, the P3P committee added a useful <JURISDICTION> extension to the <RECIPIENT> tag which makes aPDMService more easily feasible. We had previously identified the need for a Jurisdiction P3P tag, thus illustrating how development of privacy/private data Web services, and more importantly user requirements, can drive the maturity of the P3P vocabulary and vice versa.

b. SetProviderWSDL(providerID, aPDMService, nJurisdiction, WSDL) is obvious and adds/updates the WSDL entry for the corresponding supplier, service, and jurisdiction.

c. QOSProvider(aPDMService, QOS_list) returns a list of suppliers of private data related services based on quality of service (QoS) input parameters such as distance, reputation, reliability, availability, timeliness, and cost. The distance QoS parameter is perhaps the most interesting as it is intended to be the result of a distance function that measures what is the "closest" service to what is being requested.

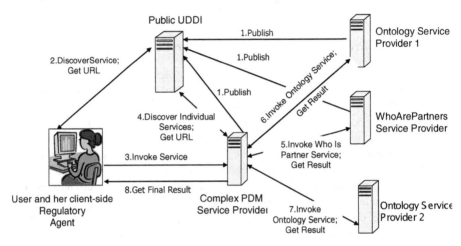

Fig. 3.3. Architectural Model of Web Services for Private Data Management.

4   Modeling Web Services for Private Data Management

Consider a user P3P agent which read in Business Technology Services (BTS) Inc.'s privacy statement that BTS "may share consumer information with its strategic partners". Also suppose that a user sets the requirement in her preferences to find out who the company's partners are. The P3P agent communicates this requirement to the regulatory agent which could then issue a query "who are BTS's partners" to an external Web Service named WhoArePartners (see Figure 4.1). The invocation of this service is not left up to the P3P agent, rather recall that one functional role of the regulatory agent is to maintain client-side knowledge about the users' trusting beliefs for various companies.

For a more complex scenario, the regulatory agent may ask "who are BTS's partners and where are BTS's partners based? " If answers include that one partner is in Japan, the other in India, and a third in England, then the regulatory agent will invoke privacy Web services to determine the level of privacy protection provided by each jurisdiction's laws. Other Web services that examine other laws that deal with the handling of private data, such as consumer protection laws, can also be invoked.

We design a Web service to perform the *three-way comparison* of user's privacy preferences, business privacy policies, and government laws relating to the handling of private data.

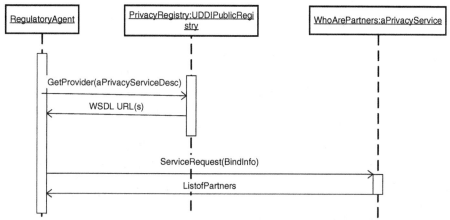

Fig. 4.1. WhoArePartners Service.

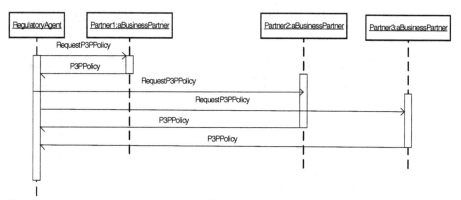

Fig. 4.2. Simultaneous matching of User BPreferences and Partners' Policies (only 3 partners shown).

We model example composition of Web services for private data management using simplified UML sequence diagrams for dynamic modeling. The three-way, or ComplexPDMService (Figure 4.4.), service is composed of two Web services, shown in 4.1, and 4.3 respectively. The first individual Web service, WhoArePartners, finds, say three, partnering companies. The simultaneous comparison of the user privacy preference with each business partner's P3P policy is designed as per Figure 4.2, and executed on the client-side. Three user P3P agents simultaneously compare the users' private data preferences with the three partners' site policies. Another Web service for comparing each partner's P3P policy with jurisdictional privacy regulations or guidelines for fair information practice is shown in Figure 4.3.

The ComplexPDMService, shown in Figure 4.4, combines findings from the other 2 Web services and P3P agents (Figures 4.1, 4.2 and 4.3) and returns the results to the user regulatory agent which then recommends an appropriate action to the user. The implementation of these Web service designs are discussed in the next section.

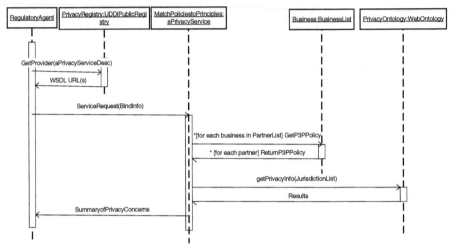

Fig. 4.3. Matching Business Policies and Jurisdictional Principles for Privacy.

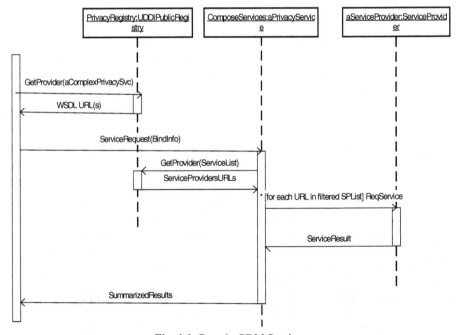

Fig. 4.4. ComplexPDM Service.

5 Implementation

Thus far we have implemented the infrastructure for the Web services described above. The P3P agents have been implemented, and user preferences and contextual information have been implemented in an OWL structure on the client-side. While P3P agents use the preference knowledge in the client-side structure, other agents can access and modify this OWL structure for automating contextual decision-making around e-privacy. This contextual decision-making is the reason we chose OWL to store preferences on the client-side, rather than use APPEL. The Web Service in Figure 4.3 retrieves regulatory information about a jurisdiction's fair information practices from an experimental regulatory privacy ontology on the Web (we created and stored this ontology in the Sesame database in the Netherlands) which returns results that are used for comparison with the business's policies.

Currently we have the Web services communication for the WhoArePartners Web service (Figure 4.1) but have not implemented full functionality. We also note that the WhoAre Partners service is particularly challenging as we may need to handle cascading sets of partners. That is, each third party partner may have in turn its third party partner. Governance in a firm or jurisdiction must be able to set limits as to whether to cascade, or to assume that the cascade level is one, as in the case when the user is assured that the original firm has a contract with its third party partner not to further share any data sent to them with other organizations. Alternatively, it would be, functionally but not organizationally, easier for P3P to be extended to encourage companies to list third party partners through addition of a PARTNERS tag. As most companies are not compelled to do partner disclosure, we are uncertain whether there could be consensus towards such a P3P extension. The case for it will be made depending on how pro-active businesses get in contributing to online trust.

The service in 4.4 is partially implemented. We do not have automatic composition of services in the ComposedPDMService as envisioned. Rather we have implemented a bouquet service where we fixed the individual services that created the aggregate. Another incremental version will add a reasonable algorithm based on fuzzy matching and QoS parameters for selecting the right aggregation of services. We will also be investigating Web Services Choreography Interface, and OWL-S, the Web Ontology Language for Services, for a more sophisticated version of our Web service shown in Figure 4.4.

We chose to implement our Web services using components of two of the major Java Web service tools, Java Web Services Developer Pack (JWSDP) version 1.3 from Sun Microsystems, and Web Service Development Kit (WSDK) version V5.1 from IBM. We used the Java API for XML-based RPC (JAX-RPC) v1.1, the Ant Build Tool 1.5.4, and Apache Tomcat v5 development container from JWSDP. From WSDK we used UDDI4J, IBM WebSphere UDDI v2.0 registry, and eclipse plug-ins to enable browsing for Web services in UDDI registries, to create Web services from WSDL definitions, and to publish and unpublish Web services to a UDDI registry. JWSDP 1.3 contains the latest versions of Java and XML technologies for building reliable and secure Web services. It also utilizes the industry well know open standard

Ant and Tomcat as the compiling and run time environment. We used IBM's UDDI 2.0 registry as it exactly meets the UDDI 2.0 specification.

We publish a tModel and service onto IBM's private UDDI directory through a graphical interface. Figure 5.1 shows the results returned from searching all the registered businesses with the name starting with "Eprivacy" from Websphere's UDDI private directory. We also did a public UDDI version.

The Web services we created are a "Complex PDM Service" (Figure 4.4) with modifications as described), multiple "Privacy Ontology Query Service" (partly Figure 4.3), and one "WhoArePartners Service" (4.1). All are implemented as Java XML RPC services which accept SOAP XML requests. Both the internal regulatory agent and the composite Web service are implemented as JAX-RPC clients. The JAX-RPC client is implemented using a dynamic proxy model which creates the proxy from WSDL file at run time. Depending on the regulatory query, the complex Web service propagates multiple threads to invoke multiple individual ontology query Web services in parallel. After this the complex Web service wraps up the answers and passes the result to the regulatory agent.

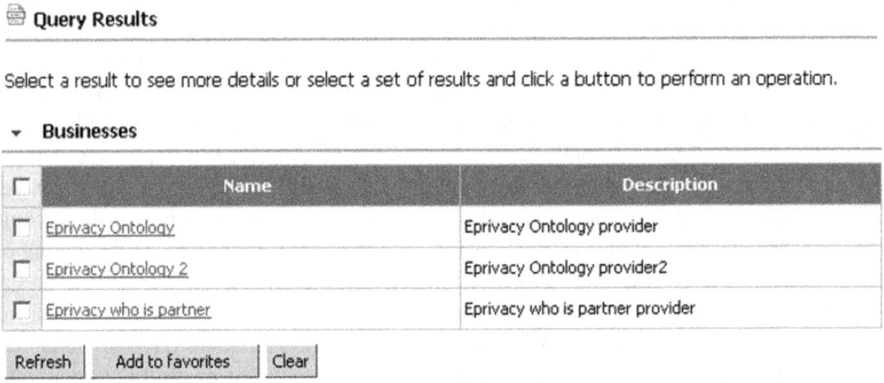

☷ **Query Results**

Select a result to see more details or select a set of results and click a button to perform an operation.

▾   **Businesses**

☐	Name	Description
☐	Eprivacy Ontology	Eprivacy Ontology provider
☐	Eprivacy Ontology 2	Eprivacy Ontology provider2
☐	Eprivacy who is partner	Eprivacy who is partner provider

| Refresh | Add to favorites | Clear |

Fig. 5.1. Services registered in Private UDDI Directory.

Our implementation of the privacy ontology sits on the Sesame server. Sesame is an open source RDF database which provides an interface for both local and remote access. In our "Privacy Ontology Query Service", we import the Sesame API 1.0 in our Web service program. The "Privacy Ontology Query Service" makes HTTP connections and then passes the RQL inquiry strings to the remote Sesame server. The Sesame server then responds with a result-table to the requester.

We created four versions of the Web Services infrastructure for the ComplexPDMService. The first version is illustrated in Figure 3.3 where all private data management services are found in a public UDDI directory. The second version was created to test the overhead difference in parallel connections to ontology service providers as opposed to serial connections. The third version is the same as the second version except that the individual services that make up a complex private data management service is found in a private UDDI directory, while the ComplexPDMService

Provider is found through public UDDI lookup as before – this is shown in Figure 5.2. Version 4 uses only private UDDI directory lookups.

Early measurements, at various times of day and week, show that the longest delay is on access to IBM's public UDDI directory. The time to access the public UDDI directory was on average 25 times slower than access to the privacy ontology stored in Sesame. Version 2 showed that parallelizing ontology searches sped up service time by 16% or approximately by 5 seconds. Version 3 shows us that access to a private UDDI directory is 40 times faster than access to IBM's public UDDI directory. In version 3, the round-trip delay for results to be returned to the regulatory agent was half that of version one (14 seconds vs. 27 seconds). Version 4 clocked the best round-trip delay (from regulatory service initiation of first UDDI lookup and return of final results from the ComplexPDMService) at 7s. These times are acceptable for informational services not on the critical path of a user transaction. However the times are expected to improve once platforms are optimized to support Web services.

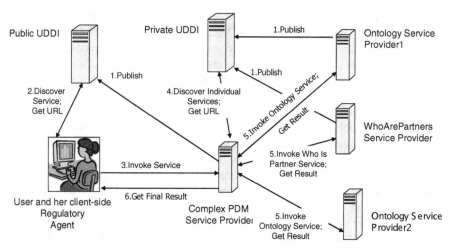

Fig. 5.2. Public UDDI Directory to find the ComplexPDMService Provider, and a Private UDDI to find Ontology and WhoArePartners Service Providers.

6 Related Work

The *Platform for Privacy Preferences (P3P)* was published by W3C in 2002 (P3P 2004) and, regardless of some shortcomings, it is the only contender on which to base privacy mechanisms. The latest working draft of P3P version 1.1 was released in April 2004. A number of tools have been developed for Web-masters to post privacy policies in P3P format. Microsoft IE6 and Netscape Navigator 7 Web browser provide basic P3P functionality. AT&T provides a P3P agent called Privacy Bird as an add-on to IE6 browser. The add-on checks for P3P policies for all content on a page visited by the user, compares them to the user preferences and reports on the match using a traffic-light metaphor in its interface. A study of users mainly over 50 year olds reports that the Privacy Bird is a useful agent (Cranor 2002). The user privacy agents simplify the task of examining the privacy policies posted by the Web-sites and determining whether or not the they are acceptable to the users/clients – a task that is cumbersome and disliked by users (Cranor 2002).

In contrast to client-side P3P agents, Agrawal et al. (2003) proposes an efficient server-based P3P-based implementation of the comparison of user preferences and a site's P3P-enabled privacy policy. Although the IBM researchers' ideas have many advantages, including convenience and performance, our main concern with it is that users' preferences must be uploaded to the server side, thus possibly enabling further user profiling. But more importantly, the server-side scheme is not suitable for e-commerce at this stage where initial online trust formation is still an issue, particularly, among on-line buyers and small and medium sized enterprises which comprise 99% of businesses in various countries. The scheme in (Agrawal et al. 2003) scheme may be more suitable for large businesses, or those businesses in trusted sectors such as the financial sector, or may get more user acceptance after e-commerce matures considerably more over the next decade.

The work that most resembles the links, between user's data and business, in our architecture is the iManager architecture (Jendricke and Markotten 2000) that contains databases for personal data, personas, URLs, and rules. The iManager does not support significant stakeholder influence or social, economic, and regulatory feeds. Usability results are not yet available for the iManager to the best of our knowledge. It does not describe how the control of the personal identity is affected by the external entities/stakeholders.

Several proposals exist for *trusted third party (TTP)* storage of user profiles and preferences. A proposal to access a user profile, anywhere and anytime, through any device, is described in [Cingil 2002]. The user is required to do a browser-login to the TTP and her surfing behavior, via click-stream, is monitored and captured locally and used to update the user's profile. The major problem is the centralized and authoritative approach that does not allow the user control over the collected information. Many users prefer their profiles to be fragmented across many devices since fragmentation provides a form of privacy protection on its own, similarly to un-synthesized databases.

Tumer et al. (2003) propose a privacy framework for Web services. This work differs considerably from ours, in that its intent is to organize mechanisms to minimize private data being handed to Web services, and to provide privacy in Web services, in general. In contrast, our Web services are informational, dedicated to providing information pertinent to the handling of private data. Our Web services avoid handing over the user's private data. However Tumer's (2003) framework can complement our Web services, or we can apply the framework to our Web services, if we should have to pay or register for access to the various ontologies and WhoArePartners services for example. It is our hope that governments will provide free read access to future privacy ontologies. We also recommend that the P3P vocabulary would benefit users if a PARTNERS tag can be added to list firms' third party partners. Then P3P agents could replace the WhoArePartners service.

Our work builds on the client-centric vs. server centric concept as evidence, both quantitative (Jutla et al. 2004, Novak et al. 2000) and qualitative (Aggarwal et al.

2004, Bodorik and Jutla 2003, Jutla 2003, Jutla and Bodorik 2004a), point to increasing users' *control* over online private data contributes to an increase in their trusting beliefs and intentions to engage in e-business behaviours with firms. We propose informational Web services for private data management including for the purposes of online privacy. We show how P3P agents can interact with these Web Services to provide the user with more information to make informed decision making about whether he/she can trust the site with which he/she is dealing.

The Resource Centre on P3P of JRC (JRCarchitecture 2004) has a basic privacy architecture that does not include access to Web-services or cooperation with *Trusted Third Parties (TTP)* as yet. However, it is an impressive platform for extended research on e-privacy that already has a demonstration site and various downloadable tools. Furthermore, an ontology for data protection is in the planning stage. It is a substantial and long-term undertaking that involves education and participation of the various stake-holders in arriving at the standard ontology (JRContology 2004).

In a two-page position paper, (Kim 2002) argues that privacy be built into the Semantic Web and stresses the need for privacy ontology. This is also one of the conclusions in (Rezgui 2003). We have proposed a high level model for a privacy ontology in Jutla and Bodorik (2004a), and implemented an ontology fragment as proof-of-concept (Xu 2004). The Web services described in this paper accesses this ontology stored on Sesame, an RDF database created in the highly regarded European OntoKnowledge project.

7 Summary and Conclusions

In this paper, we first motivate the need for informational Web services around handling of private data by describing a user scenario and identifying the user requirements. Then, we compose combinations of Web services, to form the backbone of sophisticated querying of distributed ontologies and knowledge bases, in order to provide the user with reliable advice around private data exposure. There are possibly many laws to which a business must comply when handling customer personal information such as consumer protection laws and sector-dependent laws, such as the Alberta Health Information Protection Act in the province of Alberta, Canada, or HIPAA in the US. Labor laws govern employee personal information. Depending on the circumstances of the dispute, one law can have precedence over the other. Clearly, several regulatory Web ontologies will hold semantic information to support privacy Web services. Knowledge bases for privacy need not only be about laws and acts regarding handling of private data but may provide users with industry standards, and cultural guidelines around privacy that may affect the transacting parties. We propose a novel three-way comparison using P3P tags, and suggest that these tags are embedded into the concepts and definitions within regulatory ontologies containing knowledge about the handling of private data. We designed and partially implemented a Web service to achieve the 3-way P3P comparison proposal in this paper.

We illustrate how private data management can be implemented and executed through the interaction of Web services, P3P agents, and architectural component objects in our system. Our client-side private data management system is open and already inclusive of today's P3P agents. Not unexpectedly, users are saying that they would like to have integrated PET tools (Bayers 2003). User intervention add-ons such as cookie crushers and anonymizers can be hooked in a future version of our system. Encryption is obviously assumed as included in any privacy architecture. We need security for the Web services to prevent public inferences based on what sites we visit. However much of our Web services inputs/outputs contain information that is publicly available. An advantage of our client-side private data management architecture is that user preferences are never sent out over the net.

Fledgling regulatory ontologies are becoming a reality since semantic web and ontological engineering technologies are available and maturing, and international groups are interested in their development. Once these ontologies are in place the Web service proposed in this paper will produce more sophisticated and useful results. These Web services are applicable and may form an essential part of the private data management tool kit of the future global Web user.

References

1. Agrawal, R., Kiernan J., Srikant, R., Xu, Y. Implementing P3P Using Database Technology. *19th IEEE International Conference on Data Engineering*, India, (2003) p. 595-606.
2. Aggarwal, G., Bawa, M., Ganesan, P., Garcia-Molina, H., Kenthapadi, K., Mishra, N., Motwani, R., Srivastava, U., Thomas, D., Widom, J. Vision Paper: Enabling Privacy for the Paranoids, (2004) available at http://dbpubs.stanford.edu:8090/pub/2004-11.
3. Brandt, A. Privacy Watch: A Little Bird That Guards Your Online Privacy. *PCWorld*, December, (2002). Also: http://privacybird.com
4. Bayers, S., Cranor, L., and Kormann, D. Automated Analysis of P3P-Enabled Web Sites. *Proceedings of the 5th International Conference on Electronic Commerce (ICEEC2003)*, ACM Press, (2003), http://lorrie.cranor.org/pubs/icec03.html.
5. Bayers S., Cranor L.F., Lormann D. and McDaniel P. Searching for Privacy: Desing and Implementation of a P3P-Enabled Search Engine. *Proceedings of the 2004 Workshop on Privacy Enhancing Technologies (PET 2004)*, 26-28 May, (2004), Toronto, Canada.
6. Bodorik P. and Jutla D.N. Architecture for User-controlled e-Privacy, *ACM Symposium on Applied Computing, SAC 2003*, Technical Track on E-commerce Technologies, (2003) 609-616.
7. Cingil I. Supporting Global User Profiles Through Trusted Authorities, *SIGMOD Record, Vol. 31, NO. 1*, March, (2002), 1-17.
8. Cranor F.L., Arjula M., and Guduru P. Use of a P3P User Agent by Early Adopters. *Proceedings of the ACM Workshop on Privacy in the Electronic Society*. November, (2002).
9. Cranor F.L. P3P: Making Privacy Policies More Useful, *IEEE Security & Privacy*, November/December, (2003), 50-55.
10. Consumers Will Reshape the Future of CRM Marketing, December, (2003).
11. He, Y. On-line Negotiation of Private Data. *Technical Report SMU-CIS-04*, Saint Mary's University, Halifax, Nova Scotia, (2004).
12. Jendricke U. and Gerd tom Markotten, D. Usability meets Security – The Identity-Manager as your Personal Security Agent for the Internet. *16th Annual Computer Security Applications Conference*, New Orleans, Louisiana, (2000), 11-15.
13. JRC P3P Demonstrator Project: Introduction. http://p3p.jrc.it/presentations.27May-intro.ppt, last viewed January 12, (2004).

14. JRContology (2004) -- Ontology for Data Protection: (PRONTO),.
    http://p3p.jrc.it/presentations/OntologyEOI.doc, last viewed January 12, 2004.
15. Jutla D.N. Online Trust Models:Is Privacy In or Out, ?", In *e-Business in the 21st Century,* eds. Sharma S.K., and Gupta J., IDEAS Publishing, Heidelberg Press, Australia, (2003), pp.313-336.
16. Jutla D.N., and Bodorik P. Socio-Technical Architecture for Online Privacy. *IEEE Security and Privacy*, accepted, (2004a) in press.
17. Jutla D.N. and Bodorik P. PeCAN: An Architecture for User Privacy and Profiles in Electronic Commerce Contexts on the Semantic Web. *Information Systems*, (2004b) conditionally accepted.
18. Jutla D.N., Kelloway, E.K., Saifi, S. Evaluation of the Impact of User Intervention Mechanisms for Privacy on Online SME Trust. *IEEE Conference on E-Commerce*, San Diego, (2004a), 8 pages (to appear July 2004).
19. Jutla D.N., Das H. and Weatherbee T. Adding Cultural Variables to a Web Privacy Ontology. *IADIS e-Society 2004,* Avila, Spain, (2004b), 8 pages (to appear July 2004).
20. Kim, A., Joffman, L.J., and Martin, C.D. Building Privacy into the Semantic Web: An Ontology Needed Now. *Semantic Web Workshop 2002,* Hawaii USA, (2002).
21. Novak, T.P., Hoffman, D.L., Peralta, M. Building consumer trust online. *Communications of the ACM*, (2000) 42, 4:80-85.
22. P3P (2004) Platform for Privacy Preferences Project, http://www.w3.org/P3P/, last viewed on January 12, 2004.
23. Rezgui, A.M. and Eltoweissy, M.Y. Privacy on the Web: Facts, Challenges, and Solutions. *IEEE Security and Privacy,* November/December, (2003), 40-49.
24. Spiekermann, S., Grossklags, J., Berendt, B. e-Privacy in 2nd Generation Commerce: Privacy Preferences versus Actual Behavior. *ACM Conference on Electronic Commerce*, October 14-17, 2001, Florida, USA, (2001), pp. 38-47.
25. Tumer, A., Dogac, A., Toroslu, H. A Semantic based Privacy Framework for Web Services. *WWW03 WorkShop on e-Services and the Semantic Web*, *ESSW'03*, Budapest, Hungary, (2003).
26. W3C WSDL (2003); Web Services Description Language Version 2.0 Part 1: Core Language, Working Draft, 10, November 2003, available at
    http://www.w3.org/TR/2003/WD-wsdl20-20031110/

PeerTrust: Automated Trust Negotiation for Peers on the Semantic Web

Wolfgang Nejdl[1], Daniel Olmedilla[1], and Marianne Winslett[2]

[1] L3S and University of Hannover, Germany
{nejdl,olmedilla}@l3s.de
[2] Dept. of Computer Science, University of Illinois at Urbana-Champaign, USA
winslett@cs.uiuc.edu

Abstract. Researchers have recently begun to develop and investigate policy languages to describe trust and security requirements on the Semantic Web. Such policies will be one component of a run-time system that can negotiate to establish trust on the Semantic Web. In this paper, we show how to express different kinds of access control policies and control their use at run time using PeerTrust, a new approach to trust establishment. We show how to use distributed logic programs as the basis for PeerTrust's simple yet expressive policy and trust negotiation language, built upon the rule layer of the Semantic Web layer cake. We describe the PeerTrust language based upon distributed logic programs, and compare it to other approaches to implementing policies and trust negotiation. Through examples, we show how PeerTrust can be used to support delegation, policy protection and negotiation strategies in the ELENA distributed eLearning environment. Finally, we discuss related work and identify areas for further research.

Keywords: Automated Trust Negotiation, Peer-to-Peer, Semantic Web, Policy Languages

1 Introduction

As peer-to-peer architectures start to move into use for applications based on the Semantic Web, they must address the issue of access control for sensitive resources provided by peers in the network [9, 19], such as services, documents, roles, and capabilities. For example, in the Edutella infrastructure [15, 14, 16], each peer manages distributed resources described by RDF metadata, and interfaces to the Edutella network using a Datalog-based query language. The early Edutella testbeds focussed on providing distributed learning repositories in an environment where all resources are freely available; the main research focus was efficient searching for course-related information using appropriate queries over the metadata available for that information. More recently, however, the Edutella infrastructure has been deployed in the context of the EU/IST ELENA project [18], whose participants include e-learning and e-training companies, learning technology providers, and several universities and research institutes (see also http://www.elena-project.org/). To meet the needs for access control in this peer-to-peer network that connects commercial e-learning providers and learning management systems, Edutella must also support access control policies that describe who is allowed to access each document and service.

W. Jonker and M. Petković (Eds.): SDM 2004, LNCS 3178, pp. 118–132, 2004.

For example, suppose that E-Learn Associates manages a Spanish course in the peer-to-peer network, and Alice wishes to access the course. If the course is accessible free of charge to all police officers who live in and work for the state of California, Alice can show E-Learn her digital police badge to prove that she is a state police officer, as well as her California driver's license, and subsequently can gain access to the course at no charge.

However, Alice may not feel comfortable showing her police badge to just anyone; she knows that there are Web sites on the west coast that publish the names, home addresses, and home phone numbers of police officers. We can view her police badge as an item on the Semantic Web, protected by its own release policy. For example, Alice may only be willing to show her badge to companies that belong to the Better Business Bureau of the Internet. But with the introduction of this additional policy, access control is no longer the one-shot, unilateral affair that one finds in traditional distributed systems or in recent proposals for access control and information release on the Semantic Web [9, 19]: in order to see an appropriate subset of Alice's digital credentials, E-Learn will have to show that it satisfies the release policies for each of them; and in the process of demonstrating that it satisfies those policies, it may have to disclose additional credentials of its own, but only after Alice demonstrates that she satisfies the release policies for each of *them*; and so on. Thus the use of policies and digital credentials as a basis for access control on the semantic web raises a number of challenging run-time issues:

– How can Alice and E-Learn find out about each other's relevant access control and release policies, so that they can prove that they satisfy them?
– Given that there may be many ways that Alice can prove that she satisfies a particular policy of E-Learn's (by disclosing different subsets of her credentials), how can she decide which subset to disclose?
– Often Alice may not have in her possession all the credentials she needs to satisfy one of E-Learn's policies. For example, E-Learn may offer a discounted price for its French course if Alice can demonstrate that she is a student at an accredited university. Alice probably has her student ID in hand, but how can she automatically collect the necessary credentials to show that her university is accredited?
– Traditional distributed systems security solutions (e.g., Kerberos) are centralized, which runs counter to the autonomous, peer-to-peer nature of the Semantic Web. How can we meet all the above goals without resorting to a centralized approach, while still guaranteeing individual autonomy to the extent possible and simultaneously guaranteeing that Alice and E-Learn will be able to establish trust – i.e., that Alice will be able to access E-Learn's courses – if at all possible?

In this paper, we build upon the previous work on policy-based access control and release for the Semantic Web by showing how to use *automated trust negotiation* to answer these questions, as embodied in the PeerTrust approach to access control and information release. We start by introducing the concepts behind trust negotiation in section 2. We then introduce distributed logic programs to express and implement trust negotiation in a distributed environment, in section 3 and discuss PeerTrust's trust negotiation using distributed logic programs in detail in section 4. We discuss related work in section 5 and conclude with a brief look at further research issues.

2   Trust Negotiation

In traditional distributed environments, service providers and requesters are usually known to each other. Often shared information in the environment tells which parties can provide what kind of services and which parties are entitled to make use of those services. Thus, trust between parties is a straightforward matter. Even if on some occasions there is a trust issue, as in traditional client-server systems, the question is whether the server should trust the client, and not vice versa. In this case, trust establishment is often handled by uni-directional access control methods, such as having the client log in as a pre-registered user.

In contrast, the Semantic Web provides an environment where parties may make connections and interact without being previously known to each other. In many cases, before any meaningful interaction starts, a certain level of trust must be established from scratch. Generally, trust is established through exchange of information between the two parties. Since neither party is known to the other, this trust establishment process should be bi-directional: both parties may have sensitive information that they are reluctant to disclose until the other party has proved to be trustworthy at a certain level. As there are more service providers emerging on the Web every day, and people are performing more sensitive transactions (for example, financial and health services) via the Internet, this need for building mutual trust will become more common.

In the PeerTrust approach to automated trust establishment, trust is established gradually by disclosing credentials and requests for credentials, an iterative process known as *trust negotiation*. This differs from traditional identity-based access control and release systems mainly in the following aspects:

1. Trust between two strangers is established based on parties' properties, which are proven through disclosure of digital credentials.
2. Every party can define access control and release policies (*policies*, for short) to control outsiders' access to their sensitive resources. These resources can include services accessible over the Internet, documents and other data, roles in role-based access control systems, credentials, policies, and capabilities in capability-based systems.
3. In the approaches to trust negotiation developed so far, two parties establish trust directly without involving trusted third parties, other than credential issuers. Since both parties have policies, trust negotiation is appropriate for deployment in a peer-to-peer architecture, where a client and server are treated equally. Instead of a one-shot authorization and authentication, trust is established incrementally through a sequence of bilateral credential disclosures.

A trust negotiation is triggered when one party requests to access a resource owned by another party. The goal of a trust negotiation is to find a sequence of credentials $(C_1, \ldots, C_k, R)$, where R is the resource to which access was originally requested, such that when credential C_i is disclosed, its policy has been satisfied by credentials disclosed earlier in the sequence – or to determine that no such credential disclosure sequence exists. (For uniformity of terminology, we will say that R is *disclosed* when E-Learn grants Alice access to R.)

In practice, trust negotiation is conducted by security agents who interact with each other on behalf of users. A user only needs to specify policies for credentials and other resources. The actual trust negotiation process is fully automated and transparent to users. Further, the above example used objective criteria for determining whether to allow the requested access. More subjective criteria, such as ratings from a local or remote reputation monitoring service, can also be included in a policy.

In the remainder of this paper we will show how to specify and apply policies and trust negotiation using distributed logic programs, building on the rule layer of the Semantic Web. Before we delve into details, though, let us highlight two general criteria for trust negotiation languages as well as two important features already mentioned briefly above. A more detailed discussion can be found in [17].

Well-defined semantics. Two parties must be able to agree on whether a particular set of credentials in a particular environment satisfies a policy. To enable this agreement, a policy language needs a clear, well-understood semantics.

Expression of complex conditions. A policy language for use in trust negotiation needs the expressive power of a simple query language, such as relational algebra plus transitive closure. Such a language allows one to restrict attribute values (e.g., age must be over 21) and relate values occurring in different credentials (e.g., the issuer of the student ID must be a university that ABET has accredited).

Sensitive policies. The information in a policy can reveal a lot about the resource that it protects. For example, who is allowed to see Alice's medical record – her parole officer? Her psychiatrist or social worker? Because policies can contain sensitive information, and because they may be shown to outsiders, they need to be protected like any other shared resource. Previous work on trust negotiation has looked at a variety of ways of protecting the information in policies. In this paper, we will use the protection scheme introduced in UniPro [21], which gives (opaque) names to policies and allows any named policy $P1$ to have its own policy $P2$, meaning that the contents of $P1$ can only be disclosed to parties who have shown that they satisfy $P2$. To give flexibility in assigning different levels of protection to different aspects of a policy, UniPro also allows the definition of a policy P to refer to other policy definitions by name.

Delegation. Trust negotiation research has also addressed the issue of delegation of authority. For example, rather than issuing student IDs directly, a university may delegate that authority to its registrar. Then student IDs from that university will not bear the digital signature of the university itself, but rather the signature of the registrar. To prove that Bob is a student at UIUC, then, he will have to present both his student ID and the (signed) policy from UIUC that delegates authority to the registrar to issue IDs. This level of detail will not be present in E-Learn's policy for giving student discounts, which will simply say that Bob has to be a student at UIUC. If E-Learn's policy says that Bob must be a student at an institution accredited by ABET, Bob faces additional challenges during negotiation: how can he find the credentials that show that his university is accredited, or conclude that no such credentials exist? Previous work on trust negotiation has addressed the questions of how to specify and reason about delegations of authority [11] and how to find credentials [12].

3   Distributed Logic Programs

3.1   Syntax

Definite Horn clauses. PeerTrust's language is based on first order Horn rules (definite Horn clauses), i.e., rules of the form

$$lit_0 \leftarrow lit_1, \ldots, lit_n$$

where each lit_i is a positive literal $P_j(t_1, \ldots, t_n)$, P_j is a predicate symbol, and the t_i are the arguments of this predicate. Each t_i is a term, i.e., a function symbol and its arguments, which are themselves terms. The head of a rule is lit_0, and its body is the set of lit_i. The body of a rule can be empty.

Definite Horn clauses are the basis for logic programs [13], which have been used as the basis for the rule layer of the Semantic Web and specified in the RuleML effort ([4, 5]) as well as in the recent OWL Rules Draft [7]. Definite Horn clauses can be easily extended to include negation as failure, restricted versions of classical negation, and additional constraint handling capabilities such as those used in constraint logic programming. Although all of these features can be useful in trust negotiation, we will instead focus on other more unusual required language extensions.

Definite Horn clauses are used in the Edutella infrastructure to represent each peer's knowledge about its local resources, including services, data, credentials, and the policies for its resources. Edutella also uses a restricted form of definite Horn clauses as the language peers use to query one another, as well as the language used to represent query answers. This language is a strict superset of relational algebra. On top of this definite Horn clause language, we need to add some additional features, discussed in the next sections.

References to other peers. The ability to reason about statements made by other peers is central to trust negotiation. For example, in section 2, E-Learn wants to see a statement from Alice's employer that says that she is a police officer. One can think of this as a case of E-Learn *delegating evaluation* of the query "Is Alice a police officer?" to the California State Police (CSP). Once CSP receives the query, the manner in which CSP handles it may depend on who asked the query. Thus CSP needs a way to specify which peer made each request that it receives. To express delegation of evaluation to another peer, we extend each literal lit_i with an additional *Authority* argument,

$$lit_i @ \text{Authority}$$

where *Authority* specifies the peer who is responsible for evaluating lit_i or has the authority to evaluate lit_i. For example, E-Learn's discount policy might mention policeOfficer("Alice") @ "CSP". If that literal evaluates to true, then CSP says that Alice is a California police officer. As another example, a company eOrg may have a policy that students at UIUC are preferred customers.

eOrg:
preferred(X) ← student(X) @ "UIUC".

This policy says that the UIUC peer is responsible for certifying the student status of a given person[1]. (For clarity, we prefix each rule by the peer in whose knowledge base it is included.)

The *Authority* argument can be a nested term containing a sequence of authorities, which are then evaluated starting at the outermost layer. For example, UIUC is unlikely to be willing to answer eOrg's query about whether Alice is enrolled at UIUC. A more practical approach is for eOrg to ask Alice to evaluate the query herself, i.e., to send eOrg her student ID:

eOrg:
student(X) @ "UIUC" ←
  student(X) @ "UIUC" @ X.

As mentioned earlier, CSP and UIUC may need a way of referring to the peer who asked a particular query. We accomplish this with *Context* literals that represent release policies for literals and rules, so that we now have literals and rules of the form

$$lit_i @ \text{Authority} \$ context_j$$
$$lit_i \leftarrow_{context_j} lit_1, \ldots, lit_{i-1}$$

For example, suppose that Alice has derived student("Alice") @ "UIUC" and she wishes to send this literal to eOrg. She can only do so if she is able to derive student("Alice") @ "UIUC" $ Requester = "eOrg". Here, Requester is a pseudovariable whose value is automatically set to the party that Alice is trying to send the literal or rule. If no context is specified for a literal or a rule, the default context 'Requester = Self' applies, implying that the literal or rule cannot be sent to any other peer. 'Self' is a pseudovariable whose value is a distinguished name of the local peer. The release policy for a literal can be cleanly specified in rules separate from those used to derive the literal, e.g.,

$$p(X_1, \ldots, X_n) \$ context_p (X_1, \ldots, X_n, \text{Requester, Self}) \leftarrow p(X_1, \ldots, X_n)$$

In this paper, we will strip the contexts from literals and rules when they are sent to another peer. However, sticky policies can be implemented by leaving contexts attached to literals and rules in messages and defining how to propagate contexts across modus ponens, so that a peer can control further dissemination of its released information in a non-adversarial environment.

Using the *Authority* and *Context* arguments, we can delegate evaluation of literals to other peers and also express interactions and the corresponding negotiation process between different peers. For example, consider E-Learn Associates' policy for free Spanish courses for California police officers:

E-Learn:
freeEnroll(Course, Requester) $ *true* ←
  policeOfficer(Requester) @ "CSP" @ Requester,
  spanishCourse(Course).

---

[1] In practice, this policy must be written as preferred(X) ← student(Y) @ "UIUC", authenticatesTo(X,Y), where authenticatesTo is an external predicate that allows Alice to prove at run time that she possesses the identity (i.e., the student ID number) under which she is known at UIUC.

If the user provides appropriate identification, then the policy for the free enrollment service is satisfied, and E-Learn will allow the user to access the service through a mechanism not shown here. In this example, the mechanism can transfer control directly to the enrollment service. For some services, the mechanism may instead give Alice a nontransferable token that she can use to access the service repeatedly without having to negotiate trust again until the token expires. The mechanism can also implement other security-related measures, such as creating an audit trail for the enrollment. When the policy for a negotiation-related resource such as a credential becomes satisfied, the runtime system may choose to include it directly in a message sent during the negotiation, as discussed later.

Signed rules. Each peer defines a policy for each of its resources, in the form of a set of definite Horn clause rules. These and any other rules that the peer defines on its own are its *local* rules. A peer may also have copies of rules defined by other peers, and it may use these rules in its proofs in certain situations. For example, Alice can use a rule (with an empty body in this case) that was defined by UIUC to prove that she is really a UIUC student:

Alice:
student("Alice") @ "UIUC"
   signedBy ["UIUC"].

In this example, the "signedBy" term indicates that the rule has UIUC's digital signature on it. This is very important, as E-Learn is not going to take Alice's word that she is a student; she must present a statement signed by the university to convince E-Learn. A signed rule has an additional argument that says who signed the rule. The cryptographic signature itself is not included in the logic program, because signatures are very large and are not needed by this part of the negotiation software. The signature is used to verify that the issuer really did issue the rule. We assume that when a peer receives a signed rule from another peer, the signature is verified before the rule is passed to the DLP evaluation engine. Similarly, when one peer sends a signed rule to another peer, the actual signed rule must be sent, and not just the logic programmatic representation of the signed rule.

More complex signed rules often represent delegations of authority. For example, the UIUC registrar can use a signed rule to prove that it is entitled to determine who is a student at UIUC:

"UIUC Registrar":
student(X) @ "UIUC" ←
   signedBy ["UIUC"]
  student(X) @ "UIUC Registrar".

If Alice's student ID is signed by the registrar, then she should cache a copy of the rule given above and submit both the rule and the student ID when E-Learn asks her to prove that she is a UIUC student.

3.2 Semantics

The semantics of the PeerTrust language is an extension of that of SD3 [20]. For each Authority argument that has not been specified explicitly in a rule or literal, we add the argument '@ Self'. We also add the notion of distributed *Peers* with their respective knowledge bases. The meaning of a PeerTrust program is determined by a forward chaining nondeterministic fixpoint computation process in which at each step, a nondeterministically chosen peer either applies one of its rules, sends a literal or rule in its knowledge base with context 'Requester = P' to peer P (after removing its context *and* digitally signing it), or receives a context-free signed rule or literal from another party. Axioms not shown here allow peers to convert signed literals 'lit [signedBy A]' to unsigned literals 'lit @ A' that can be used in applications of rules, and to strip signatures off rules as well. Entailment rules not shown here allow peers to apply modus ponens using rules and literals of their own ('@ Self') or that they have obtained from other peers ('@ Alice'), so that they can mimic the reasoning processes of other peers. Due to space constraints, we omit all details in this paper. We also omit a discussion of query syntax; queries are needed for PeerTrust sites that use backward chaining.

In PeerTrust, many true statements will be underivable at a particular peer at runtime, because peers will not be willing to devote unlimited time and effort to trying to answer the queries of other peers. Each peer can control how much effort it is willing to exert to help other peers; most peers will only be willing to answer a few kinds of queries, and those only for a few kinds of requesters. In this paper, we do not present possible evaluation schemes for peers, but obvious choices include a forward-chaining 'push' paradigm and a backward-chaining paradigm based on an extension of SLD resolution. Also, in practice, it is not necessary for the contents of every message to be signed (e.g., there is no real need for Alice to sign her UIUC student ID before sending it to eOrg), but space constraints impel us to omit a discussion of the syntax and semantics that can be used to avoid message signatures in some cases.

4 Automated Trust Negotiation in Detail: Examples and DLPs

We will now extend the PeerTrust examples presented informally in the preceding sections and show how to represent the appropriate policies and negotiation rules for automated trust negotiation using distributed logic programs.

4.1 Scenario 1: Alice & E-Learn

E-Learn Associates sells learning resources and gives special offers to some users. For example, E-Learn clients can get a discount if they are preferred customers at the ELENA consortium. This is represented by the following two rules that govern access to the "discountEnroll" service:

E-Learn:
discountEnroll(Course, Party) $ Requester = Party ←
  discountEnroll(Course, Party).
discountEnroll(Course, Party) ←
  eligibleForDiscount(Party, Course).
eligibleForDiscount(X, Course) ← preferred(X) @ "ELENA".

At run time, E-Learn could ask ELENA whether each E-Learn client is a preferred ELENA customer, but that is not necessary because ELENA has given E-Learn a signed rule specifying how ELENA computes the "preferred" status of individuals.

preferred(X) @ "ELENA" ←
    signedBy ["ELENA"]
    student(X) @ "UIUC".

E-Learn could also ask the university directly about the student status of its customers, but UIUC's release policies are unlikely to allow release of student information to E-Learn. So instead E-Learn will ask students themselves to provide full proof of their student status, as hinted at by the following rule:

student(X) @ University ←
    student(X) @ University @ X.

This rule follows directly from PeerTrust axioms, but its inclusion directly in E-Learn's program is a hint to E-Learn's runtime evaluation engine (not shown here) that the engine should not try to evaluate the rule itself. In the current implementation of PeerTrust, each '@ authority' argument is taken as a directive to the runtime engine regarding who should try to evaluate that particular literal.

E-Learn is a member of the Better Business Bureau, and can prove it through an appropriate release policy (not shown) and signed rule:

member("E-Learn") @ "BBB"
    signedBy ["BBB"].

UIUC employs a registrar to whom it delegates student status certification. This is expressed by an appropriate delegation rule from UIUC to the UIUC registrar.

UIUC:
student(X) $ Requester = "UIUC Registrar" ←
    student(X) @ "UIUC Registrar".

UIUC does not directly respond to queries about student status, or release its delegation rule to anyone other than the registrar. Students get a credential from the UIUC registrar certifying their student status, and a copy of the delegation rule that UIUC gave to the UIUC registrar. Alice has both of these. Her policy is to give out her credentials only to members of the Better Business Bureau, and she expects them to produce a proof of this membership themselves, as hinted at by her inclusion of multiple levels of required signatures in her (publicly releasable) release policy for student literals:

Alice:
student(X) @ Y $ member(Requester) @ "BBB" @ Requester ←$_{true}$
    student(X) @ Y

With the current implementation of the PeerTrust run-time system and this set of policies, Alice will be able to access the discounted enrollment service at E-Learn.

4.2 Scenario 2: Signing Up for Learning Services

The following scenario uses policies to control access to ELENA Web services, including course enrollment and delivery. Bob works for the HR department of IBM, and is in charge of buying new e-learning courses. He has the authority to buy courses costing up to $2000. He is only willing to disclose this authorization to ELENA members.

Bob:
email("Bob", "Bob@ibm.com").
employee("Bob") @ X $ member(Requester) @ "ELENA" $\leftarrow_{true}$
  employee("Bob") @ X.
employee("Bob") @ "IBM" $\leftarrow$
    signedBy ["IBM"].
authorized("Bob", Price) @ X $ member(Requester) @ "ELENA" $\leftarrow_{true}$
  authorized("Bob", Price) @ X.
authorized("Bob", Price) @ "IBM" $\leftarrow$
    signedBy["IBM"]
    Price < 2000.
member(Requester) @ "ELENA" $\leftarrow_{true}$
  member(Requester) @ "ELENA" @ Requester.

Bob pays with his company's credit card, but will not even discuss the existence of the card with non-members of ELENA. He will only disclose the card to ELENA members who are authorized by VISA to accept VISA cards. The credit card is signed by VISA and includes many fields; for conciseness we show only a name field, containing "IBM". From previous interactions, Bob also knows that IBM and E-Learn are members of the ELENA consortium.

visaCard("IBM")
    signedBy ["VISA"].
visaCard("IBM") $ policy27(Requester) $\leftarrow_{true}$
  visaCard("IBM").
policy27(Requester) $\leftarrow$
  authorizedMerchant(Requester) @ "VISA" @ Requester,
  member(Requester) @ "ELENA".
member("IBM") @ "ELENA"
    signedBy ["ELENA"].
member("E-Learn") @ "ELENA"
    signedBy ["ELENA"].

E-Learn Associates offers free courses and pay-per-use courses. Free courses are available to employees of ELENA network members. Pay-per-use courses require an authorization from the company as well as the company's VISA information for billing. When a course is made available, a notification is sent to the requester, and the requester is billed if appropriate. Notification and billing are handled by an external mechanism; the "extra" variables in some rule heads are needed by those external functions.

"E-Learn":
enroll(Course, Requester, Company, Email, 0) $\leftarrow_{true}$
  freeCourse(Course),
  freebieEligible(Course, Requester, Company, EMail).
enroll(Course, Requester, Company, Email, Price) $\leftarrow_{true}$
  policy49(Course, Requester, Company, Price)

The following rules express the policies for free and pay-per-use courses:

freebieEligible(Course, Requester, Company, EMail) $\leftarrow$
  email(Requester, EMail) @ Requester,
  employee(Requester) @ Company @ Requester,
  member(Company) @ "ELENA" @ Requester.
policy49(Course, Requester, Company, Price) $\leftarrow_{true}$
  price(Course, Price),
  authorized(Requester, Price) @ Company @ Requester,
  visaCard(Company) @ "VISA" @ Requester.

The use of policy names and contexts in the above example allows us to protect policies in the same way as other resources. For example, E-Learn's partner agreements and customer list are privileged business information. Without additional protection, anyone can learn that E-Learn's only partner agreement that involves free course registration is with ELENA. To avoid disclosing this sensitive information during negotiation, the definition of freebieEligible has the default context (Requester = Self). ELENA member companies can disseminate the definition of freebieEligible to their employees, so the employees know to push the appropriate credentials to E-Learn to satisfy the private rule and gain access to free courses.

Finally, E-Learn has a database of course information, and may have cached other signed rules and credentials from other peers (e.g., to speed up negotiation, or for use in the private rule for determining eligibility for free course enrollment). For example:

freeCourse(cs101).
freeCourse(cs102).
price(cs411, 1000).
member("IBM") @ "ELENA".
  signedBy ["ELENA"]
authorizedMerchant("E-Learn")
  signedBy["VISA"].

To check if a requester's VISA card has been revoked, E-Learn must make an external function call to a VISA card revocation authority. (This approach provides a run-time interpretation for the revocation speech acts mentioned in [9].) E-Learn can implement this as an extension of policy49, where E-Learn checks for credit card revocation directly with VISA and ensures that the purchase price will not cause the account balance to exceed its credit limit.

policy49(Course, Requester, Company, Price) $\leftarrow_{true}$
    price(Course, Price),
    authorized(Requester, Price) @ Company @ Requester,
    visaCard(Company) @ "VISA" @ Requester,
    purchaseApproved(Company, Price) @ "VISA".

To help E-Learn decide where to send a particular query, it can keep a database list-ing authoritative peers for various topics. At run time, unbound *Authority* arguments can be instantiated from this database. In this case E-Learn might have a list of authorities it can ask about specific predicates:

policy49(Course, Requester, Company, Price) $\leftarrow_{true}$
    price(Course, Price),
    authorized(Requester, Price) @ Company @ Requester,
    visaCard(Company) @ "VISA" @ Requester,
    authority(purchaseApproved, Authority),
    purchaseApproved(Company, Price) @ Authority.

These lists of authorities can also come from a broker:

policy49(Course, Requester, Company, Price) $\leftarrow_{true}$
    price(Course, Price),
    authorized(Requester, Price) @ Company @ Requester,
    visaCard(Company) @ "VISA" @ Requester,
    authority(purchaseApproved, Authority) @ myBroker,
    purchaseApproved(Company, Price) @ Authority.

With the PeerTrust run-time system and these policies, IBM employees will be able to enroll in free courses at E-Learn. If IBM were not a member of ELENA, then IBM employees would not be eligible for free courses, but Bob would be able to purchase courses for them from E-Learn.

Bob might want to delegate authority to another peer to carry out a negotiation on his behalf. For example, handheld devices may not have enough power to carry out trust negotiation directly. In this case, Bob's device can forward any queries it receives to a another peer that Bob trusts, such as his home or office computer. This trusted peer has access to Bob's policies and credentials, performs the negotiation on his behalf, and returns the final results to the handheld device. If desired, this can be implemented in a manner that allows Bob's private keys to reside only on his handheld device, to reduce the amount of trust that Bob must place in the other peers.

5   Related Work

The Secure Dynamically Distributed Datalog (SD3) trust management system [8] is closely related to PeerTrust. SD3 allows users to specify high level security policies through a policy language. The detailed policy evaluation and certificate verification is handled by SD3. Since the policy language in SD3 is an extension of Datalog, security policies are a set of assumptions and inference rules. SD3 literals include a "site" argu-ment similar to our "Authority" argument, though this argument cannot be nested. SD3 does not have the concept of a context, which is appropriate for SD3's target application of DNS, but restricts SD3's expressiveness too much for our purposes. SD3 does not have a mechanism to allow the information in policies to be kept private from certain parties, which we accomplish with contexts. The newly proposed policy language Cassandra [2] combines many of the features of SD3 and RT [10], and is also close to PeerTrust.

Yu et al. [21] have investigated issues relating to autonomy and privacy during trust negotiation. The work on autonomy focuses on allowing each party in a negotiation maximal freedom in choosing what to disclose, from among all possible safe disclosures. Their approach is to predefine a large set of negotiation *strategies*, each of which chooses the set of disclosures in a different way, and prove that each pair of strategies in the set has the property that if Alice and E-Learn independently pick any two strategies from the set, then their negotiation is guaranteed to establish trust if there is any safe sequence of disclosures that leads to the disclosure of the target resource. Then Alice and E-Learn only have to agree on which set of strategies they will use. Similar concepts will be needed in PeerTrust. Yu et al.'s approach to protecting sensitive information in policies is UniPro, which is supported by the run-time environment we have presented in this paper.

Recent work in the context of the Semantic Web has focussed on how to describe security requirements, leading to the KAoS and Rei policy languages [9, 19]. KAoS and Rei investigate the use of ontologies for modeling speech acts, objects, and access types necessary for specifying security policies on the Semantic Web. PeerTrust complements these approaches by targeting trust establishment between strangers and the dynamic exchange of certificates during an iterative trust negotiation process that can be declaratively expressed and implemented based on distributed logic programs.

Similar to the situated courteous logic programs of [5] that describe agent contracts and business rules, PeerTrust builds upon a logic programming foundation to declaratively represent policy rules and iterative trust establishment. The extensions described in [5] are orthogonal to the ones described in this paper; an interesting addition to PeerTrust's distributed logic programs would be the notion of prioritized rules to explicitly express preferences between different policy rules.

6   Conclusion and Further Work

In this paper, we have used discussed the PeerTrust policy language and how to use it for negotiating and establishing trust in a distributed elearning environment investigated in the EU/IST ELENA project (another scenario of using PeerTrust in a Grid environment is described in [1]). PeerTrust harnesses a network of semi-cooperative peers to automatically create, in a distributed fashion, a certified proof that a party is entitled to access a particular resource on the Semantic Web. We have also shown how to use a declarative policy and credential language to support crucial trust negotiation features such as delegation, bilateral iterative disclosure of credentials, and policy protection.

For readers interested in experimenting with PeerTrust, the PeerTrust 1.0 prototype is freely available at http://www.learninglab.de/english/projects/peertrust.html and https://sourceforge.net/projects/peertrust/. Like the earlier prototype described in [3], PeerTrust 1.0's outer layer is a signed Java application or applet program, which keeps queues of propositions that are in the process of being proved, parses incoming queries, translates them to the PeerTrust language, and passes them to the inner layer. Its inner layer answers queries by reasoning about PeerTrust policy rules and certificates using Prolog metainterpreters (in MINERVA Prolog, whose Java implementation offers excellent portability), and returns the answers to the outer layer. PeerTrust 1.0 imports RDF metadata to represent policies for access to resources, and uses X.509 certificates and the Java Cryptography Architecture for signatures. It employs secure socket connections between negotiating parties, and its facilities for communication and access to security related libraries are in Java. PeerTrust 1.0 implements an earlier version of the policy language presented in this paper; in particular, contexts are just simple Requester arguments, rather than arbitrary predicates; and DLPs are used to provide policy protection.

There are many compelling directions for future work on the use of distributed certified proofs as a basis for trust negotiation. Due to space limitations, we will single out only two of these directions. First, one would like to see formal guarantees that trust negotiations will always terminate and will succeed (i.e., result in access to the desired resource) when possible. Further, one would like to see an analysis of the autonomy available to each peer (e.g., "If I refuse to answer this query, could it cause the negotiation to fail?") and the information that can be leaked by a peer's behavior during negotiation. The first three kinds of guarantees are preordained for all meta interpreters that implement the negotiation protocols and strategies proposed in [21], which are more complex than the simple meta interpreters presented in this paper, but offer peers a much higher degree of autonomy. Thus one interesting future direction is the extension of these strategies, which were designed for negotiations that involve exactly two peers, to work with the n peers that may take part in a negotiation under PeerTrust.

Second, the example policies in this paper each protect a single resource and a single type of access to that resource. For scalability, Semantic Web access control policies must support an intensional specification of the resources and types of access affected by a policy, e.g., as a query over the relevant resource attributes ("the ability to print color documents on all printers on the third floor"). This capability, already present in policy languages such as Rei, KAoS, and Ponder, is supported at run time by the *content-triggered* variety of trust negotiation [6]. We are currently working to adapt content-triggered trust negotiation to the context of the Semantic Web.

Acknowledgments

The research of Nejdl and Olmedilla was partially supported by the projects ELENA (http://www.elena-project.org, IST-2001-37264) and REWERSE (http://rewerse.net, IST-506779). The research of Winslett was supported by DARPA (N66001-01-1-8908), the National Science Foundation (CCR-0325951,IIS-0331707) and The Regents of the University of California.

References

1. J. Basney, W. Nejdl, D. Olmedilla, V. Welch, and M. Winslett. Negotiating trust on the grid. In *2nd SemPGRID Workshop*, New York, USA, May 2004. co-located with WWW'2004.

2. M. Y. Becker and P. Sewell. Cassandra: distributed access control policies with tunable expressiveness. In *Policies in Distributed Systems and Networks*, June 2004.

3. R. Gavriloaie, W. Nejdl, D. Olmedilla, K. Seamons, and M. Winslett. No registration needed: How to use declarative policies and negotiation to access sensitive resources on the semantic web. In *European Semantic Web Symposium*, Heraklion, Greece, May 2004.

4. B. Grosof. Representing e-business rules for the semantic web: Situated courteous logic programs in RuleML. In *Proceedings of the Workshop on Information Technologies and Systems (WITS)*, New Orleans, LA, USA, Dec. 2001.

5. B. Grosof and T. Poon. SweetDeal: Representing agent contracts with exceptions using XML rules, ontologies, and process descriptions. In *WWW12*, 2003.

6. A. Hess and K. E. Seamons. An Access Control Model for Dynamic Client Content. In *8th ACM Symposium on Access Control Models and Technologies*, Como, Italy, June 2003.

7. I. Horrocks and P. Patel-Schneider. A proposal for an owl rules language. http://www.cs.man.ac.uk/ horrocks/DAML/Rules/, Oct. 2003.

8. T. Jim. SD3: A Trust Management System With Certified Evaluation. In *IEEE Symposium on Security and Privacy*, Oakland, CA, May 2001.

9. L. Kagal, T. Finin, and A. Joshi. A policy based approach to security for the semantic web. In *International Semantic Web Conference*, Sanibel Island, Oct. 2003.

10. N. Li and J. Mitchell. RT: A Role-based Trust-management Framework. In *DARPA Information Survivability Conference and Exposition (DISCEX)*, Washington, D.C., Apr. 2003.

11. N. Li, J. Mitchell, and W. Winsborough. Design of a Role-based Trust-management Framework. In *IEEE Symposium on Security and Privacy*, Berkeley, California, May 2002.

12. N. Li, W. Winsborough, and J. Mitchell. Distributed Credential Chain Discovery in Trust Management. *Journal of Computer Security*, 11(1), Feb. 2003.

13. J. W. Lloyd. *Foundations of Logic Programming*. Springer, 2nd edition edition, 1987.

14. W. Nejdl, W. Siberski, and M. Sintek. Design issues and challenges for RDF- and schema-based peer-to-peer systems. *SIGMOD Record*, 32(3), 2003.

15. W. Nejdl, B. Wolf, C. Qu, S. Decker, M. Sintek, A. Naeve, M. Nilsson, M. Palmér, and T. Risch. Edutella: A P2P networking infrastructure based on RDF. In *Proceedings of the 11th International World Wide Web Conference (WWW2002)*, Hawaii, USA, June 2002.

16. W. Nejdl, M. Wolpers, W. Siberski, C. Schmitz, M. Schlosser, I. Brunkhorst, and A. Loser. Super-peer-based routing and clustering strategies for rdf-based peer-to-peer networks. In *Proceedings of the International World Wide Web Conference*, Budapest, Hungary, May 2003.

17. K. Seamons, M. Winslett, T. Yu, B. Smith, E. Child, J. Jacobsen, H. Mills, and L. Yu. Requirements for Policy Languages for Trust Negotiation. In *3rd International Workshop on Policies for Distributed Systems and Networks*, Monterey, CA, June 2002.

18. B. Simon, Z. Miklós, W. Nejdl, M. Sintek, and J. Salvachua. Smart space for learning: A mediation infrastructure for learning services. In *Proceedings of the Twelfth International Conference on World Wide Web*, Budapest, Hungary, May 2003.

19. G. Tonti, J. M. Bradshaw, R. Jeffers, R. Montanari, N. Suri, and A. Uszok. Semantic web languages for policy representation and reasoning: A comparison of KAoS, Rei and Ponder. In *Proceedings of the International Semantic Web Conference*, Sanibel Island, Oct. 2003.

20. J. Trevor and D. Suciu. Dynamically distributed query evaluation. In *PODS*, 2001.

21. T. Yu, M. Winslett, and K. Seamons. Supporting Structured Credentials and Sensitive Policies through Interoperable Strategies in Automated Trust Negotiation. *ACM Transactions on Information and System Security*, 6(1), Feb. 2003.

A Flexible Framework for Architecting XML Access Control Enforcement Mechanisms

Bo Luo, Dongwon Lee, Wang-Chien Lee, and Peng Liu

The Pennsylvania State University
University Park, PA, 16802, USA
{bluo,dlee,wlee,pliu}@ist.psu.edu

Abstract. Due to the growing interest in XML security, various access control schemes have been proposed recently. However, little effort has been put forth to facilitate a uniform analysis and comparison of these schemes under the same framework. This paper presents a first attempt toward a flexible framework that can capture the design principles and operations of existing XML access control mechanisms. Under this framework, we observe that most existing XML access control mechanisms share the same design principle with slightly different orderings of underlying building blocks (i.e., data, query, and access control rule). Furthermore, according to the framework, we identify four plausible approaches to implement XML access controls, namely built-in, view-based, pre-processing and post-processing. Finally, we compare the actual performance of different approaches.

1   Introduction

The eXtensible Markup Language (XML) [2] has emerged as the de facto standard for storing and exchanging information in the Internet Age. As the distribution and sharing of information over the World Wide Web becomes increasingly important, the needs for efficient yet secure access of XML data naturally arise. It is necessary to tailor information in XML documents for various user and application requirements, preserving confidentiality and efficiency at the same time. Thus, it is critical to specify and enforce access control over XML data to ensure that only authorized users have an access to the data they are allowed to access. Toward this goal, recently, many research and industrial proposals have appeared (e.g., [1, 3, 4, 8]).

However, there has been little effort to facilitate a uniform analysis and comparison of these proposals. Therefore, in this paper, we made such an attempt to identify necessary building blocks and operations under the framework. Having such a framework brings several benefits: (1) Without a uniform view, comparing different XML access control mechanisms is somewhat similar to comparing apples with oranges. By having a flexible framework that can represent many proposals, one can easily compare different approaches from the same and "fair" perspective; (2) The framework can help users see the architectural uniqueness of an approach in an intuitive manner. That is, once one understands the basic

W. Jonker and M. Petković (Eds.): SDM 2004, LNCS 3178, pp. 133–147, 2004.
© Springer-Verlag Berlin Heidelberg 2004

building blocks of the framework, it is intuitive to view other proposals in terms of the building blocks; (3) By combining different building blocks in different orders, one can devise novel approaches (or implementations) of XML access control mechanisms that are not known before.

In summary, the **contributions** of this paper are as follows:

- We present a flexible framework that consists of three building blocks (i.e., data, query, access control rules) and a set of operations (e.g., evaluate, merge, etc). Based on these elements, we present different ways of implementing XML access controls with their pros and cons, namely built-in, pre-processing, post-processing, etc. To our best knowledge, this is the first attempt to model and compare different XML access control mechanisms under the same roof (Section 3).
- We demonstrate that the proposed framework can easily capture majority of the known XML access control mechanisms (e.g., [8, 9, 1, 4]) in a succinct and consistent way (Section 4).
- Finally, after implementing four representative XML access control mechanisms, we present experimental result from a performance study of those mechanisms (Section 5). In general, the pre-processing approach outperforms the others.

The rest of the paper is organized as follows: Section 2 presents related works of this paper. Section 3 presents the main framework that we propose, and Section 4 discusses architectures of some of the existing XML access control mechanisms under the proposed framework. Section 5 provides a performance comparison of four representative XML access control mechanisms. Finally, a conclusion is drawn in Section 6.

2   Related Work

XML access control in general has two aspects: *access control models* and *enforcement mechanisms*. The focus of this paper is on the latter.

Several authorization-based XML access control models are proposed. In [11], authorizations are specified on portions of HTML documents, but no semantic context similar to that provided by XML can be supported. In [5], a specific authorization sheet is associated with each XML document/DTD expressing the authorizations on the document. In [4], the model proposed in [5] is extended by enriching the authorization types supported by the model, providing a complete description of the specification and enforcement mechanism. Among comparable proposals, in [1], an access control environment for XML documents and some techniques to deal with authorization priorities and conflict resolution issues are proposed. Finally, the use of authorization priorities with propagation and overriding, which is an important aspect of XML access control, may recall approaches in the context of object-oriented databases, like [7] and [10]. Although our proposal is based on existing XML authorization models such as [4], we focus on how to architect and implement XML access control mechanisms on top of XML engines without security support.

From the enforcement mechanism perspective, existing XML access control methods are either view-based or relying on the XML engine to enforce node-level access control. The idea of view-based enforcement is to create and maintain a *view* for each user who is authorized to access a specific portion of an XML document. The view contains exactly the set of data nodes that the user is authorized to access. The view is generated by using the set of authorizations granted to the user to filter off the nodes that the user should not access. During run time, each user can simply run his queries against his view. In [5] and [4], a detailed view-based enforcement mechanism is proposed. Although views can be prepared offline, view-based enforcement has two serious limitations: (1) not scalable in managing and maintaining views when there are a large number of roles (or users), (2) high storage cost. To tackle this problem, [15] proposes a method to compress XML views. However, view-independent enforcement mechanisms are sometimes more desirable.

Letting XML engines enforce access control at the node-level is a view-independent enforcement mechanism, but the complexity of managing and maintaining authorizations can be too significant to make this enforcement mechanism practical. The idea is to associate an access-control-list with each node of the XML document. The major complexities are: (1) whenever a user is created or removed, or an authorization is granted or revoked, the XML engine has to "refresh" its access control lists; (2) the query processing overhead can be substantial; (3) this enforcement mechanism is useless when XML data are managed by a RDBMS, as many real world applications do; (4) how to manage the authorization inheritance relationships among data nodes? [3] addresses this issue by mitigating the problem (2), but cannot solve the other two problems; (5) when XML documents are huge, using XML engines to enforce access control may not be cost-effective.

To further reduce the overhead of the XML engine, [9] proposed an automata-based static analysis that identifies XML queries that are either "entirely" authorized or "entirely" prohibited before the queries are submitted to an XML engine. Therefore, if a query Q is completely prohibited by access control rules, then there is no need to submit Q to an XML engine, and Q can be simply thrown away outright. Conversely, if one is certain that Q does not have any conflicts with access control rules, Q may be processed as if it is a regular query without security concern. However, for the "partially" authorized XML queries, [9] still relies on an XML engine to filter out the data nodes that users do not have authorizations to read or write. The proposed solution in [8] removes this problem so that query processing as well as security enforcement are optimized regardless of the query or access control types. That is, our solution is independent of the underlying XML engine or the usage of views, solving the above enforcement problems naturally.

3   A Framework for XML Access Control Enforcement

3.1   XML Security Model

Since the focus of our framework is on *how to enforce access controls*, rather than on *how to define a security model* itself, the choice of a particular XML security model that we use in this paper is insignificant. Nevertheless, to simplify the presentation of the paper, let us first define a model as follows.

In short, we adopt an XML access control model from [4] and incorporate role-based access control from [12] to make our access control mechanisms more pragmatic. In this model, users are assigned to roles and thus can exercise certain access rights characterized by their roles. An XML document can be represented as a hierarchy of nested nodes (i.e., elements and attributes) so that fine-grained access controls at node level are established. XPath (or XQuery) is used for specification of queries as well as identification of nodes. The node-level authorization is specified via access control rules (ACR), each of which is a 5-tuple: $ACR = \{subject, object, action, sign, type\}$, where (1) *subject* is to whom an authorization is granted (e.g., user or role); (2) *object* is part of an XML data specified by an XPath expression; (3) *action* consists of read, write, and update[1]; (4) *sign* $\in \{+, -\}$ refers to either access "granted" or "denied", respectively; and (5) *type* $\in \{LC, RC\}$ refers to either local check (i.e., authorization is applied to nodes in context only) or recursive check (i.e., authorization is applied to current nodes and propagated to all their descendants), respectively.

In general, all nodes whose authorization is not explicitly specified in ACR are considered to be "access denied". It is possible for a node to have more than one relevant access control rule. If conflicts occur among such rules, denial takes precedence. When an answer returned from databases does not contain any security-violating data in it, the answer is called *safe answer (SA)*, and *un-safe answer (UA)* otherwise. Similarly, if a query produces only safe answers, then the query is called *safe query (SQ)*, and *un-safe query (UQ)* otherwise.

3.2   Building Blocks

We view the XML access control mechanism as the interplay of three building blocks – *data*, *query*, and *access control rule* as follows:

- **Data (D)** indicates the XML data (or document) that contains the answers users are looking for. Often the data are stored in native XML engines or RDBMS, but the choice of storage system is irrelevant to the discussion of this paper.
- **Query (Q)** describes the information that users want, and can be viewed as a conceptual pointer to the desired data in D. In XML domain, query is often written in either XPath or XQuery language. When a Q is issued by a user, Q has the same security role as what the user has.

---

[1] In this paper, we focus on the read action since write/update operations for XML model are still being designed by W3C.

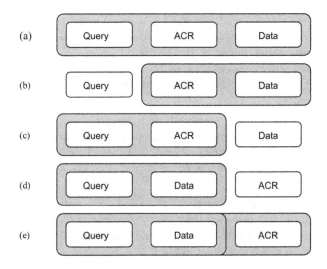

Fig. 1. Different combinations of building blocks in the framework.

- **Access Control Rules (ACR)** is a list of 5-tuple access control rule, describing the security policy of some roles. When a portion of data in D that does not violate policies of ACR are returned, it is a "safe" answer.

Note that D, Q and ACR are independent components, and thus can be located independently and processed separately. Figure 1 illustrates various combinations of the three building blocks, where gray box implies that building blocks in it are (1) co-located (in a spatial sense); and/or co-processed (in a temporal sense). For instance, (a) can be interpreted as: all three building blocks must be (1) co-located in a single system; and/or (2) processed at the same time. Below, we will consider both aspects of the framework.

- (a) indicates a scenario where all three building blocks are co-located in a single system. For instance, conventional RDBMS supports relational access control via the embedded support of GRANT/REVOKE. In such a setting, Q is issued against both D and ACR which are stored together;
- (b) is a slight modification of (a) in that Q can be issued remotely while ACR must be stored together with D in a system. Typical example of this scenario includes the client-server model such as web-based database interface. On the other hand, from the temporal aspect, (b) illustrates the view-based XML access control mechanism where ACR and D are processed first (yielding a safe view), and then Q is evaluated against the view. Whichever case it is, the data provider must be able to support XML access control mechanism;
- In the spatial sense, (c) indicates a scenario where one party holds Q and ACR, while D is stored elsewhere. For instance, D is provided by a data provider while ACR is provided by a data mediator who connects end users

with raw data sources with marginal fees. Once acquiring an adequate security role from the mediator by paying the fee, end users can issue a query to D. On the other hand, in the temporal sense, (c) implies that Q and ACR can be pre-processed prior to D. Therefore, for optimization, one can "merge" Q and ACR such that new output Q' can be processed against D more efficiently;

- (d) shows a scenario where only ACR is stored elsewhere. Since Q and D are stored together, conventional databases without access control support can be used to first evaluate Q against D. When ACR itself carries security-conscious information and has to be stored securely, this approach can be adopted; and

- Lastly, (e) is a conceptual merge of (b) and (d). Since the final "safe" answers are those data that can pass through constraints of Q as well as ACR, one can do intersection of two data sets – one from evaluating Q against D, and the other from enforcing ACR against D.

3.3   Operators

By viewing the three building blocks of the previous section as "operands", here, we present a few core "operators", thus forming an Algebra in a sense.

- **D' = evalQuery(Q, D).** This operator takes a query Q issued by a user and a data D, and returns a data D' as the answer. If either input Q is a "safe query" or D is a "safe data", then the output D' is also a "safe data".

- **D' = evalRule(ACR, D).** This operator applies the 5-tuple access control rules ACR against D, and produce a set of data D' (i.e., D'_1, ..., D'_n) as return, one for each role. That is, each returned D' is a portion of data in D that a role is entitled to access. Note that D' can be a virtual concept. For instance, D'_1 and D'_2 can exist as augmented taggings to D', instead of being physically-returned data.

- **Q' = merge(Q, ACR).** This operator "re-writes" the input query Q using ACR such that parts of Q that violate the security policies specified in ACR are pruned. The output query Q' is thus a conceptual merge of Q and ACR. For instance, suppose a manager "John" issues the following query `Q://dept[@loc='East']//salary` when ACR has only 1 rule in it: `<manager, //member/salary, +, read, LC>` (i.e., managers can read any member's salary information). Then, $merge(Q, ACR)$ would generate: `Q'=//dept[@loc='East']//member/salary`.

Note that the proposed three operators can be nested in an arbitrary manner, together with the traditional set operators (i.e., $\cap$, $\cup$, and $-$). Now, let us see how different scenarios of Figure 1 can be captured using the operators.

- **Figure 1(a) and 1(b).** Since all of our operators are binary, both scenarios (a) and (b) can be captured as "$evalQuery(Q, evalRule(ACR, D))$". Note that since $evalRule(ACR, D)$ returns a list of D', instead of a single D', in order to use it in a nested fashion, there needs to be another operator that lets us pick one of the D' such as "$evalQuery(Q, pickOne(evalRule(ACR, D)))$". However, for simplicity, we omit this operator.

- **Figure 1(c).** The operation "$evalQuery(merge(Q, ACR), D)$" captures the scenario (c). Note that how individual operator is "implemented" in practice is not discussed yet, and to be explored in Section 4. For instance, $merge(Q, ACR)$ operator is implemented in two ways in [8], called primitive and QFilter.

- **Figure 1(d).** The operation "$evalRule(ACR, evalQuery(Q, D))$" captures the scenario (d). Note the potential inefficiency stems from the fact that $evalQuery(Q, D)$ is processed first so that intermediate (possibly un-safe) data must be carried to the second step of $evalRule(ACR, D)$. In this scenario, the first $evalQuery(Q, D)$ may need to do extra task of keeping ancestor tags or predicates. For instance, after the `Q:/a/b` returns `<b>` nodes, when an access control rule has `/a[c]/b`, it cannot be checked since necessary tags are already stripped out.

- **Figure 1(e).** This scenario can be captured as the operation "$evalQuery(Q, D) \cap evalRule(ACR, D)$" if the domain compatibility of the $\cap$ operator is provided. Consider the following case: `Q://a` and `ACR:<admin, //b, +, read, RC>` (i.e., administrators can read all b elements and their descendants). Furthermore, suppose the first operator $evalQuery(Q, D)$ returns an answer $\{a_1, a_5, a_7\}$, while the second operator $evalRule(ACR, D)$ returns a subtree rooted at b_2 that contains $\{a_3, a_5, a_7, a_{10}\}$ as sub-elements. In this case, the first sub-answer has the type of `<a>` while the second sub-answer has the type of `<b>`, and therefore, their domains are not compatible. However, two elements of `<a>` – a_5 and a_7 – must be returned as the final answer since they satisfy both constraints of Q and ACR. How to achieve this intelligent intersection is beyond the scope of this paper, and for instance explored in [8].

4   Current XML Access Control Enforcement Mechanisms Under the Framework

In this section, we discuss the current XML access control approaches, and show/compare how they are architected under our framework.

4.1   Available Approaches

- **RDBMS-Style Approach.** Typical RDBMS uses the role-based access control (RBAC) model where users are assigned a certain role which has predetermined GRANT/REVOKE privileges. Access control rules are stored in the access control tables (ACT), along with data. Therefore, architecturally, they typically adopt the scenario of Figure 1(a) (although queries can be issued remotely using database interfaces such as ODBC). To our best knowledge, there is no commercially available native XML databases with full access control support at this point.

– **Instance-Tagging Approach.** When ACR and D are available together like in Figure 1(b), one can traverse entire XML data tree, and tag each (element and attribute) node by its corresponding security information. [3], for instance, uses this approach although their focus is on optimizing the query evaluation, not the access control mechanism itself. With the two rules `<user1, //a//c, read, +, LC>` and `<user2, //b//c, read, +, LC>`, the `<c>` elements in the tree would have taggings, specifying that they are readable by both "user1" and "user2". Assuming there is some kind of index on this tagged information, then secure query evaluation can be provided. That is, when "John" with a "user1" role issues a query "$//c$", databases can retrieve all `<c>` elements under `<a>`, but not under `<b>` using the index. In some sense, this approach is related to the subsequent view-based approach.

– **View-Based Approach.** By adopting the architecture of Figure 1(b), view-based approach takes advantage of the fact that ACR and D are either co-located or co-processed. By processing $evalRule(ACR, D)$ first, therefore, this approach produces a set of data, D'_1, ..., D'_n for each role, thus creating a number of "views". Since each view contains only "safe" data for that particular role, query can be processed on this view without any further special care, making the query processing very efficient. The examples of view-based approaches recently proposed include [15, 4, 1], and is one of the most popular XML access control mechanisms. Depending on the details of the algorithms, the views can be maintained either physically or virtually.

Since the I/O and space costs for constructing views are amount to evaluating $evalRule(ACR, D)$, it is dependent on the number of roles in ACR and the size of D. However, often, this view construction is performed off-line, and thus the cost issue becomes less important. When the space cost becomes a major issue due to large number of views (e.g., million roles in Internet environment), then one may mitigate the problem using the compression-based techniques suggested in [15]. However, this approach still has to take extra burden to maintain the views. When update occurs to either ACR or D, synchronization must be performed to views. Overall, the view-based approach is fast in answering user queries but may have to pay high I/O and storage cost, and the extra complexity of view maintenance. Another drawback of this approach is that since ACR must be processed against D first, the database engines must be aware of the security aspect. That is, one cannot implement this approach using off-the-shelf databases that do not have built-in security support.

– **Pre-processing Approach.** Scenarios depicted in Figure 1(c) allows the handling of Q and ACR prior to D. Since the D are de-coupled from ACR, databases do not need to understand ACR. To exploit this property, one can probe only Q and ACR to do optimization. Known approaches in this category include two proposals from [8] and a proposal from [9].

In [8], we proposed *primitive* and *QFilter* as a pre-processing approach. The primitive approach simply merges Q and ACR with $\cap$ operator to construct $Q' = Q \cap ACR^2$. This Q' is then passed to the XML database capable of handling the set operator. Although simple to implement, its performance is highly dependent on the capability of underlying XML database. To remedy the problem of the primitive approach, QFilter tries to produce a more "optimized" Q' by pruning unnecessary parts as early as possible. It performs the "intersection" of ACR and Q using the extended non-deterministic finite automata (NFA). Informally, suppose we have the query Q:`//dept[@loc='East']//salary` when ACR has 2 rules in it: `<manager,` `//member/salary, +, read, LC>` (i.e., managers can read any member's salary), and `<manager, //member[@proj-type='secret']/salary, -,` `read, LC>` (i.e., managers cannot read member's salary if they work for a secret project). Then, the primitive approach would produce an output query Q' as: "`//dept[@loc='East']//salary` $\cap$ `//member/salary` $-$ `//member[@proj-type='secret']/salary`." However, the QFilter approach would instead produce Q' as:

"`//dept[@loc='East']//member[@proj-type<>'secret']/salary`",

which is often processed much faster. More importantly, since the new query Q' fully preserves both constraints of Q and ACR, even if Q' is processed by normal databases that do not support access controls, the output of $evalQuery(Q', D)$ is the "safe" answer. The details of the QFilter algorithm to achieve this optimization is beyond the scope of this paper, and can be found in [8].

On the other hand, [9] proposed another approach called *static analysis*, which is a hybrid of pre-processing and internal XML database security check. The idea is to recognize two cases in the pre-processing stage: "access-fully-granted" and "access-fully-denied". That is, in our framework, (1) access-full-granted occurs when $evalQuery(Q, D) \subseteq evalRule(ACR, D)$. Since all answers returned from Q are fully allowed by ACR, then $Q' = Q$ holds. This means that the original user query can be processed by databases without any special care; and (2) access-fully-denied occurs when $evalQuery(Q, D) \cap evalRule(ACR, D) = \emptyset$. That is, all the answers that the user is asking for are prohibited to access by ACR. In this case, there is no point of sending any query to databases, and thus system simply returns null to the user right away. Compared to the QFilter approach, the static analysis method lacks of the capability to handle the case: $evalQuery(Q, D) \cap evalRule(ACR, D) \neq \emptyset$, i.e., some parts of the answers that the user is asking for are blocked, but other parts are accessible. Mainly due to this reason, [8]

---

[2] In reality, the primitive algorithm is a bit more complicated to take care of the subtle differences in the semantics of "$+/-$" sign and "LC/RC" type.

demonstrated the QFilter method can outperform the static analysis method by significant margin.

- **Post-processing Approach.** Figure 1(d) illustrates the post-processing scenario, where Q is applied to D first (where no security enforcement is engaged), and then ACR is examined second. Since the first and second step may be temporally and spatially far apart, the risk of carrying unnecessary intermediate data in the middle can hamper this approach significantly. One may use data filter techniques such as YFilter [6] in the second step to remove the forbidden contents from the unsafe answers. The cost to construct YFilter depends on ACR only, thus could be performed off-line efficiently. The final step of data filtering is the major performance bottleneck if the intermediate data contains a large volume of forbidden data in them. In additions, the post-processing filters often require the intermediate answers (after $evalQuery(Q, D)$) to retain full path to the nodes that query requested. However, current XML database engine such as Galax returns only requested nodes without their ancestors. Therefore, to implement XML access controls using the post-processing approach, one has an extra burden to recover all the ancestor tags to the root.

Let us emphasize that all of the aforementioned approaches are well captured in our framework, usually in a slight different orderings. For instance, note the slight difference of the view-based, pre-processing, and post-processing approaches:

- View-based: $SA = evalQuery(Q, evalRule(ACR, D))$
- Pre-processing: $SA = evalQuery(merge(Q, ACR), D)$
- Post-processing: $SA = evalRule(ACR, evalQuery(Q, D))$

Note that at the end, users always get the "safe answer" (SA) back. Figure 2 depicts details of three XML access control enforcement mechanisms using our framework.

4.2   Qualitative Comparison

In this section, let us do a close examination on the three (important) categories: view-based of Figure 1(b), pre-processing of Figure 1(c), and post-processing of Figure 1(b). End-to-end processing time of these approaches are illustrated in Figure 3. We observe that typically an XML access control mechanism involves three separate operations: (1) off-line service preparation, (2) on-line query processing, and (3) service maintenance.

- **Off-Line Service Preparation.** This step is typically devoted on tasks to help speed-up the subsequent query processing step, and done off-line. Obviously, view-based approach would need to generate views per roles in this step. Similarly, the pre-processing approach like QFilter or static analysis method spends this time on constructing needed data structures (e.g., NFA). For the post-processing approach, one can build up some kind of index on ACR (e.g., given a "role", quickly retrieve all relevant rules from

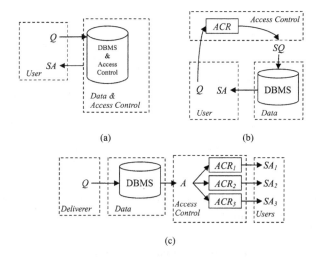

Fig. 2. Illustration of three XML access control approaches under our framework: (a) view-based, (b) QFilter, and (c) YFilter.

ACR) so that later post-filtering process can run faster. Note that in this stage, Q from users are not known, and both ACR and D are the sole resources. Therefore, often the cost for service preparation depends on the size of ACR and D. Moreover, when the preparation requires non-trivial probing of ACR such as QFilter case, the complexity of ACR also does affect the cost. However, overall, since these tasks are done off-line, they do not contribute much to the performance of whole XML access control mechanisms, and thus omitted in our experimental comparisons of Section 5.

- **On-Line Query Processing.** Once Q is issued, the task of evaluating Q while ensuring security policies in ACR is done in this step, and must be done on-line (unless the submitted query is part of batch-process). The end output of this task must be the "safe answers". Thus, the end-to-end on-line query processing time is the time-line between Q and SA in Figure 3.

For the view-based approach, the query processing can be efficient since there is no need for additional security check (i.e., each view contains only safe data for the role, after all). For the pre-processing approach, the performance largely depends on the quality of the re-written query from the pre-processing. For instance, if the primitive method generates a re-written query Q' as "$s_1 \cap \ldots \cap s_n - t_1 \ldots - t_m$" ($n$, $m \gg 1$), then the evaluation of the Q' can be quite slow. Other pre-processing approaches like QFilter or static analysis method improve it drastically via early-pruning of access-full-granted or access-fully-denied cases and via improved query re-writing in $merge(Q, ACR)$. For the post-processing approach, the security check is pipelined after the query evaluation, and thus can be disadvantageous in terms of performance. Post-filtering time is highly dependent on the size of unsafe answer set.

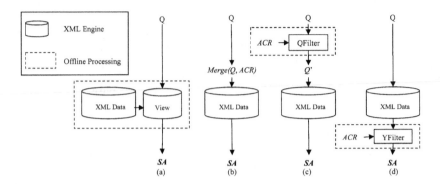

Fig. 3. Processing flow of XML access control mechanisms: (a) view-based approach, (b) primitive pre-processing, (c) QFilter-based pre-processing, and (d) YFilter-based post-processing.

Table 1. Qualitative comparison of different XML access control mechanisms.

Approach	Preparation	Processing	Maintenance
View-based	Medium	Good	Medium
Pre-processing	Good	Medium/Good	Good
Post-processing	Good	Bad/Medium	Good

– **Service Maintenance.** In general, any service preparations done off-line need to be maintained when update occurs. For instance, when D is changed (e.g., new sub-tree is inserted to D), view-based approach needs to (incrementally) re-construct relevant views. However, the changes to D do not affect the pre-processing or post-processing approach. On the other hand, when ACR is changed, it affects the pre-processing (e.g., an NFA needs to be updated) and post-processing approach (e.g., index on ACR needs to be updated).

The summary of the qualitative comparison of three scenarios of Figure 1 is summarized in Table 1. Note that the query processing cost of the post-processing approach heavily depends on the size of intermediate un-safe data and/or the complexity of rules in ACR.

5   Performance Evaluation

Now we validate the analysis of Section 4 with the experimental results. We use Galax 0.3.1 [14] as the underlying XML engine, and XMark [13] schema and data set. Overall, we experimented with: (1) for Q, user-denied and synthetic XPath queries. Depending on the complexities of queries, we identified 8 categories; (2) for ACR, user-defined and synthetic access control rules in the range of $0 - 500$ rules ; and (3) for D, the sizes range from 500KB – 2.5MB. Among all these, here we present a simple case of: 32 rules (of 4 roles) in ACR and 200 synthetic

Table 2. Summary of roles and rules.

Role	Policy	Size (KB)	# of + rules	# of − rules
#1	Can view all information, except auction.	1,525	6	0
#2	Can view all category, north America item, and user information except for their private ones.	1,279	8	2
#3	Can view all the closed auctions, basic item and user information except for their private ones.	1,256	8	2
#4	Can view all the open auctions and basic item information.	1,352	6	0

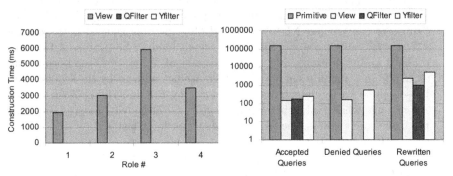

Fig. 4. Performance comparison: (a) Service preparation time (ms); and (b) Query evaluation time (ms).

queries against 2.5MB data. Note that other results not shown here are still consistent with the presented case, and are available in [8].

We did not really implement the view-based approach. Instead, we simulate it by evaluating ACR on data to create answer set as views, and then evaluate queries on these views. Same as the situation in the YFilter approach, answer set of evaluating ACR on the document do not have ancestor tags and special care was taken to trace back the ancestor axis to recover full path. However, this step is not included in the comparison below.

Figure 4(a) shows the service preparation time of view-based, QFilter, and YFilter. The view-based approach takes the longest time while both QFilter and YFilter approaches are quite fast (appears to be 0 in the graph). The end-to-end query processing time is shown in Figure 4(b) (in logarithmic scale) for the 200 synthetic queries of the role #1. One can clearly observe:

− The primitive pre-processing approach performs the slowest since the underlying XML engine (i.e., Galax)'s performance degrades as the number of set operators such as ∩ or ∪ in the re-written query Q' increases when it evaluates $Q' = merge(Q, ACR)$. On the contrary, YFilter-based post-processing approach turns out to be faster than the primitive pre-processing since the intermediate data after evaluating $evalQuery(Q, D)$ was significantly small, incurring little cost to post-processing task. However, when the size of intermediate (unsafe) data increases, the post-processing approach often becomes slower than the primitive pre-processing.

- The view-based and QFilter pre-processing approaches are the fastest. For fully-accepted queries (i.e., $evalQuery(Q, D) \subseteq evalRule(ACR, D)$), "$Q' = Q$" holds, and thus the view-based approach is faster than even the QFilter approach, as it evaluates the query on a smaller data set of "views". For fully-denied queries (i.e., $evalQuery(Q, D) \cap evalRule(ACR, D) = \emptyset$), the QFilter approach takes almost no time since the query is rejected outright without being sent to databases for evaluation. For re-written queries (i.e., $evalQuery(Q, D) \cap evalRule(ACR, D) \neq \emptyset$), the QFilter approach exhibits a better performance mainly due to its good query rewriting algorithm utilizing pre-constructed NFA. Often, QFilter rewrites general paths having "*" or "//" into more specific paths, which tend to be processed faster in evaluation. In additions, due to the existence of "*" and "//" in both Q and ACR, Q' may include some paths which are not allowed by the schema, and those can be easily detected and ruled out by the underlying XML engine. As a result, while evaluating $evalQuery(Q', D)$ and $evalQuery(Q, V)$ yields the same safe answers, the former tends to perform faster.

6   Conclusion

In this paper, we proposed a flexible framework that can capture most of the current XML access control enforcement mechanisms using the same set of building blocks (query Q, access control rules ACR, and data D) and operators ($evalQuery(Q, D)$, $evalRule(ACR, D)$, $merge(Q, ACR)$). Using the framework, we have identified various architectural settings of access control scenarios. Especially, by focusing on three representative approaches – view-based, preprocessing, and post-processing, we showed and compared the pros and cons of each scenario. Furthermore, by examining many existing XML access control mechanisms, we identified which belongs to which category, providing easy and intuitive platform to understand and compare different proposals. Finally, experimental validations to confirm our qualitative comparison are presented. In short, pre-processing approach such as QFilter or static analysis method is promising due to its low maintenance cost and high performance.

Acknowledgment

Authors would like to thank Yanlei Diao and Michael Franklin for providing the YFilter software package. Peng Liu is partially supported by NSF CCR-0233324 and DOE Early Career PI Award.

References

1. E. Bertino and E. Ferrari. "Secure and Selective Dissemination of XML Documents". *ACM Trans. on Information and System Security (TISSEC)*, 5(3):290–331, Aug. 2002.
2. T. Bray, J. Paoli, and C. M. Sperberg-McQueen (Eds). "Extensible Markup Language (XML) 1.0 (2nd Ed.)". W3C Recommendation, Oct. 2000. http://www.w3.org/TR/2000/REC-xml-20001006.
3. S. Cho, S. Amer-Yahia, L. V.S. Lakshmanan, and D. Srivastava. "Optimizing the Secure Evaluation of Twig Queries". In *VLDB*, Hong Kong, China, Aug. 2002.
4. E. Damiani, S. De Capitani di Vimercati, S. Paraboschi, and P. Samarati. "A Fine-Grained Access Control System for XML Documents". *ACM Trans. on Information and System Security (TISSEC)*, 5(2):169–202, May 2002.
5. E. Damiani, S. De Capitani Di Vimercati, S. Paraboschi, and P. Samarati. "Design and Implementation of an Access Control Processor for XML Documents". *Computer Networks*, 33(6):59–75, 2000.
6. Y. Diao and M. J. Franklin. "High-Performance XML Filtering: An Overview of YFilter". *IEEE Data Eng. Bulletin*, Mar. 2003.
7. E. Fernandez, E. Gudes, and H. Song. "A Model of Evaluation and Administration of Security in Object-Oriented Databases". *IEEE Trans. on Knowledge and Data Engineering (TKDE)*, 6(2):275–292, 1994.
8. B. Luo, D. Lee, W.-C. Lee, and P. Liu. "QFilter: Fine-Grained Run-Time XML Access Control via NFA-based Query Rewriting". Technical report, Penn State University, Jan. 2004. (Submitted for publication).
9. M. Murata, A. Tozawa, and M. Kudo. "XML Access Control using Static Analysis". In *ACM Conf. on Computer and Communications Security (CCS)*, Washington D.C., 2003.
10. Fausto Rabitti, Elisa Bertino, Won Kim, and Darrell Woelk. "A Model of Authorization for Next-Generation Database Systems". *ACM Trans. on Database Systems (TODS)*, 16(1):88–131, 1991.
11. P. Samarati, E. Bertino, and S. Jajodia. "An Authorization Model for a Distributed Hypertext System". *IEEE Trans. on Knowledge and Data Engineering (TKDE)*, 8(4):555–562, 1996.
12. R. Sandhu, E. Coyne, H. Feinstein, and C. Youman. "Role-Based Access Control Models". *IEEE Computer*, 29(2), 1996.
13. A. R. Schmidt, F. Waas, M. L. Kersten, D. Florescu, I. Manolescu, M. J. Carey, and R. Busse. "The XML Benchmark Project". Technical Report INS-R0103, CWI, April 2001.
14. J. Simeon and M. Fernandez. "Galax V 0.3.5", Jan. 2004. http://db.bell-labs.com/galax/.
15. T. Yu, D. Srivastava, L. V.S. Lakshmanan, and H. V. Jagadish. "Compressed Accessibility Map: Efficient Access Control for XML". In *VLDB*, Hong Kong, China, Aug. 2002.

Abstracting and Refining Authorization in SQL*

Arnon Rosenthal[1] and Edward Sciore[2]

[1] The MITRE Corporation, 202 Burlington Road, Bedford MA, USA
arnie@mitre.org
http://www.mitre.org/resources/centers/it/staffpages/arnie/
[2] Boston College, Chestnut Hill, MA, USA and The MITRE Corporation
sciore@bc.edu

Abstract. The SQL standard specifies authorization via a large set of rather opaque rules, which are difficult to understand and dangerous to change. To make the model easier to work with, we formalize the implicit principles behind SQL authorization. We then discuss two extensions, for explicit metadata privileges and general privilege inference on derived objects. Although these are quite simple and easily implemented, we show how together, they help solve several administrative problems with existing SQL security. This sort of abstraction is also an important step towards having DBMSs that simultaneously support security policies over SQL, XML, RDF, and other forms of data.

Keywords: SQL Authorization, Views, Privilege Inference

1 Introduction

When SQL was first introduced, its authorization semantics were clean and elegant. Over time, as triggers, objects, and other features were introduced into the language, the security semantics were greatly extended. The result of these piecemeal changes is an authorization mechanism that has numerous special cases, unnecessary restrictions, and different treatments of similar constructs. This situation is exemplified in the SQL standard [18], which specifies authorization via a large number of detailed rules, whose behavior can be extremely difficult to understand.

In addition to language extensions, today's administrators must cope with diverse user communities, each with their own external schemas and services. The imperfections of SQL authorization exacerbate this administrative burden. They cause unexpected behaviors that administrators must consider (e.g., covert channels that can occasionally be significant), raise costs for administrator training, and DBMS implementation (because there are few reusable abstractions), and limit automation for deriving privileges on derived objects. Moreover, the restrictions encourage having the DBA do all of the table administration, increasing vulnerability to insider threats.

Our goal is to return SQL to the state where authorization is consistent, and to show that this base makes it easier to provide useful extensions. We aim to reduce the (seemingly) ad hoc nature of authorization semantics, replacing it with explicit, simple principles. To that end, this paper makes the following contributions:

- We formalize the intuition behind the authorization rules in the SQL standard, and give a definition of correctness.

---

* Approved for Public Release. The opinions are the authors, not the corporation's.

W. Jonker and M. Petković (Eds.): SDM 2004, LNCS 3178, pp. 148–162, 2004.
© Springer-Verlag Berlin Heidelberg 2004

- We state a fundamental underlying principle for inferring privileges on derived data, and prove that SQL (and our later extensions) obey it.
- We propose two *small* extensions to the SQL security model that provide *very* useful additional capabilities for derived objects and metadata, and show how they work together to correct several deficiencies of current SQL systems.

The novelty of this work consists of providing an abstract model of a substantial portion of SQL security, and using that model to guide incremental improvements, again crafted to fit SQL. The basic ideas (inferring privileges to derived objects, protecting metadata, ownership) have been in SQL for decades; our contribution is in the detailed analysis.

This paper belongs to an unusual genre – abstraction and simplification starting from practice. We believe that abstracting from practice can be a valuable form of database research. To quote the head of data management at Microsoft Research [12]:

> A database industry would be alive and well ... even if researchers had never entered the database arena. ... Industry identified the problems and provided the early impetus. Researchers came along later and provided the clean abstractions and the elegant solutions. These are what enables database technology to be readily transmitted to new practitioners and to become solid engineering, not just arcane craft.

We know of only one other published abstraction of SQL authorization [9]. That paper formalized SQL cascade delete, and then went on to propose an alternative model.[1] In [13], query semantics was formalized using a three valued predicate calculus; however, this formalization does not help provide the intuition needed for understanding security. Moreover, it does not address updates, procedures, or views. In [1], the attention is on major, controversial extensions, rather than abstraction, underlying correctness criteria, or detailed compatibility with SQL systems. Within the chunk of SQL that we address – tables and columns, views and procedures, metadata – we have gone into more detail, and provide useful abstractions. Our success criterion is to simplify something, not everything.

The more common research approach is to examine consequences of new ideas in models that highlight the ideas but have little industrial presence. Although such a strategy is worthwhile, it complicates technology transfer. For example, consider the "derived data" ideas from [10]. To enhance SQL with these ideas, one would need to disentangle them from their object model (which is not SQL's object model), examine interactions with SQL capabilities such as column privileges and metadata protection. (discovering that the proposed rules seem incompatible with SQL security's design decisions for metadata visibility), and then add a major new capability (negative privileges).

One might ask whether the focus on SQL is warranted; perhaps it is more appropriate to create a new security model, e.g., security for XML (e.g., [1, 6]) or for semantic web knowledge formalisms such as RDF or OWL. However, over a million SQL DBMSs have been sold, and they will not go away soon; anything that simplifies

---

[1] That model, which SQL did not adopt, had the elegant "global" semantics that revoking a grant was equivalent to the grant never existing. However, the local semantics were awkward, requiring an administrator to examine Grant timestamps to determine the (cascade) consequences of a Revoke.

their security administration is important. In addition, well-defined abstractions can help guide future extensions to SQL.

Apart from its benefit to SQL, our abstractions also help with the future development of these other formalisms. Any future XML (or RDF, etc.) security standard will need to be compatible with the installed base, and as it matures, is likely to become as feature-rich as SQL. Moreover, it is likely that future standards will have support for multiple models. For example, major DBMS vendors have indicated that their systems will simultaneously support relational and XML views of the same data. Security administration and implementation will clearly need to span both models, as one integrated treatment, and will need to be consistent across all the formalisms. The best hope is to define most security semantics and implementation in terms of abstractions that span both models.

2 Abstracting Authorization in Standard SQL

The descriptions of SQL authorization that appear in most database texts and SQL reference guides are relatively straightforward, but the simplicity disappears when one examines details of the language. The current SQL standard [15] requires a myriad of rules and special cases to handle constructs such as views, stored routines, column-level operations, and triggers. This complexity is exacerbated by vendors, who extend the standard. (Oracle's treatment of triggers, stored procedures, and update privileges on views are good examples.)   This section describes and abstracts key portions of SQL security semantics.

2.1 Operations, IDs, and Privileges

A database consists of a set of *objects*, such as schemas, base tables, views, columns, and procedures. Each object has a well-defined set of *actions* that can be performed on it. Base table and view actions include SELECT, UPDATE, INSERT, and DELETE; procedures have the action EXECUTE.

An *operation*, denoted by the pair (α, O), specifies a particular action α on a particular object O. Each operation abstracts a generic activity that the database can perform. For example, the operation (SELECT, T) corresponds to reading one or more records of table T, and the operation (UPDATE, T.A) corresponds to modifying the A-value of one or more records of T.

An *ID* is an individual user, a role, or the (pseudo)role PUBLIC. A *privilege* allows an ID to perform an operation. We write a privilege as the pair (τ, θ), where τ is an ID and θ is an operation. If θ is the operation (α, O), then we say that τ *has privilege for θ*, or that τ *has α privilege on O*. (Facilities for grouping IDs into roles and attaching an ID to a run-time session are orthogonal to our concerns, and not covered here.)

2.2 Statements and Authorization

IDs interact with database objects by issuing *statements*. Given a statement S, SQL implicitly defines a set of operations, which we denote *OPS(S)*, to be used in checking authorizations. We say that an ID τ is *authorized* to perform S iff τ has a privilege for every operation in OPS(S).

The SQL standard defines OPS(S) implicitly by means of an exhaustive set of rules, case-by-case for each kind of statement. Although this approach specifies exact behavior, it does not justify (or even motivate) its correctness. It thus gives no guide to how new features should behave. Consequently, in this section we introduce an alternative, more easily understood definition of OPS(S).

Intuitively, an operation θ should be in OPS(S) if the "natural" execution of S effectively performs θ. A somewhat more abstract treatment can be based on data lineage [5], which expresses whether S *requires* the activity denoted by θ. The meaning of "requires" can be formalized for each kind of action. For example, operation (SELECT, T.A) is in OPS(S) if changing one or more A-values of T can produce a different output for S; and operation (INSERT, T.A) is in OPS(S) if executing S could insert at least one tuple into T with a non-null A-value. The definitions for other actions are defined similarly. As a concrete example, let S be the following update statement:

```
update T set A = C+2 where B1 in (select B2 from V)
```

Then:

```
OPS(S) = {(SELECT, T.B1),(SELECT, T.C),
          (SELECT, V.B2),(UPDATE, T.A)}
```

Although the above paragraph specifies what operations ought to be in OPS(S), it provides no practical means for determining this set. SQL contains many kinds of statement, which can nest inside of each other. If the structure of S is relatively simple, then OPS(S) may be computed automatically from the above definition, using the techniques of [5] (extended to updates). For example, the following rules can be easily deduced:

- If S is a query, then OPS(S) contains (SELECT, A) for all columns A mentioned in S.
- If S is an update command, then OPS(S) contains (UPDATE, A) for each column A being updated, plus (SELECT, B) for all columns B mentioned elsewhere in S.
- If S is a call to routine P, then OPS(S) contains (EXECUTE, P), plus (SELECT, A) for all columns A mentioned in the argument list of the call.
- If S contains a nested statement S′, then OPS(S) contains all operations in OPS(S′).

If S is more complex, however, the computation of OPS(S) may be less straightforward. The computations defined in the SQL standard satisfy our definition of OPS(S) when S is simple, and we believe it is satisfied for all S. But the sheer volume of the rules, combined with the difficulty of the standard's formal execution semantics (expressed as tuple-at-a-time interpretation) are so daunting that nobody is likely to attempt a compete proof.

One complicating issue involves unnecessary predicates. For example, suppose S is the following query:

```
select T.A from T where T.B is null or T.B*T.B >= 0
```

It is easy to see that the entire WHERE-clause predicate is a tautology, and thus unnecessary. The value of T.B does not affect the output of S, so the operation (SELECT, T.B) should not be in OPS(S). Constraints (such as referential integrity) may also cause predicates to be unnecessary. Since the detection of such predicates is not decidable in general, we cannot expect OPS(S) to be computed exactly. Instead, we opt for the pragmatic simplification that tautologies and constraints not be considered when determining OPS(S).

2.3 Explicit Privileges via Grants

An ID receives privileges explicitly via *grant* statements. An ID is able to issue a grant statement for an operation if its privileges include a *grant-option* privilege for the operation. For ease of exposition, we model grant-option capability as a separate privilege that is required to execute Grant statements. In particular, for each action A we assume that there is a corresponding action *grantA*. For example, the grant statement

```
grant SELECT on T to amy with grant option
```

creates the two privileges (amy, (SELECT, T)) and (amy, (grantSELECT, T)).

2.4 Ownership

When an object is created, SQL gives the creator administrative authority over use of the object; informally, this authority is usually called "ownership" of the object. We observe that ownership has two distinct aspects: rights over the defining metadata; and rights over the instance population. In standard SQL, these rights are defined as follows.

- *Base tables:* The creator of a base table is given all possible privileges on it – that is, full rights to access and modify both the instance population and the metadata.
- *Derived objects:* The creator of a derived object gets full rights on the object's metadata. The creator also gets limited rights over the derived object's population, as explained in Section 2.5.

Standard SQL intertwines these two aspects of ownership; in particular, there are no explicit privileges on metadata. Consequently, SQL neither requires nor permits administrators to control metadata access directly. Instead, an ID is allowed to access an object's metadata iff the ID has any privilege on an object.

By intertwining the two aspects, SQL gives creators of base tables more power than they need, and requires that an ID be granted substantial power before it can create a useful derived object. These issues (and our solution to them) will be addressed in Sections 3-5.

2.5 Derived Objects

In this section we abstract SQL's rules for derived objects, in a way that unifies views and stored procedures.

We say that procedures and views are *derived objects*. Each derived object Z has a *defining statement*, which we denote by *DEF(Z)*. Views are defined by queries, and procedures typically are defined by compound statements. Derived objects differ from base tables in that the creator does not automatically receive privileges on all possible operations. Instead, the database system infers the appropriate privileges, based on what privileges the creator has on the underlying objects.

Let ID τ be the creator of derived object Z. The SQL standard states that τ is the only ID that can automatically receive privileges on Z. But which operations should τ receive? Our general principle is that it is safe to infer privileges for tasks the user could accomplish by other means. That is, inference may increase convenience, but not power. SQL applies this principle for the derived object's creator. We now give a more formal statement.

The SQL Inference Principle: Let θ be an operation on derived object Z. Then Z's creator τ should automatically receive privilege on θ provided that τ's ability to access and modify data does not increase.

In other words, inferred privileges on a derived object Z ought to increase convenience but not power. The additional privileges merely allow the creator to issue statements that include Z, instead of issuing equivalent statements on the underlying tables.

For example, suppose that Z is a view, defined as follows:

```
create view Z as select A, C from T where T.B > 2
```

Suppose that the creator τ has privileges on (SELECT, T) and (UPDATE, T.A). Then it would be wrong to give τ the privilege on (UPDATE, Z), since doing so would suddenly give τ the ability to modify additional columns of T. However, (UPDATE, Z.A) is reasonable, since this operation reads B and updates T.A, and both operations for which τ is authorized. Moreover, now suppose τ loses privilege on (SELECT, T.C). Then τ should lose privilege on (SELECT, Z.C), but should keep privilege on (SELECT, Z.A).

The approach we use to justify inferences on derived objects is to use *query modification*. Query modification takes a statement S involving derived object Z, and produces an equivalent statement S' by replacing references to Z by references to tables in DEF(Z). For example, consider the following query on the above view:

```
select Z.A from Z
```

Query modification produces the following equivalent query:

```
select T.A from T where T.B > 2
```

From this equivalence, we know that it would be incorrect to give τ an inferred privilege on (SELECT, Z.A) unless τ already has privileges on (SELECT, T.A) and (SELECT, T.B); otherwise, τ would be able to execute the first query in lieu of the forbidden second one.

Analying the modification of a single statement can provide a counterexample (demonstrating that inference would increase power), but it cannot directly tell us if an inference is correct. The SQL inference principle states that the creator τ should receive privilege on θ if the following condition is true: *For every statement S involving Z, if after adding privilege for θ, τ is authorized for S then τ is also authorized for an equivalent statement that does not mention Z.* To test this condition directly, we would have to examine every possible statement S involving Z, which is clearly infeasible.

In order to provide conditions that are independent of S, we need to know, for a given operation θ, which other operations affect it. We introduce the following definition.

Let Z be a derived object, and let θ be an operation on Z. We define *OPS(θ)* to be the set of operations that in effect, implement θ. This set is defined for each action individually:

- OPS((SELECT, Z.B)) consists of those operations (SELECT, T.A) such that changing some A-value of T can change the B-values of Z.
- OPS((INSERT, Z.B)) consists of those operations (INSERT, T.A) if inserting into Z can cause an insertion into T, and Z.B is derived from T.A.
- OPS((DELETE, Z)) consists of (DELETE, T) if deleting from Z can cause a deletion from T.
- OPS((UPDATE, Z.B)) consists of those operations (UPDATE, T.A) if updating the B-value of Z can cause a change in the A-value of T.
- OPS((EXECUTE, P)) consists of the operations required to execute the body of procedure P. That is, it contains each operation in OPS(DEF(P)).

Lemma: Let statement S be a query, update, or procedure call that mentions derived object Z. Let S′ be an equivalent statement that does not mention Z, resulting from query modification. Suppose that $\theta' \in$ OPS(S′). Then either $\theta' \in$ OPS(S), or there exists a θ in OPS(S) such that $\theta' \in$ OPS(θ).

Proof: Query modification for Z, by definition, replaces only references to Z. Therefore, all operations in OPS(S) that do not involve Z must also be in OPS(S′). Moreover, any other operation in OPS(S′) must have resulted from query modification. So consider any operation θ' in OPS(S′). We analyze it according to its action.

- Suppose θ' = (SELECT, T.A). Then by definition, changing the A-value of T changes the result of S′, and thus S as well. Let B be an attribute of S whose values change when T.A changes. If B does not come from Z, then the reference to B must carry over to S′. In other words, θ' must also be in OPS(S). So suppose B does come from Z. Since changing T.A changes Z.B, it must be that (SELECT, Z.B) is in OPS(S), and θ' must be in OPS((SELECT, Z.B)). In either case, the lemma holds.
- Suppose θ' = (INSERT, T.A). Then S′ (and S) insert a tuple into T having a non-null A-value. If S is an "insert into T" statement, then θ' would be in OPS(S). Otherwise, S must be an "insert into Z" statement. Moreover, since T.A is non-null, there must be a corresponding Z.B that maps to it. Thus θ' must be in OPS((INSERT, Z.B)) and (INSERT, Z.B) must be in OPS(S). Again the lemma holds.
- The proofs for the actions DELETE and UPDATE are similar to that for INSERT, and are omitted.

End of Proof.

The following rule shows how OPS(θ) can be calculated. The theorem following it shows that this rule is correct.

The SQL Privilege Inference Rule: Let τ be the creator of derived object Z, and let θ be an operation on Z.

- *Infer the privilege (τ, θ) if τ has a privilege for every operation in OPS(θ).*
- *Infer the privilege (τ, grantθ) if τ has grant-option privilege for every operation in OPS(θ).*

Theorem: The privileges inferred by this rule satisfy the SQL Inference Principle.

Proof: Let S be a statement involving derived object Z, and suppose that the creator τ is authorized for S due to privileges inferred from the inference rule. We show that τ is also authorized for an equivalent statement S' that does not mention Z. There are two cases.

The first case is when S is a query, update, or procedure call. Let S' be the equivalent statement resulting from query modification. If τ is not authorized for S', then there must be an operation θ' in OPS(S') that τ does not have privilege on. The above lemma states that θ' is either in OPS(S) or in OPS(θ) for some θ in OPS(S). If it is in OPS(S), then τ is not authorized for S. If it is in OPS(θ), then τ would not have inferred privilege on θ. Consequently, τ must be authorized for S'.

The second case is when S is a grant statement. Suppose S is:

```
grant select on Z.A to x [with grant option]
```

In order for τ to be authorized for this statement, τ must have grant-option privileges for each operation in OPS((SELECT, Z.A)). Suppose that this set is {(SELECT, T1.A1),..., (SELECT, Tn.An)}. The equivalent statement S' is thus the compound statement:

```
grant select on T1.A1 to x [with grant option];
...
grant select on Tn.An to x [with grant option]
```

By executing S', ID τ has empowered subject x to create his own version of Z' of Z. Once Z' is created, the SQL inference rule would then grant privilege on (SELECT, Z'.B) to x, which has the same effect as executing S. The cases where τ grants other actions to x are handled similarly.

End of proof.

This theorem shows that the above inference rule, together with our definition of OPS(θ), infers reasonable and correct privileges on derived objects. The SQL standard has a similar inference rule but does not have a correctness proof. The standard defines OPS(θ) implicitly, via numerous case-by-case rules similar to those for OPS(S). We believe that our definition is equivalent to that of the standard, but (just like the situation with defining OPS(S)) the task of proving it is daunting.

3   Inferred Privileges on Derived Objects

The SQL model, and many researchers' models, provide for inferred privileges on derived objects. Our contribution is to extend derived privileges *in a SQL-friendly way* to non-creators. We first present the extension. Section 4 identifies a wide range of benefits.

Our proposed extension to SQL is to allow privileges on a derived object to be inferred for any ID, not just the object's creator. This extension is formalized as follows:

The Inference Principle: Let θ be an operation on derived object Z. An ID τ should receive privilege on θ as long as τ's ability to access and modify data does not increase.

In order to apply this principle to the SQL model, three issues must be addressed:

- Lift the SQL restriction on who may create a derived object.
- Define simple controls on SQL metadata privileges.
- Allow users to infer privileges on derived objects, if they have privileges on underlying operations *and they have adequate metadata privileges.*

The following subsections address these issues.

3.1 Creation and Visibility

In standard SQL, all privileges on a derived object stem from the creator. Consequently there is no reason for SQL to allow an ID to create an object unless the creator receives a reasonable number of privileges. However, this rationale collapses once we allow privileges to be inferred by the general user population – the creator may have few privileges on the object, but other users may receive substantially more, via inference.

We therefore propose to drop this restriction, and to allow *every* ID to create a derived object *regardless of the resulting inferred privileges.* The creator will receive whatever privileges the system can infer.

A problem now arises with metadata visibility. The simple SQL inference rule is concerned with only the object creator's privileges, and of course the creator knows the object definition. We now must be concerned with users who, even if they have access to underlying data, might not deserve access to the view definition, or even be told what attributes it references. We thus propose that metadata privileges be explicit. In particular, we define a new action on derived objects, called VISIBLE. Privilege on (VISIBLE, Z) allows the ID to see Z's definition.

The creator of a derived object automatically receives privileges on VISIBLE, with grant option, and can grant these privileges to others, as desired. For example, a user might have use of a view (i.e., the right to execute some operation on it), but no ability to see its defining query. Conversely, one might want to make derived object interfaces visible to users who then, if interested, could negotiate permission to use the view. For example, one might advertise services, and allow usage after a payment is received. Finally, many organizations may prefer to make metadata visible as a default.

3.2 Privilege Inference

The following rule extends the SQL Privilege Inference Rule of Section 2.5 to all subjects. Its simplicity testifies to the utility of our abstractions.

The Privilege Inference Rule: Let Z be a derived object, τ denote any ID, and θ be an operation on Z.

- *Infer the privilege (τ, θ) if τ has privilege for every operation in OPS(θ) and also has (VISIBLE, Z)*
- *Infer the privilege (τ, grantθ) if τ has grant-option privilege for every operation in OPS(θ), and also has (grantVISIBLE, Z).*

Theorem: The Privilege Inference Rule satisfies the Inference Principle.

Proof: The proof is exactly the same as the proof of the corresponding theorem in Section 2.5. That proof showed that if giving ID τ privilege on θ allows τ to execute statement S, then there is an equivalent statement S' that τ is already authorized for. The only wrinkle is that the construction of S' requires knowledge of DEF(Z), and if S is a grant statement, the ability to convey DEF(Z) to the grantee as well. In other words, τ must have VISIBLE privilege on Z so that S' can be constructed; if S is a grant statement, then τ must also have grantVISIBLE privilege.

The inference rule for procedures adapts easily to handle composite web services, e.g., expressed as workflows: The inference rule infers the right to execute the workflow for users who can read its definition, and have rights for all services requested. Inference is useful for two different approaches to privilege checking:

- *Authorizations may enable execution of the entire workflow* (exactly as is done for a database procedure). The semantics are conservative, since an execution may invoke only a subset of the services mentioned in its definition.
- *Authorization may be done at run time, for each service the workflow invokes.* Additional executions may be possible, depending on conditions in the code. However, some situations require guarantees that a service will be available; inference helps the administrator determine whether a guarantee is possible.

4 Benefits of Our Extensions

The Inference Principle provides for *automated, well-founded,* and *sound* inference of privileges for all users of a database system. In particular, the above theorem shows that the privileges inferred by the Inference Rule are guaranteed to satisfy the Inference Principle, and are thus reasonable and correct. In the following subsections we discuss how our extensions are able to overcome the following weaknesses in SQL.

4.1 Creators Need Not Be Administrators

In SQL, every privilege on a derived object must stem from a chain of grants starting from the object's creator. If the creator does not wish to administer and has no willing designee, the object won't be shared. If the creator does not have grant-option privileges on the object, then it can't be shared at all. In our model, subjects with (VISIBLE, Z) and privileges on OPS(θ) are immediately able to use θ without any explicit grant by the creator. For example, the creator could give access on Z to "anyone who has sufficient authorization on the underlying tables" simply by granting (VISIBLE, Z) to PUBLIC.

In fact, any combination of controls is possible. A proprietary service could be applied to data the user already owns (and does not share with the service creator), by granting VISIBLE. Alternatively, the creator could negotiate for access to proprietary data, and then delegate his privileges.

4.2 Privileges Can Be Kept Consistent Automatically

Consider a data warehouse, whose contents are in effect a materialized view of its underlying source databases[2]. In current systems, the warehouse DBA is responsible

---

[2] In this example, we assume the user has rights to execute on the warehouse machine, and just needs data rights. In [14] we confront the issue of execution autonomy.

for granting privileges on the warehouse data. The DBA is trusted to protect the interests of data providers, but the system has no way to enforce consistency between the warehouse privileges and the source privileges. Moreover, when the sources' decisions change, there may not be an obvious way for the DBA to derive corresponding changes to the warehouse privileges. Consider, for example, where a user persuades the DBA that he already had rights on the underlying data, so it is legitimate to allow access to the copy in the warehouse. If the user loses their rights on the underlying data, how likely is it that the warehouse DBA will be informed, deduce the consequences, and immediately revoke the rights in the warehouse?

In our model, the Inference Rule establishes and maintains consistency. Privileges can be defined once and inferred on views, eliminating the need for redundant grant specifications. The warehouse could automatically infer privileges consistent with the underlying source privileges, so that its DBA need only administer the explicit grants (if any) that go beyond the inferred ones.

4.3 Explicit Control Over Metadata Privileges

SQL's metadata visibility philosophy emphasizes convenience and simplicity over accuracy. By allowing an ID having any privilege on an object has the ability to see all metadata about the object, more metadata is revealed than is required:

- A user with SELECT privileges on one column can see all columns' metadata.
- A user with only SELECT privileges can see the constraints.
- A user who can execute a derived object can see its definition.

In some cases, the wider accessibility is desirable. It lets users browse schema information related to what they already use. They may discover additional useful resources, and negotiate for access. But in some cases, it may be undesirable. The need seems particularly strong for view definitions, which may embody confidential thresholds and weighting parameters. Our introduction of the VISIBLE action allows administrators to fine-tune the availability of their metadata. (Withholding access to metadata prevents inference, as a side effect. "Do you want inference to occur" is a question with no clear criteria – it seems better to focus on the fundamental notion of metadata access, and derive inference privileges from that).

This "gap" in treatment of metadata privileges illustrates the value of having a model that conforms to theoretical principles. Many papers, (e.g., [2, 8]), including our own [13], have proposed inferring view or federated view privileges from privileges on underlying operations. These proposals "almost" conform to the Inference Principle, but still allow users to indirectly discover information about the view definition. For example, unrestricted inference can allow attackers to determine what tables are mentioned in the view query. When one adds query simplification strategies that replace a query by an equivalent [13], the gap becomes more serious, because privilege inference may permit attackers to guess WHERE clause predicates. This "covert channel" illustrates how a small gap in a model can cause significant costs (if the product is widely used), and how what seemed a decent approximation originally becomes inappropriate when the system is extended. Our theory closes the gap.

4.4 Untrusted IDs can Create Useful Derived Objects

In standard SQL, the creator of a derived object is the source of all delegatees' privileges. Consequently, only someone trusted with the underlying objects can create a useful view. Either the view-creator must be given privileges on underlying data, or some trusted administrator must act as the "official" creator. We allow modes where the creator merely provides the container. Our privilege inference democratizes the capability to create useful derived objects, Other IDs can access or administer the object if the creator is too busy, or untrusted (e.g., the programmer should not get to read medical records).

4.5 Invoker Rights Are Integrated into the Model

The SQL standard requires that the creator of a procedure have grant-option privileges on all operations used in the procedure's code. This situation has not been acceptable to the user community, and vendors have responded by adding additional security options to procedures. For example, Oracle procedures can be executed using an *invoker-rights* mechanism. An invoker-rights procedure not only requires an EXECUTE privilege, but the invoker must also be authorized to execute the procedure's body. That is, invoker-rights procedures are conveniences, and privileges on them do not confer additional database power. Thus a contract programmer can write a complex procedure, and grant EXECUTE privilege to PUBLIC (say); then only those users having sufficient authorization on the objects accessed are allowed to call the procedure.

Our work extends invoker-right features beyond procedure execution, to any operation θ on a derived object Z. In our model, an administrator can simulate invoker-rights mode on θ by refusing to explicitly grant privileges on it, and instead selectively granting VISIBLE privileges on Z. Only those subjects having privilege for (VISIBLE, Z) plus all privileges in OPS(θ) will be given privilege on θ.

In our model, invoker-rights and traditional administration modes are orthogonal – they can be combined arbitrarily. An administrator can choose to grant explicit privileges on θ to some IDs, and to allow possible inference of θ to other IDs by granting VISIBLE privilege to them.

4.6 Support for Other Data Models

The major DBMS vendors have announced plans to provide both XML and SQL services in the same DBMS, and to allow data stored in one model to be viewed in the other. Authorization semantics should therefore be consistent wherever possible – preferably by building over shared abstractions. Our "derived data" abstraction, explicit treatment of metadata visibility, and (in next section) transferring ownership will be useful both within and across the data models.

5 Base Table Ownership

The last two sections have demonstrated the benefit of separating the metadata privileges on a derived object from the privileges on its contents. In this section we consider whether similar benefits are possible for base tables.

It is clear that the creator of a base table deserves all metadata privileges. The question is how to assign the privileges on the table's contents. For example, a programmer or DBA who creates a table to hold medical data should probably not have the right to see that data. Instead, privileges on the table data should belong to the medical community.

There are various tricks that can be used to work around this issue, such as calling the medical privacy officer to do the actual creation, denying programmers access to operational systems, and using a predicate in middleware or in an audit system to enforce that DBAs not abuse their privileges. Some models have separate "administer" and "access" rights, and impose a constraint to prevent an administrator from granting themselves access rights [16]. This approach has much to recommend it, but might be seen as too big a step for SQL; also, it requires a powerful, path-following constraint mechanism.

A simple, direct treatment would be better – a way to say simply "user X no longer has rights" without affecting their delegatees. The barrier in current SQL is that one cannot remove the creator's rights, because deletion cascades [7] – that is, each privilege must be supported by a path from the object creator.

We therefore propose that an ID τ possessing privilege on an operation should be able to *renounce* that privilege, while allowing grantees to retain it. For example, suppose that operation $\theta = $ (SELECT, T); the SQL syntax to renounce θ might look something like this:

```
renounce select on T
```

The effect of this statement is that τ loses the privilege on θ, as well as grantθ if applicable. In addition, the provenance for grantees from τ are adjusted. Supposing that τ granted privilege on θ (or grantθ) to ID τ', we reconnect the grant graph in the obvious way:

- If τ received the privilege from some other ID, then create a direct grant from that ID to τ'. (That is, connect up the graph).
- If τ received the grant by inference or as object creator, then label τ's privilege as "inferred" or "system-granted".

A larger *transfer* command can be provided. It would first grant to the recipients, and then call *renounce*. To guarantee correctness, one should also give the *transfer* command the precondition that τ has no unrevoked grants of θ. Transfer of privileges also is supported in [2], with a richer set of capabilities, including explicit acceptance of responsibility. (We omit acceptance because it seemed hard to resolve ambiguity about exactly what responsibility is being accepted). The simplicity of the Renounce primitive also appears useful, e.g., when analyzing possible behaviors of a system. Many flavors of Transfer can then be built using Grant followed by Renounce.

6 Open Problems

We have shown that a careful analysis of SQL authorization can point out its limitations and inconsistencies. This analysis also led us to the discovery of a few extensions to SQL that not only resolve these limitations, but also streamline the overall semantics and simplify administration. The fact that these extensions can be small is significant – not only do they have a greater chance of being implemented by vendors, but they also indicate that the (hidden) elegance of the SQL authorization model.

This paper focused primarily on derived objects in SQL. In this section we will briefly discuss three other areas where analysis is needed.

SQL has become an object relational language, with IS-A relationships and complex attributes, expressed in a table-friendly way that differs from traditional object models. Object security rules are mixed with other aspects (e.g., views), in procedural specifications. Several researchers have proposed security semantics for object models that include IS-A or complex object relationships [8, 11], but these object models and security models differ from SQL's. An important open problem is to extend the results of this paper to adapt their insights to SQL. The goals would be to simplify the current treatment, and perhaps provide additional capabilities.

Relational systems are quickly moving to include XML capabilities. Many researchers are proposing security models for XML [6, 9]. Generally these proposals examine the model's power and implementability in an XML-specific way. Analysis would help to integrate XML and SQL security, perhaps by expressing both in terms of common foundational abstractions. Not only would such an analysis simplify the semantics of a combined SQL/XML model, if would also contribute to the understanding of XML-based middleware. In particular, security policies will be needed so that SQL data can be shared with XML-oriented administrators at the middleware level, and vice versa. Again, a common core would greatly simplify the mappings.

XML security is still a work in progress, and easier to change than relational systems. As argued above, there are strong gains if it is compatible with SQL. Furthermore, semantic web formalisms such as RDF and OWL are on the near horizon, and they too will need security models. The results of this paper suggest that compatibility with SQL security should be an additional goal when developing a new model, and that security policies should be expressed in terms of abstract language constructs (e.g., containment, derivation). This situation is depicted below. In this way, we can greatly reduce the costs of learning, implementing, and maintaining consistency among security models for XML, SQL, RDF, and OWL.

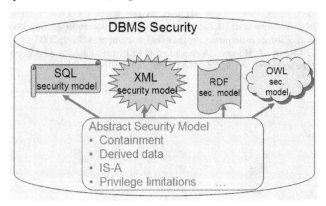

References

1. E. Bertino, P. Samarati, S. Jajodia, "An extended authorization model for relational databases", *IEEE TKDE,* 1997
2. E. Bertino, E. Ferrari, "Administration Policies in a Multipolicy Authorization System", *Database Security XI - Status and Prospects, Proc. of Tenth Annual IFIP Working Conference on Database Security,* 1997
3. R. Bhatti, E. Bertino, A. Ghafoor, J. Joshi, "XML-Based Specification for Web Services Document Security", *IEEE Computer,* April 2004.
4. S. Castano, S. De Capitani di Vimercati, M.G. Fugini, Automated Derivation of Global Authorizations for Database Federations, *Journal of Computer Security*, vol. 5, n. 4, 1997, pp. 271-301.

5. S. De Capitani di Vimercati, P. Samarati, "Authorization Specification and Enforcement in Federated Database Systems", *Journal of Computer Security*, vol. 5, n. 2, 1997, pp. 155-188.
6. S. Castano, M. Fugini, G. Martella, P. Samarati, *Database Security*, Addison-Wesley 1995.
7. Y. Cui, J. Widom, J. Weiner, "Tracing the lineage of view data in a warehousing environment" *ACM Transactions on Database Systems (TODS)* Volume 25 Issue 2 (June 2000)
8. E. Damiani, S. De Capitani di Vimercati, S. Paraboschi, P. Samarati, " A Fine-Grained Access Control System for XML Documents," *ACM Transactions on Information and System Security (TISSEC)*, vol. 5, n. 2, May 2002, pp. 169-202.
9. R. Fagin, "On an Authorization Mechanism", *ACM Transactions on Database Systems*, Vol. 3, No. 3, September 1978, Pages 310-319.
10. E Gudes and MS Olivier, "Security Policies in Replicated and Autonomous Databases," in S. Jajodia (ed), *Database Security XII: Status and Prospects*, 93-107, Kluwer, 1999
11. S. Jajodia, P. Samarati, M. Sapino, V. S. Subrahmanian, "Flexible Support for Multiple Access Control Policies", *ACM Trans. Database Systems*, 2001.
12. D. Lomet "A Role for Research in the Database Industry" *ACM Computing Surveys* 28(4es), December 1996.
13. M. Negri, G. Pelagatti, L. Sbattella, "Formal Semantics of SQL Queries" ACM TODS 17(3), September 1991
14. F. Rabitti, E. Bertino, W. Kim, D. Woelk, "A model of authorization for next generation database systems", *ACM Trans. Database Systems*, 16(1) March 1991.
15. S. Rizvi, A. Mendelzon, S. Sudarshan, P. Roy "Extending Query Rewriting Techniques for Fine-Grained Access Control", *ACM SIGMOD Conf.*, Paris, 2004.
16. A. Rosenthal, E. Sciore, "First-Class Views: A Key to User-Centered Computing", *SIGMOD Record*, Sept. 1999.
17. A. Rosenthal, E. Sciore, "View Security as the Basis for Data Warehouse Security", *CAiSE Workshop on Design and Management of Data Warehouses*, Stockholm, 2000.
18. *SQL Standard, Part 2 (Foundations)*, ISO/IEC document 9075-2, 2003.
19. W. Yao, K. Moody, J. Bacon, "A model of OASIS role-based access control and its support for active security", *ACM SACMAT Conf.*, Chantilly VA, 2001.

A Classifier-Based Approach
to User-Role Assignment for Web Applications

Shengli Sheng and Sylvia L. Osborn

Dept. of Computer Science
The University of Western Ontario
London, Ontario, Canada
ssheng@uwo.ca/sylvia@csd.uwo.ca

Abstract. Role-based access control (RBAC) can be used to design a security system for on-line applications. The Role Graph Model is the only RBAC system which has the notion of a group graph. We show how using the group graph to assign users to groups rather than directly to roles helps with this security design. We also show how a machine-learning based classifier can be used to do user-group assignment.

1 Introduction

Recently, role-based access control (RBAC) models have been introduced to control access to resources when there are a large number of resources and a large number of users [SCFY96,NO99]. Roles model a set of privileges as a single unit, which can then be easily assigned to one or more users in a single operation. Role models include the Sandhu model [SCFY96], the NIST standard [FSG+01] and the role graph model [NO99]. Of these the role graph model also provides a way to put users into groups, which the others do not emphasize.

Role design can take place in different kinds of environments. In a large company, the task of role design involves both deciding what privileges the roles should have and which users are assigned to roles. The users in this case are company employees whose job titles and personalities are known to the company and to the security designers. In a web application environment, the users are on-line customers from the far corners of the world. They are unknown to the company providing the service, but nevertheless have to be assigned to roles when they enter the web application of the company. Not only are they unknown to the site administrators, but the cardinality of the user set is unbounded.

In this paper we propose using classification techniques from the data mining field to assign users to groups. We will begin by describing RBAC models and the role graph model in particular. This is followed in Section 3 by a comparison with other research. Section 4 provides a motivating example. The use of a classifier for user-group assignment is explained in Section 5. Section 6 summarizes the paper.

W. Jonker and M. Petković (Eds.): SDM 2004, LNCS 3178, pp. 163–171, 2004.

2   Role-Based Access Control

As we have noted above, several RBAC models have been introduced in the past decade. In the RBAC96 model [SCFY96], the major model components are the roles, R, the permissions, P, users, U and sessions, S. Permissions are composed of a data object and an access mode or operation on the object. Access modes can be read, write, append, etc. Objects are the items which are being protected by the access control model. Roles are arranged in a role hierarchy. The role hierarchy provides a many-to-many relationship among roles. There are also many-to-many relationships between users and roles, and between roles and permissions. Sessions model the activities of a single user and may map to many roles, but only to one user. Constraints can be defined on all of the components as well as the relationships. We will see how constraints can be used later in an example. The Sandhu model also has an administrative component [OS02] which is not germane to the discussion in this paper.

The role graph model [NO94,NO99] enhances the role hierarchy (called the role graph here) with algorithms for role insertion and deletion, privilege addition and deletion and graph edge insertion and deletion (which corresponds to adding/deleting relationships between roles). As well, the role graph is required to be acyclic; operations that would violate this requirement are rejected. The algorithms are implemented in a tool which provides feedback to the role designer [OHL03]. Within the tool, senior roles are shown above their juniors in the display. An edge from a role r_i to r_j indicates that the permissions assigned to r_i are a proper subset of the permissions assigned to r_j.

One enhancement of the role graph model over the Sandhu and Nist models is the presence of the group graph [OG00]. Groups are organized in a group graph, with an edge representing the fact that one group is a proper subset of the other. Each group represents a set of users. Individual users can be represented by a group of cardinality 1, although in the web application scenario where there are thousands of users, it is not feasible to display individual nodes for each user. Groups are assigned to roles in a many-to-many relationship similar to the way in which users are assigned to roles in the other models.

We feel that the separation of groups and roles is important to modeling. The design of roles focuses on what privileges or permissions should correspond to each role; in some environments the structure of the roles and the relationships between them might be almost static once the initial design is complete. The design of the groups, on the other hand, focuses on which users have something in common. Users will have, in general, more than one user-role assignment. In an enterprise environment, there might be a group for all engineers based on some qualifications of individual users. This Engineer group would be assigned to a basic role for engineers. As well, there might be a steering committee which is composed of one engineer, a manager, a staff member, etc. One of the engineers would be a member of this group, which is then assigned to a role which encapsulates the permissions necessary for the steering committee to carry out its function. Deciding which users should be on the steering committee is a separate modeling activity from deciding on the rights and privileges that should belong to the steering committee role; furthermore, role design and user-role assignment might be carried out by different managers.

The third aspect of the role graph model is the consideration of privileges or permissions [IO03]. In a complex environment, say where the objects are deeply nested, the privilege to read a large object may imply the privilege to read all its components (this can, for example, be applied to XML documents). The role graph model also has an administrative component [WO03].

3   Related Work

There has been previous work in this area, relating to using knowledge about users and reasoning to assign users to roles. All use some kind of rules, which have to be specified by the system administrators in advance.

Zhong et al. [ZBM01] describe assigning roles to web service users in terms based on information on trustworthiness. The trustworthiness information can be collected in different ways. It can be provided by trusted third parties or by users themselves through interactive dialogues. It can also be obtained through analysis of web logs. After the trustworthiness information is assessed, users are assigned a set of roles automatically according to a pre-defined policy.

Herzberg et. al [HMM00] define the Trust Policy Language (TPL) for mapping web service users to predefined business roles, based on the certificates issued by third parties. The XML-Based TPL allows complex policies. The certificate contains a public key and properties of the owner of the corresponding secret key. The properties include the identity of the owner and a collection of attribute values. The certificate authentication component outputs the entire certificate to the TE system. The TE system identifies a role, based on a policy that maps a certificate to roles.

Al-Kahtani and Sandhu [AKS02,AKS03] describe a Rule-Based RBAC model which assigns users to a set of roles based on a finite set of rules defined by an enterprise. The rules are built using attribute expressions and constraints. Since users have a lot of attributes and an enterprise has its business polices, how to predefine the rules and the constraints is an issue. They define a Rule-Based RBAC language, which they call RB-RBAC. They introduce a seniority levels concept to explain the rule-rule relationships and the relations between rules and roles, such as which rule is senior to which rule under what conditions, and how a senior rule inherits the roles produced by its juniors. RB-RBAC assigns roles to users in terms of the attribute expressions and the constraints predefined in an enterprise.

All of this previous research focuses on assigning users directly to roles. We advocate, instead, using such mechanisms to assign users to groups based on their properties and credentials. Thus when changes have to be made to the role hierarchy, it should be clear what new role existing groups should be assigned to, and the users credentials will not have to be reevaluated to decide which new roles are appropriate. In other words, separating the formation of user groups from the role hierarchy could also be applied to these existing proposals. In the next section we will carry this one step further by showing an alternative way of assigning strangers to groups.

4   Example

We now present a simplified example for an on-line store, which allows customers to borrow, donate, or buy and sell videos or books which might have adult-only content. A group graph and a role graph for this example are shown in Figure 1. Users will be classified into the groups shown in the group graph. The role graph has roles which correspond to different aspects of the company's user interface, so the roles deal with donating materials, borrowing youth materials, borrowing adult materials and buying and selling, both regular merchandise and special editions which are a lot more expensive. Based on the information provided by the users, they will be classified into various groups: Youth, Adult, Silver, and Gold. All users can be put in the Anyone group.

The edges in the role graph indicate that any privileges assigned to the role at the tail of the edge are inherited by the role at the head of the edge. Thus, the YouthBorrow role inherits any privileges in the Browse role, etc. Moreover, if the privileges included in the YouthBorrow role are a subset of the privileges of the AdultBorrow role (i.e. the access modes in both cases are just "borrow" but the objects in the YouthBorrow case are a subset of the objects available through the AdultBorrow role), the role graph algorithms will make YouthBorrow a junior role to AdultBorrow, as shown in Figure 1. Role design can be carried out in such a way that the roles reflect useful packages of privileges which may correspond to parts of the code in the system being implemented. It is not necessary to have users or groups assigned to all roles.

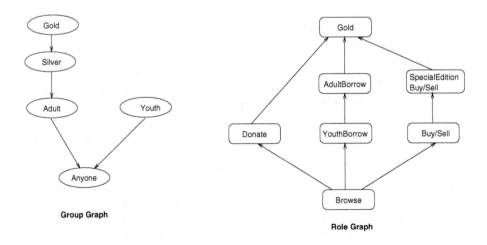

Fig. 1. Example Group Graph and Role Graph for an On-Line Store

In the Group graph, an edge indicates that the group at the tail of the edge is a proper subset of the group at the head of the edge. Thus all Gold members are also Silver members, and in turn all Silver members are also Adult members.

The user-role assignment for the example is the following: the Anyone group is assigned to the Browse role; the Youth group is assigned to Donate and Youth-Borrow. The Adult group is assigned to Donate and AdultBorrow. The Gold group is assigned to the Gold role, which inherits all the privileges of the other roles in the graph, including the SpecialEdition Buy/Sell role. The Silver group is assigned to the Buy/Sell role. Note that the SpecialEdition Buy/Sell role has no direct group assignments. These direct group-role assignments are summarized in Table 1. Note that any user who is a member of the Silver group, because they are also in the Adult group according to the group graph, also is able to perform the Donate and AdultBorrow roles.

Table 1. Summary of Direct Group-Role Assignments

Group	Role
Anyone	Browse
Youth	Donate, YouthBorrow
Adult	Donate, AdultBorrow
Silver	Buy/Sell
Gold	Gold

Such a model also needs constraints. As noted in [NO99], constraints arise for various reasons. There might be conflict of interest constraints between groups or between roles. Such constraints can be used, for example, to say that a user who is a member of the Youth group cannot also be a member of the Gold (or Adult) group. Constraints can also be put on user/group to role assignment; an example of this would be that a user who is assigned to the Donate role should not also be assigned to the Buy/Sell role. Such a constraint can be static, which means that this is a constraint on all user/role assignments, so that no user can ever be assigned to these two roles (note that this makes the Gold role unassignable because if a user is assigned to Gold, they would be able to perform both junior roles, which has been deemed impossible by the constraint). We can also have dynamic conflict of interest constraints which constrain what roles can be active simultaneously in a session. An example of this is perhaps that we do not want users from the Adult group doing donations (i.e. activating the Donate role) and borrowing (activating the AdultBorrow role) in the same session.

Another type of constraint is illustrated by the next example. Suppose the store wants a policy that once an adult or youth has borrowed two items, they should not borrow anything more until those items are returned. They could still perform other privileges such as those involving donating items. This could be modeled by adding groups to the group graph, such as AdultCan'tBorrow and YouthCan'tBorrow, and not assigning those groups to the corresponding Borrow roles. However, this solution would involve moving users around into different groups part way through a session if they have borrowed the two items during the session. Another way to handle this situation is to have a constraint on sessions, or group-role activation, which checks the number of items borrowed and prevents the user from activating the Borrow role or deactivates it if their quota is full.

5   Classifier-Based User-Group Assignment

A classifier is a software tool based on a machine learning algorithm such as decision trees, neural networks, Bayesian networks, etc. [Mit97]. Objects, for example the customers of the simple on-line store, who possess attribute values such as age, sex, occupation, citizenship and so on, are presented to the system. The goal of the classifier used in the model is to eventually put all objects into classes. Machine learning techniques start with a set of given instances with class labels supplied and use this learning set to construct the classifier. The classifier is then used to predict the class for new instances with known attribute values but unknown class labels.

We will explain how a classifier can be used to construct groups, by discussing a classifier based on a decision tree. Decision tree learning is the learning algorithm most commonly used for constructing a classifier. This classifier is also called a decion tree, as it represents a set of if-then rules which are mined from the training examples. The internal nodes of the tree, called attribute nodes, denote the attributes of customers. The branches of each attribute node represent the possible values of the attribute. The leaves of the decision tree represent groups. When a new instance is presented, it can be classified into a related group in terms of these rules by comparing it with the node contents in the tree from root to leaf. The resulting leaf represents a group in which it can be classified.

A decision tree is learned from a set of training examples, which are objects (here it would be data representing the users of our system) with attribute values and a predetermined classification value. The decision tree construction algorithm builds the tree top-down. First it selects the attribute which is best at classifying the training examples, from among the attributes of the users, to be used in the root node of the tree. The possible branches represent the values the attribute can take on. The descendants of the root node are selected from the remaining attributes in the same way, given the root attribute value on the relevant path from the root node. The entire process is repeated until the full tree is built. The decision tree construction algorithms also employ pruning techniques to prune parts of the tree where the attribute values no longer contribute to useful splitting of the data sets. The result of the pruning is that not all the leaves are at one level. The leaves of the decision tree represent the resulting classes. It might be that there are, say, 20 leaves but only 3 classes. The classes then are made up of the union of all the instances which fall into one of the leaf nodes with a given class label. The classes thus obtained are mutually disjoint. A example of a simple decision tree for our retail store is shown in Figure 2.

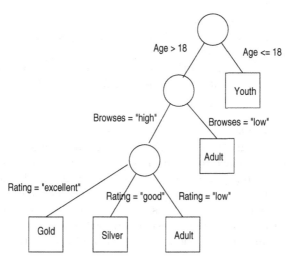

Fig. 2. Example Decision Tree

Given the results of the classification exercise, we then have to consider the correspondence between the resulting classes produced and the groups already designed for the group graph. Note that in the decision tree, the classes are considered to be disjoint. However, in the group graph, we wish to consider anyone who is a Gold customer to also be Silver, and anyone who is Silver is also considered to be adult.

The modeling that is done in the group graph is different from that carried out by the decision tree classifier. Suppose that rather than the group graph in Figure 1, we instead had the group graph shown in Figure 3. Then with the same user-role assignments as given in Table 1, the Silver group can now only perform the directly assigned BuySell role, whereas the total set of privileges available to Gold members is the same, because, given the structure of the role graph, the gold role inherits all the privilege of the other roles.

Fig. 3. Alternative Group Graph

This example shows why we believe that there are three kinds of modeling necessary in an application such as this. In designing the role graph, one determines the useful units of privilege, which may correspond to different aspects of the business. With the machine learning classifier, one is deciding how trustworthy certain users are. By designing the group graph, one is deciding that say, any user who can be trusted, say as a Silver member, should be able to do whatever an adult can do, and that therefore we should make the set of Silver users a subset of the Adult users as in Figure 1. It is important that whatever tools one uses to design the group and role graphs give feedback so that the designer can see the consequences of making a group graph a certain shape, or of constructing the role graph in a certain way.

There is also a difference in the timing and volatility of the three kinds of information. The role graph design reflects business units, and would change only when new aspects are added to the business. The group graph also is fairly static, as it reflect an understanding of how we want to do business. The classifier reflects how we assess trustworthiness; we might change the classifier (i.e. recompute the decision tree) when new attributes become available concerning users. Each time a user returns to our on-line business, we will probably reclassify them by running them through the decision tree, as some of their attribute values may have changed.

6   Conclusions

We have shown several things in this paper. The first was to emphasize that, even with the other techniques surveyed in section 3, it is important to have a group graph separate from the role graph or role hierarchy. In a traditional business environment, the human resources department may do user-group assignment, while the security system designers determine the shape of the role and group graphs and the group-role assignments. In the web application environment, where the users are strangers, the consideration of user-group assignment has to do with determination of trustworthyness of the user, whereas the design of the group and role graphs has the same considerations as any security design.

The second point we have made in this paper is that machine-learning based classifiers can be used to determine user-group assignment. We have shown how the classes generated by a classifier can be put in correspondence with the group graph. Building the classifier requires some expertise. Usually a domain expert collects the training data and decides which attributes are probably useful in classifying the data. We contend that expressing the policies in the other models also requires expertise, and that if the company already has someone familiar with machine learning, then using a classifier to do user-group assignment should be seriously considered.

We noted that the classification of users would take place far more frequently than the redesign of the group graph and role graph. The two graphs should be relatively stable in an on-line application – they should only change if major business policies change (which would affect group-role assignments) or if aspects of the business change (which would affect role graph design). Redesigning the classifier would happen rarely as well, but classifying users as they enter the on-line application would happen more frequently if their attributes change. We also noted that there are many aspects of such a system which are best modeled by constraints.

References

[AKS02]   M.A. Al-Kahtani and R. Sandhu. A model for attribute-based user-role assignment. In *ACSAC 2002*, 2002.

[AKS03]   M.A. Al-Kahtani and R. Sandhu. Induced role hierarchies with attribute-based rbac. In *Proceedings ACM SACMAT*, 2003.

[FSG+01] D.F. Ferraiolo, R. Sandhu, S. Gavrila, D.R. Kuhn, and R. Chandramouli. Proposed NIST standard for role-based access control. *ACM TISSEC*, 4(3):224–275, 2001.

[HMM00]   A Herzberg, Y. Mass, and J. Mihaeli. Access control meets public key infrastructure, or: Assigning roles to strangers. In *IEEE Symposium on Security and Privacy*, May 2000.

[IO03]   Cecilia M. Ionita and Sylvia L. Osborn. Privilege administration for the role graph model. In *Research Directions in Data and Applications Security, Proc. IFIP WG11.3 Working Conference on Database Security*, pages 15–25. Kluwer Academic Publishers, 2003.

[Mit97]   T. Mitchell. *Machine Learning*. McGraw-Hill, 1997.

[NO94]   M. Nyanchama and S. L. Osborn. Access rights administration in role-based security systems. In J. Biskup, M. Morgenstern, and C. E. Landwehr, editors, *Database Security, VIII, Status and Prospects WG11.3 Working Conference on Database Security*, pages 37–56. North-Holland, 1994.

[NO99]   M. Nyanchama and S. L. Osborn. The role graph model and conflict of interest. *ACM TISSEC*, 2(1):3–33, 1999.

[OG00]   S. Osborn and Y. Guo. Modeling users in role-based access control. In *Fifth ACM Workshop on Role-Based Access Control*, pages 31–38, Berlin, Germany, July 2000.

[OHL03]   Sylvia L. Osborn, Yan Han, and Jun Liu. A methodology for managing roles in legacy systems. In *Proc. 8th ACM SACMAT*, pages 33–40, 2003.

[OS02]   Sejong Oh and Ravi Sandhu. A model of role administration using organization structure. In *Proc. 7th ACM SACMAT*, pages 155–162, 2002.

[SCFY96] R. Sandhu, E.J. Coyne, H.L. Feinstein, and C.E. Youman. Role-based access control models. *IEEE Computer*, 29:38–47, Feb. 1996.

[WO03]   He Wang and Sylvia Osborn. An administrative model for role graphs. In *Proc. IFIP WG11.3 Working Conference on Database Security, Estes Park, Colorado*, 2003.

[ZBM01]   Y. Zhong, B. Bhargava, and M. Mahoui. Trustworthiness based authorization on WWW. In *IEEE workshop on Security in Distributed Data Warehousing*, 2001.

LTAM:
A Location-Temporal Authorization Model

Hai Yu and Ee-Peng Lim

Center for Advanced Information Systems,
Nanyang Technological University, Singapore
yuhai@pmail.ntu.edu.sg, aseplim@ntu.edu.sg

Abstract. This paper describes an authorization model for specifying access privileges of users who make requests to access a set of locations in a building or more generally a physical or virtual infrastructure. In the model, primitive locations can be grouped into composite locations and the connectivities among locations are represented in a multilevel location graph. Authorizations are defined with temporal constraints on the time to enter and leave a location and constraints on the number of times users can access a location. Access control enforcement is conducted by monitoring user movement and checking access requests against an authorization database. The authorization model also includes rules that define the relationships among authorizations. We also describe the problem of finding inaccessible locations given a set of user specified authorizations and a multilevel location graph, and outline a solution algorithm.

1   Introduction

Access control is an important aspect of computer security. It provides a framework for protecting resources within a system by restricting the accesses to *objects* (or resources) by *subjects* (or users). Other than objects and subjects, a basic access control model consists of *rules* that govern the way subjects are granted accesses to objects. Access control models can be discretionary or mandatory. In *discretionary access control* (DAC), owners of objects may grant access to others and are responsible for protecting the objects they own. In contrast, *mandatory access control* (MAC) assigns each object a security label that is used as the basis of restricting accesses of the users to the object. DAC has been widely adopted by commercial applications and databases systems. Due to its rather constrained way of granting access, the use of MAC has not been popular among commercial applications.

As wireless devices (e.g., RFIDs, handphones) become ubiquitous and are often equipped with positioning capabilities, they have been increasingly used for tracking user and object movements to support a wide range of applications[1–3]. For example, Singapore has used RFIDs to track movements of hospital users during the outbreaks of SARS (Severe Acute Respiratory Syndrome), a highly contagious and deadly disease. From the user movement data, users who were in

W. Jonker and M. Petković (Eds.): SDM 2004, LNCS 3178, pp. 172–186, 2004.

contact with diagnosed SARS patients could be traced and placed in quarantine or observations[4].

In homeland security, preventive measures are highly critical. As part of the efforts to safeguard the security of physical infrastructure, movements of users within a secured building can be tracked and their accesses to various locations in the building can be controlled by a security system that supports flexible access control. The ability of user tracking is also assumed in this research on authorization model.

In this paper, we propose a location-temporal authorization (LTAM) model that allows locations to be treated as objects and user accesses to these locations are restricted. The enforcement of such an authorization model requires maintaining the current locations of users and processing their access requests. Based on this model, computation and reasoning can be conducted on the authorizations to derive useful properties and knowledge about the location and time where authorizations are given.

Our proposed LTAM model differs from the existing office security systems that involve the use of card readers to authenticate and register user access requests for entering a room. The key differences are:

- The existing systems only enforce access control upon access requests while LTAM monitors the user movement at all times. This eliminates situation where a group of users enters a restricted location based on a single user authorization.
- LTAM can support more expressive access control restrictions. For example, one may be authorized to leave a location only during a certain time interval. Should this restriction be violated, security alerts can be triggered.
- LTAM can support an interesting range of queries on the authorizations and these queries are necessary to implement applications that manage movement and accesses to locations in a secure infrastructure. This is clearly a large improvement over the existing ad-hoc implementations.
- LTAM provides a framework for analyzing the security shortfalls due to human errors in specifying authorizations.
- LTAM protects the location privacy [5] of the users by restricting the location information in the central control station and not releasing it to other applications.

1.1   Outline of Paper

The rest of the paper is organized as follows. Section 2 reviews the existing work in temporal authorization models and context-aware information security. Our proposed authorization model is defined in Section 3 followed by the enforcement of the model described in Section 5. The authorization rules that allow new authorizations to be derived will be defined in Section 4. The problem of finding inaccessible locations and its solution are given in Section 6. Finally, Section 7 concludes the paper.

2   Related Work

Our proposed location-temporal authorization model falls under the area of spatio-temporal access control. Our literature survey however has found very little research work on this topic. We therefore examine some of the related work in temporal access control and spatial access control.

One of the first papers about temporal authorization model came from Bertino, Bettini and Samarati[6]. In their proposed authorization model known as TAM, each authorization for a user to access an object is augmented with a temporal interval of validity. In other words, the user is only able to access the object during the specified temporal interval and the dependencies among temporal authorizations can be specified within the proposed model. In [7], Gal and Atluri proposed another temporal authorization model called TDAM to support discretionary access control based on the temporal attributes of the objects themselves. Both TAM and TDAM are complementary models and can be used together.

An authorization model that specifically addresses access control issues of geospatial objects was proposed by Atluri and Mazzoleni[8]. This model known as GSAM can authorize users to view specific *region* within a satellite image object with a certain *resolution*. An indexing structure supporting efficient retrieval and enforcement of GSAM authorizations on satellite image has been developed. GSAM however does not include spatial locations of users and temporal dimension in the specification of authorizations.

In the area of pervasive computing, context aware role-based access control was proposed to model transitions of user roles and object states due to contextual changes and to grant users access privileges to objects based on the context at the time of access requests[9]. This proposed model however does not include the temporal and location dimensions of authorizations. Jiang and Landay further defined the notion of *information space* to organize information objects and services into different boundaries for better privacy control[10]. The boundaries can be defined by physical space, social grouping, or activity. By granting access privileges differently for different information spaces, authorizations can be made more context aware. We believe that information space can be viewed as some kind of locations in our proposed authorization model. Using our proposed model, information spaces can be linked together representing their relationships, and users are required to be authorized before entering an information space or moving from one information space to another.

Finally, a location and user authentication architecture was given in [11]. The paper however did not provide a comprehensive model to represent authorizations that involve both time and locations.

3   Location-Temporal Authorization Model

In this section we describe our Location-Temporal Authorization model (LTAM) in detail.

3.1   Preliminaries

Locations in LTAM are both *semantic* and *physical*. When represented physically, a location is described by its absolute spatial coordinates. In [12], Pradhan describes semantic locations as objects with unique identifiers so as to give semantic meanings to the locations. The physical location information are used to define the spatial boundaries of location so that it is possible to track users in different locations. A location can be *primitive* or *composite*. A *primitive location* is a location that cannot be further divided into other smaller locations. A *composite location* is a collection of related primitive, composite, or a mix of both locations. For instance, a room in a building is a primitive location, and the building which consists of a number of rooms is a composite location. All rooms in the building forms a *location graph* that represents the building. The building together with other buildings form a *multilevel location graph*. Formally, we define location graph and multilevel location graph as follows.

Definition 1 (Location Graph). *A location graph is defined as (L,E) where*

– *L is a set of primitive locations*
– *E is a set of edges connecting pairs of locations*

Within a location graph, if (l_1, l_2) is an edge e, it implies that l_2 can be reached from l_1 directly without going through other locations, and vice versa. By definition, an edge is bidirectional.

Definition 2 (Multilevel Location Graph).
  If $G_1, ..., G_k$ are location graphs or multilevel location graphs with mutually disjoint locations, then (L', E) is a multilevel location graph where $L' = \{G_1, ..., G_k\}$ and $E \subseteq L' \times L'$

Each location graph or multilevel location graph must have at least one location designated as *entry location*. An entry location serves as the first location a user must visit before visiting other locations within the graph. A entry location also serves as the last location where the user may visit before his/her exit. In some cases it is possible that the entry and exit locations have to be treated separately, which we have not considered in this paper. We believe our proposed model can be easily extended to deal with these cases.
  Let H be a multilevel location graph and l_i be a primitive location (or composite location), we say that l_i is *part of* H if l_i is a primitive location (or composite location) that directly or indirectly belongs to H.
  Fig. 1 depicts the location layout of School of Computer Engineering and School of Electrical and Electronic Engineering in Nanyang Technological University. Fig. 2 shows the corresponding multilevel location graph, where NTU is a multilevel location graph and SCE, EEE, CCE, SME, NBS[1] are all location graphs. The locations with double lines denote the entry locations.

---

[1] SCE, EEE, CCE, SME, NBS are the schools in the university

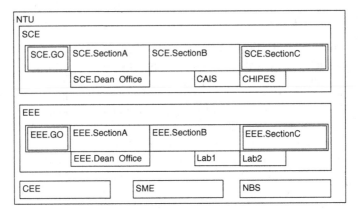

Fig. 1. A Location Layout

In Fig. 2, primitive locations SCE.GO, SCE.Dean's Office, CAIS, CHIPES, SCE.SectionA, SCE.SectionB, SCE.SectionC[2] form a location graph named SCE. The entry locations of SCE are SCE.GO and SCE.SectionC. To access any location that is part of SCE, one has to go through at least one of these two entry locations. The edge between SCE.SectionB and SCE.CAIS shows one to go from SCE.SectionB to CAIS directly and vice versa.

A *simple route* in a location graph, (G, E), refers to a series of primitive locations $\langle l_1, l_2, ..., l_k \rangle$ ($l_i's \in G$) through which a subject can move from location l_1 to location l_k, i.e., $(l_i, l_{i+1}) \in E, \forall 1 \leqslant i < k$. For example, $\langle$ SCE.Dean's Office, SCE.SectionA, SCE.SectionB, CAIS $\rangle$ is a simple route.

A *complex route* in a multilevel location graph (G, E) refers to a series of primitive locations $\langle l_1, l_2, ..., l_k \rangle$ through which a subject can move from l_1 to location l_k such that $\forall 1 \leqslant i < k$,

- (l_i, l_{i+1}) is an edge in some location graph; or
- l_i and l_{i+1} are entry locations in two different location graphs G_i and G_{i+1} respectively. G_i and G_{i+1} are multilevel location graphs of two composite locations l'_i and l'_{i+1}, respectively, such that (l'_i, l'_{i+1}) is an edge in some multilevel location graph G' that contains both G_i and G_{i+1}.

For example in Fig. 2, $\langle$ EEE.Dean's Office, EEE.SectionA, EEE.GO, SCE.GO, SCE.SectionA, SCE.Dean's Office $\rangle$ is a complex route.

In a route $r, \langle l_1, l_2, ..., l_n \rangle$, l_1 and l_n are called the *source* and the *destination* of r, respectively. Note that there can be multiple routes from a source to a destination.

Location graphs are connected graphs. For a given location graph (L, E), there exist a route r such that l_d can be reached from l_s, for any $l_s, l_d \in L$. Similarly multilevel location graphs are also connected graphs.

---

[2] SCE.GO denotes the general office of SCE. CAIS and CHIPES are research centers in SCE

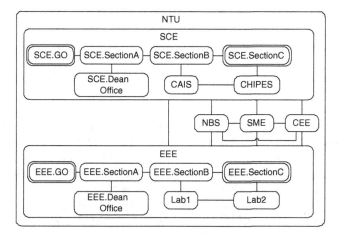

Fig. 2. A Multilevel Location Graph

Time is another important concept in the access control. We adopt the approach similar to that in [6]. A time unit is a *chronon* or a fixed number of chronons, where a chronon refers to the smallest invisible unit of time. A *time interval* is a set of consecutive time units. The size of the time interval is the number of time units in the time interval.

3.2   Location-Temporal Authorization

Location Authorizations are policies created by security officers for defining the accesses that the users have over the locations. *Location-Temporal authorizations* are location authorizations augmented with temporal conditions to limit the period during which the authorization is valid. Formally, they are defined as follows.

Definition 3 (Location Authorization). *A location authorization is a pair* (s, l) *where*

- *s is a subject (user) who requests authorizations; and*
- *l is a primitive location*

A location authorization (s,l) means that user s is authorized to enter the primitive location l. For example, (Alice, CAIS) denotes that Alice is authorized to access location CAIS.

Definition 4 (Location-Temporal Authorization). *A location-temporal authorization is a quadruple* (entry duration, exit duration, auth, entry) *where*

- entry duration *is a time interval* $[t_s^i, t_e^i]$ *during which a subject can enter a primitive location*
- exit duration *is a time interval* $[t_s^o, t_e^o]$ *during which a subject can leave a primitive location, where* $t_s^o \geqslant t_s^i$ *and* $t_e^o \geqslant t_e^i$

- auth *is an location authorization*
- entry *is the number of accesses that the subject can exercise within entry duration. The range of entry is* $[1, \infty)$.

A Location-Temporal Authorization imposes temporal constraints on a location authorization. An authorization $([t_1^i, t_2^i], [t_1^o, t_2^o], (s,l), n)$ indicates that user s is authorized to enter primitive location l during $[t_1^i, t_2^i]$ and exit during $[t_1^o, t_2^o]$, for a maximum number of n times. If the entry duration is not specified, it means the subject can enter a location at any time after the creation of the authorization. On the other hand, if the exit duration is not specified, the default value will be $[t_1^i, \infty]$ which means that the subject can exit any time after entering the location. The default entry value is ∞.

Consider the authorization $([5, 40], [20, 100], (\text{Alice}, \text{CAIS}), 1)$. Alice is allowed to enter location CAIS once during the period $[5, 40]$, and to exit during the period $[20, 100]$. If she does not exit CAIS during the exit duration, a warning signal to the security guards will be generated.

4   Authorization Rules

In large organizations, it is impractical to define authorizations for individual users on every location. In addition, some authorizations may only be valid when certain conditions are satisfied. Manually specifying all the authorizations is a very tedious and error-prone job. *Authorization rules* are therefore introduced to automate the work of deriving additional authorizations based on the existing authorizations. An authorization rule can also be viewed as a kind of relationship between authorizations. An authorization rule generates a number of authorizations based on an input authorization. The input authorization is called the *base authorization*. The generated authorizations are called the *derived authorizations*. The formal definition of authorization rule is as follows.

Definition 5 (Authorization Rule). *An authorization rule is defined as* $\langle t_r : (a, OP) \rangle$, *where*

- t_r *is the time from when the authorization rule is valid.*
- $a = ([t_s^i, t_e^i], [t_s^o, t_e^o], (s,l), n)$ *is the base authorization*
- *OP is a tuple of operators* $(op_{\text{entry}}, op_{\text{exit}}, op_{\text{subject}}, op_{\text{location}}, exp_n)$, *where*
  - op_{entry} *and* op_{exit} *are temporal operators, which take* $[t_s^i, t_e^i]$ *and* $[t_s^o, t_e^o]$ *of a as inputs, and generate the entry and exit durations for the derived authorizations, respectively.*
    The temporal operators can be one of the following:
    * WHENEVER
      WHENEVER *is a unary operator which returns the same time interval as the input.*
    * WHENEVERNOT
      Given an input time interval, $[t_0, t_1]$, *the unary operator* WHENEVERNOT *operator returns* $[t_r, t_0 - 1]$ *and* $[t_1 + 1, \infty]$.

* UNION

  UNION *is a binary operator. Given two input time intervals* $[t_0, t_1]$ *and* $[t_2, t_3]$, UNION *returns* $[t_0, t_3]$ *if* $t_2 \leqslant t_1$; *or* $[t_0, t_1]$ *and* $[t_2, t_3]$ *if* $t_2 > t_1$.

* INTERSECTION

  INTERSECTION *is a binary operator. Given two input time intervals* $[t_0, t_1]$ *and* $[t_2, t_3]$, INTERSECTION *returns* $[t_2, t_1]$ *if* $t_2 \leqslant t_1$; *Otherwise it returns* NULL.

- op_{subject} *takes subject s of a, and derives the subjects for the derived authorizations based on some relationships between subjects.*
- op_{location} *is a location operator, which generates a set of primitive locations for the derived authorizations, given the primitive location l of a.*
- exp_n *specifies a numeric expression on the number of entries.*

If any of the rule elements is not specified in a rule, the default value will be copied from the base authorization.

Example 1. Consider the following authorization.

a1: $([5, 20], [15, 50], (\text{Alice}, \text{CAIS}), 2)$

If we want the supervisor of `Alice` to have the same authorization on `CAIS` as that of Alice, we can define the following rule.

r1: $\langle 7\text{:a1}, (\text{WHENEVER}, \text{WHENEVER}, \text{Supervisor\_Of}, \text{CAIS}, 2) \rangle$

The $op_{subject}$ operator `Supervisor_Of` returns the supervisor of a user by querying the *user profile database* described in the next section. Suppose `Alice`'s supervisor is `Bob`, the following authorization can be derived.

a2: $([5, 20], [15, 50], (\text{Bob}, \text{CAIS}), 2)$

By specifying this rule, it is not necessary to create new authorizations if `Alice` is assigned a different supervisor. The system is able to automatically derive the authorizations for the new supervisor while the authorization for `Bob` will be revoked.

Example 2. If we modify rule `r1` slightly as follows.

r2: $\langle 7\text{:a1}, (\text{INTERSECTION}([10, 30]), \text{WHENEVER}, \text{Supervisor\_Of},$
    $\text{CAIS}, 2) \rangle$

The derived authorization of `r2` is

a3: $([10, 20], [15, 50], (\text{Bob}, \text{CAIS}), 2)$

Rule `r2` specifies that the supervisor of `Alice` is supposed to access `CAIS` during $[10, 30]$, however, only when `Alice` is also authorized to access `CAIS`.

Example 3. Now given authorization a1, we would like to grant Alice access to all locations on the route from SCE.GO to CAIS. The following authorization rule can be specified for this purpose.

r3:⟨7:a1,(WHENEVER, WHENEVER,, all_route_from(SCE.GO),2)⟩

The location operator all_route_from returns all the locations on the route from source SCE.GO to destination CAIS, which are {SCE.GO, SCE.SectionA, SCE.SectionB, SCE.SectionC, SCE.CHIPES}. An authorization will be derived for each of these locations as the result of rule r2.

Besides the operators aforementioned, customized operators can be defined as well, which leads to greater degree of flexibility.

It is worth noting that the authorization rules may introduce conflicts of authorizations, which means the derived authorizations may contradict with other authorizations. For example, a derived authorization may say that Alice can enter CAIS during $[5, 10]$. However, another authorization (either existing or derived) may state that Alice is authorized to enter CAIS during $[10, 11]$. This conflict should be resolved either by combining the two authorizations, or discarding one of them. The problem is left for future work.

5   Location-Temporal Authorization Enforcement

The authorizations are checked when an *access request* is posed by a subject. Formally, we define access request as follows.

Definition 6 (Access Request). *An access request is a triple (t, s, l) where*

- *t is the time instant at which the access request is made*
- *s is the user who requests the access*
- *l is the location where the user requests to access*

For example, a triple (10,Alice,CAIS) denotes that at time 10, Alice issued an access request to location CAIS.

An access request is checked against the set of authorizations in the system. If an authorization exists at time t, the access request is authorized. We define *authorized access request* as follows.

Definition 7 (Authorized Access Request). *An access request (t, s, l) is authorized if there exists at least one location temporal authorization $A : ([t^i_s, t^i_e], s, l, [t^o_s, t^o_e], n)$ such that*

- *$t^i_s \leqslant t \leqslant t^i_e$*
- *s has entered l during $[t^i_s, t^i_e]$ for less than n times.*

For example, suppose that the system contains the following authorizations.

- A1: $([10, 20], [10, 50], (\text{Alice},\text{CAIS}),2)$
- A2: $([5, 35], [20, 100], (\text{Bob},\text{CHIPES}),1)$

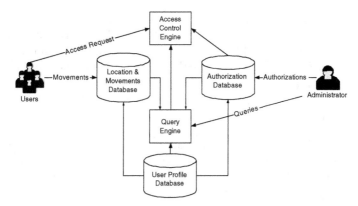

Fig. 3. System Architecture for Authorization Enforcement

Assume that each subject has not entered any location yet, we have

- At time 10, access request (10,Alice,CAIS) is granted according to A1.
- At time 15, access request (15,Bob,CAIS) is not authorized because there is no authorization specifies Bob's access to CAIS.
- At time 16, access request (15,Bob,CHIPES) is authorized based on A2.
- At time 20, Bob leaves CHIPES.
- At time 30, access request (30,Bob,CHIPES) is not authorized because Bob has only one entry to CHIPES.

Fig. 3 shows the system architecture for location-temporal authorization enforcement. The system has five major components.

- **Authorization Database**
  The authorization database stores all authorizations defined by the system administrators.
- **Location & Movements Database**
  The location & movements database stores the location layout, as well as users' movements. These data are then used for authorization validation, system status checking, etc..
- **User Profile Database**
  As its name indicates, the user profile database stores user profiles, which are used for creating authorizations, or deriving authorizations, etc..
- **Access Control Engine**
  The access control engine is the core of the authorization enforcement. When a user issues an access request, the access control engine have to perform a few tasks.
  1. It checks the authorization database to search for any authorization that has been defined for the user and the location that the user request access to.
  2. It invokes the query engine to find out whether the user has violated any authorization due to unauthorized access requests or over-staying.

3. Access control engine is also responsible for authorization derivation. When the administrator specifies new rules, the access control engine will evaluate the new rules on the existing authorizations and user profiles. The derived authorizations are then added to the authorization database.

- **Query Engine**
  The query engine evaluates queries by the system administrators and the access control engine based on the information stored in all of the databases.

The design of a query language for our proposed authorization model will be part of our future work. Some of these questions can be complex. In the following section, we will present a query that find all locations inaccessible (or accessible) to a given subject.

6   Finding Inaccessible Locations

Given a set of LTAM authorizations, one can query and conduct reasoning or computation on them to derive useful knowledge. In this section, we will describe the problem of finding inaccessible locations and develop the corresponding solution algorithm.

Given an access request duration $[t_p, t_q]$ from a user s to a location l and a location-temporal authorization $a = ([t_s^i, t_e^i], [t_s^o, t_e^o], (s, l), entry)$, the *grant duration* of s for l in the access request duration is defined by $[\max(t_p, t_s^i), \min(t_q, t_e^i)]$, and the *departure duration* of s for l in the access request duration is defined by $[\max(t_p, t_s^o), t_e^o]$.

A route $r = \langle l_1, l_2, ..., l_k \rangle$ is *authorized* for a subject s with access request duration $[t_p, t_q]$ if,

- The grant duration of s for l_1 in $[t_p, t_q]$, denoted by $[t_{p_1}^g, t_{q_1}^g]$, is not null;
- The departure duration of s for l_1 in $[t_p, t_q]$, denoted by $[t_{p_1}^d, t_{q_1}^d]$, is not null;
- The grant duration of s for l_i in $[t_{p_{i-1}}^d, t_{q_{i-1}}^d]$, denoted by $[t_{p_i}^g, t_{q_i}^g]$, is not null $\forall 2 \leqslant i < k$;
- The departure duration of s for l_i in $[t_{p_{i-1}}^d, t_{q_{i-1}}^d]$, denoted by $[t_{p_i}^d, t_{q_i}^d]$, is not null $\forall 2 \leqslant i < k$; and
- The grant duration of s for l_k in $[t_{p_{k-1}}^d, t_{q_{k-1}}^d]$, denoted by $[t_{p_k}^g, t_{q_k}^g]$, is not null.

The grant duration and departure duration of s for the route r are therefore $[t_{p_1}^g, t_{q_1}^g]$ and $[t_{p_k}^d, t_{p_k}^d]$ respectively.

Definition 8. *Given a subject s, a set of authorizations D and a location graph (or multilevel location graph) $G = (L, E)$, a location (or composite) l is known to be* inaccessible *by s if there is no authorized route for s with an access request duration $[0, \infty)$ that covers l from every entry location of G.*

Following the above definition, an entry location is inaccessible to a subject s if it has null exit duration for its authorization.

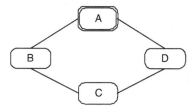

Fig. 4. An example of finding the inaccessible locations

From the above definition, we also know that a location can be make inaccessible to a subject by directly defining appropriate authorizations for that location, or by blocking all routes to the location. Hence, to ensure that a subject can visit a location, one should check that the location is not inaccessible instead of just defining the authorizations for that location.

The inaccessible location finding problem is thus defined as follows:

Definition 9. *(Inaccessible Location Finding Problem) Given a subject s, a set of authorizations D and a location graph (or multilevel location graph) G = (L, E), find all inaccessible locations in G.*

We now outline a solution algorithm to the above problem. Our algorithm has been developed based on the following lemma which can be easily proven.

Lemma 1. *Given a composite location l with a location graph or multilevel location graph (L, E), if a location l' in L is inaccessible to a subject s considering only the entry locations in L, then the location l' is also inaccessible to s from every entry location in the multilevel location graph containing l.*

The inaccessible location finding algorithm is shown in Algorithm 1. The algorithm first associates to each location l an *overall grant time* and a *overall departure time*, denoted by T^g and T^d respectively. Each of them consists of a set of time intervals. The overall grant time of each location is initialized to be null. As the algorithm assigns a location a new overall grant time, a new overall departure time is derived and the neighboring locations will adjust their overall grant and departure times accordingly. To indicate whether a location should be assigned a new overall grant and departure time, a boolean flag (denoted by $flag$) is associated with every location.

For example, consider the location graph in Fig. 4, consisting of locations A, B, C, and D, where A is the entry location. Suppose that a number of location-temporal authorizations have been defined for these locations as shown in Table 1. The steps of finding the inaccessible locations are shown in Table 2

The algorithm starts from the entry location A, by setting its grant duration T_A^g to $[2, 35]$ and departure duration T_A^d to $[20, 50]$. In the next step, its neighboring locations B and D are to be examined since their flags are set to true. B's grant duration T_B^g is assigned $[\max(20, 40), \min(50, 60)] = [40, 50]$ and its departure duration T_B^d is assigned $[\max(20, 55), 80] = [55, 80]$. Similarly, we can obtain D's grant duration T_D^g and the departure duration T_D^d, which are $[20, 25]$

Algorithm 1 FindInaccessible(G,s)

Input: location graph $G = (L, E)$, subject s
output: set of inaccessible locations

1: initialise $l.T^g := l.T^d := null$ and $l.flag := false$ for each $l \in L$
2: **for** each entry location $l_{entry} \in L$ **do**
3:     **for** each location-temporal authorization a of l_{entry} **do**
4:         $l_{entry}.T^g := l_{entry}.T^g \cup [a.t_s^i, a.t_e^i]$
5:         $l_{entry}.T^d := l_{entry}.T^d \cup [a.t_s^o, a.t_e^o]$
6:     **end for**
7:     $l_{entry}.flag := false$ // their admissible time will not change further
8:     **if** $l_{entry}.T^d \neq null$ **then**
9:         **for** each l next to l_{entry} **do**
10:            $l.flag := true$
11:        **end for**
12:    **end if**
13: **end for**
14: **while** $\exists l \in L$ where $l.flag = true$ **do**
15:    **for** each $l \in L$ where $l.flag = true$ **do**
16:        $l.flag := false$
17:        $l.T^{old\_d} := l.T^d$
18:        $T := \cup_{l_i \ next \ to \ l} l_i.T^d$
19:        **for** each $[t_p, t_q] \in T$ **do**
20:            **for** each location-temporal authorization a of l **do**
21:                $t := [\max(t_p, a.t_s^i), \min(t_q, a.t_e^i)]$
22:                **if** $t \neq null$ **then**
23:                    $l.T^g := l.T^g \cup t$
24:                    $l.T^d := l.T^d \cup [\max(t_p, a.t_s^o), a.t_e^o]$
25:                **end if**
26:            **end for**
27:        **end for**
28:        **if** $l.T^d \neq l.T^{old\_d}$ **then**
29:            **for** each l' next to l **do**
30:                $l'.flag := true$
31:            **end for**
32:        **end if**
33:    **end for**
34: **end while**
35: **Return** $\{l | l \in L$ and $l.T^g = null\}$

---

and $[20, 30]$, respectively. After processing B and D, the flags of A and C are set to true because they are the neighbors of B and D. For C, both the grant duration T_C^g and the departure duration T_C^d are null. For A, it updates its T_A^g and T_A^d to $[2, 35] \cup [20, 35] = [2, 35]$ and $[20, 50] \cup [30, 50] = [20, 50]$, respectively, according to the new values of the grant and departure durations of its neighbors. Since there is no change to both durations, A will not update its neighbors. Therefore the whole process stops because no location has a flag set to true.

Table 1. A set of authorizations

Location	Authorization
A	$([2, 35], [20, 50], (\texttt{Alice,A}), 1)$
B	$([40, 60], [55, 80], (\texttt{Alice,B}), 1)$
C	$([38, 45], [70, 90], (\texttt{Alice,C}), 1)$
D	$([5, 25], [10, 30], (\texttt{Alice,D}), 1)$

Table 2. An illustration of the example

Location	A			B			C			D		
	flag	T_A^g	T_A^d	flag	T_B^g	T_B^d	flag	T_C^g	T_C^d	flag	T_D^g	T_D^d
Initiation	F	ϕ	ϕ	F	ϕ	ϕ	F	ϕ	ϕ	F	ϕ	ϕ
Update A	F	$[2, 35]$	$[20, 50]$	T	ϕ	ϕ	F	ϕ	ϕ	T	ϕ	ϕ
Update B	T	$[2, 35]$	$[20, 50]$	F	$[40, 50]$	$[55, 80]$	T	ϕ	ϕ	T	ϕ	ϕ
Update D	T	$[2, 35]$	$[20, 50]$	F	$[40, 50]$	$[55, 80]$	T	ϕ	ϕ	F	$[20, 25]$	$[20, 30]$
Update C	T	$[2, 35]$	$[20, 50]$	F	$[40, 50]$	$[55, 80]$	F	ϕ	ϕ	F	$[20, 25]$	$[20, 30]$
Update A	F	$[2, 35] \cup [20, 35] = [2, 35]$	$[20, 50] \cup [20, 50] = [20, 50]$	F	$[40, 50]$	$[55, 80]$	F	ϕ	ϕ	F	$[20, 25]$	$[20, 30]$

T – True   F – False ϕ – null

The above algorithm has the time complexity of $O(N_L^2 \cdot N_d \cdot N_a)$ where N_L denotes the number of locations in L, N_d denotes the maximum degree of locations, and N_a denotes the maximum number of authorizations for each location. Though the complexity is of a relatively high order, it should not cause any problem considering the fact that the number of locations in a building is limited in most cases. Note that the algorithm covers the possibility that there may exist multiple routes between two locations, by considering the grant and departure durations of all neighbors of every location.

7 Conclusions

We have defined a new authorization model for granting accesses to locations with temporal considerations. This model, LTAM, can represent the location layout using a location graph or multilevel graph. By monitoring a user's movement and evaluating location access requests against user specified authorizations, one can determine if the user can be granted access to a location and if the user should leave the location. We also describe based on the proposed model the interesting problem of finding inaccessible locations within a (multilevel) location graph given a database of authorizations. A solution algorithm that explores authorized routes to locations in a (multilevel) location graph has been developed.

As part of the future work, we plan to expand the location-temporal authorization definition to include more access constraints. More authorization rules will be explored to represent more expressive rules. The consistency issues among the rules will be studied. A query language and the corresponding query operators will also be studied. Lastly, we would like to further integrate other context about data objects and subjects into our model to provide more comprehensive mechanisms to support applications with advanced security requirement.

References

1. Hightower, J., Borriello, G.: A survey and taxonomy of location systems for ubiquitous computing. IEEE Computer **34** (2001) 57–66
2. Pitoura, E., Samaras, G.: Locating objects in mobile computing. Knowledge and Data Engineering **13** (2001) 571–592
3. Awerbuch, B., Peleg, D.: Online tracking of mobile users. In: Proceedings of the ACM SIGCOMM Symposium on Communication Architectures and Protocols. (1991)
4. RFiD Journal: Singapore fights SARS with RFID. RFiD Journal, `http://www.rfidjournal.com/article/articleview/446/1/1/` (2003)
5. Beresford, A.R., Stajano, F.: Location privacy in pervasive computing. IEEE Pervasive Computing **2** (2003) 46 – 55
6. Bertino, E., Bettini, C., Samarati, P.: A temporal authorization model. In: Proceedings of the 2nd ACM Conference on Computer and Communications Security (CCS '94). (1994) 126–135
7. Gal, A., Atluri, V.: An authorization model for temporal data. In: Proceedings of the 7th ACM Conference on Computer and Communications Security (CCS2000). (2000) 144–153
8. Atluri, V., Mazzoleni, P.: A uniform indexing scheme for geospatial data and authorizations. In: IFIP WG 11.3 Sixteenth International Conference on Data and Applications Security (DBSec2002). (2002)
9. Zhang, G., Parashar, M.: Context-aware dynamic access control for pervasive applications. In: Proceedings of the Communication Networks and Distributed Systems Modeling and Simulation Conference (CNDS2004). (2004)
10. Jiang, X., Landay, J.A.: Modeling privacy control in context-aware systems. IEEE Pervasive Computing **1** (2002) 59–63
11. Michalakis, N.: PAC: Location aware access control for pervasive computing environments. In: MIT Student Oxygen Workshop. (2002)
12. Pradhan, S.: Semantic location. HP, `http://cooltown.hp.com/dev/wpapers/semantic/sematnic.asp` (2002)

Identifying Sensitive Associations in Databases for Release Control

Claudio Bettini[1], Xiaoyang Sean Wang[2], and Sushil Jajodia[3]

[1] DICO, Università di Milano, Italy
bettini@dico.unimi.it
[2] Department of Computer Science, University of Vermont, Vermont
xywang@cs.uvm.edu
[3] Center for Secure Information Systems,George Mason University, Virginia
jajodia@gmu.edu

Abstract. In a database system, authorization-based access-control is generally the first line of defense, preventing unauthorized accesses to secret or sensitive data. However, this mechanism is susceptible to security breaches due to improper authorization (e.g., the general public is mistakenly granted access to a copy of sensitive data) and cannot block insider attacks (an authorized user accidentally or intentionally discloses secrets to outsiders). Supplementary to access-control, the release-control mechanism is to check all the outgoing documents for any leak of secret or sensitive information. This paper reports preliminary results on a specific release-control task, namely, how to deal with sensitive associations that need to be restricted from releasing. A sensitive association refers to a pair of values whose connection involves some secrets. The disclosure of such a pair may reveal the secretive connection and therefore should be controlled. The release control of sensitive associations is a very challenging and long term research problem. This paper introduces techniques to identify and represent sensitive associations hidden in a database.

1 Introduction

Security in databases means "protecting the data against unauthorized users" [3]. In relational DBMS, such a protection is provided by an authorization subsystem, in which a user must have explicitly granted privileges in order to access a part of the database, such as a table, a column of a table, or a view. From a system manager's perspective, data security translates to identifying sensitive parts of the database and assigning users' privileges accordingly.

The above approach often works well; however, when a database grows more complex, the task of a system manager becomes more difficult. The ease of access to data by users and the security concerns of who has access to data are always two competing aspects, and human errors are sometimes unavoidable that cause misclassification of data and/or wrong assignments of privileges (see [11]).

W. Jonker and M. Petković (Eds.): SDM 2004, LNCS 3178, pp. 187–201, 2004.

Compounding the issue, "insider attacks" are a major security problem[1]. While insider attacks take various forms, intentional and unintentional disclosure of secret information, to which a user has the privilege to access, is one problem that the current authorization-based access control does not address.

Release control is a supplemental mechanism used to deal with the above problems [8, 1]. Instead of controlling how information is accessed, a release control subsystem checks the outgoing information to decide if any improper release is occurring. Since release control acts independently of access control, mistakes made by access privilege assignments may be caught and insider attacks curbed.

Our long term research plan involves the study of release control techniques for checking *documents* being released over an organization boundary. These documents may be simply answers to database queries, semi-structured, or unstructured documents containing data from different data sources within the organization. The general architecture we propose for release control has been illustrated in [1]. Among the major tasks we have: i) identifying *controlled items*, i.e., sensitive terms and sensitive associations between terms; ii) specifying *release constraints*, i.e., rules to search for sensitive associations in the documents[2]; Finally, (iii) devising efficient *matching* techniques to check release constraints over the outgoing documents. In [1] we reported preliminary results on tasks ii) and iii) and proposed a learning-based approach. This paper focuses on the first task listed above: identifying and representing sensitive associations. While part of these associations may be explicitly given by security officers, we believe that when some of the data sources are databases a significant portion of sensitive associations can be automatically derived.

A specific problem not dealt with by the current database authorization subsystem is that of sensitive associations. A *sensitive association* refers to a pair of values whose connection involves some secret data. The disclosure of such a pair may reveal the secretive connection and should be controlled.

Consider an example database with three tables, **Employees**, **Projects** and **Assignments** (of employees to projects). (See Fig. 1.) Assume the information in the **Assignment** table is secret while the other two tables contain public information. Hence, a particular employee's name (say, **John**) and a particular project name (say, **Trace**) may be given to the general public, separately. However, the appearance of these two names (**John** and **Trace**) together in some form may be considered sensitive since **John** is assigned to the project **Trace**. Indeed, for example, from this assignment and people's knowledge of **John**'s background, people may be able to deduce what project **Trace** is about. Another way of looking at this problem is that since the only "natural" way we can obtain the

---

[1] Forty-five percent of respondents to the eighth annual Computer Crime and Security Survey of the Computer Security Institute (May 2003) stated to have detected unauthorized access by insiders. See http://www.gocsi.com/press/20030528.jhtml

[2] Note that the appearance of the two values of an association in an outgoing document not necessarily implies the release of the association. For example, we may be looking at two separate listing of the employees and projects in the document, which should not be considered problematic even if **John** and **Trace** both appear.

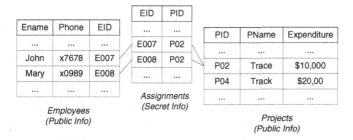

Fig. 1. An example database.

association of **John** and **Trace** is through a join with a secret table, we must consider this association sensitive.

The authorization-based access control will prevent an unauthorized user from obtaining the association via the natural join. However, it is possible to derive the association without using the secret table but through special handling of public data. For example, a user may simply pick up **John** from the **Employees** table, **Trace** from the **Projects** table, and use cross-product to obtain the pair (**John**, **Trace**). This special handling of public data is suspicious since the end result is an association that may imply some secret in the secret table. Therefore, even if the query does *not* touch the secret table, the appearance of the association in an outgoing document should raise an alarm. Access control does not handle this kind of issue.

Making **Employees** and **Projects** as secret may seem to be a plausible solution. However, this creates an accessibility problem: a user must have the privilege to access secret tables in order to obtain the public information about employees and projects. Clearly, this is not a viable solution. It is pointing again at the weakness of authorization-based access control. Furthermore, an insider with access rights to the secret table can easily obtain the association and pass it to the outside. This too is not addressed by the access control.

In contrast, release control simply looks for the appearance of **John** and **Trace** together in the outgoing document in some form (e.g., in one tuple, one sentence, and so on) and thus prevent the security breach. This is what we term *sensitive association release control*.

The above example points to a general model for sensitive associations. For each pair of tables, we decide the "allowed" join between these tables. The most common type of allowed join conditions are based on referential constraints. That is, if attribute A in table T refers (foreign key) to attribute B in table S, we allow $T.A = S.B$ to be part of the join condition. System managers can add explicit join conditions to make the link between tables, and create view definitions to take care of special semantics of the database.

Roughly speaking, we consider a sequence of such joins among multiple tables and if this sequence of tables contains a secret table, then each pair of values from a tuple in the result of join (first value from the first table in the sequence and the second value from the last table) form a sensitive association. This definition captures pairs of values whose connections contain some secret.

In order to deal with the possibly large number of sensitive associations we first define different levels of accuracy in the semantic characterization of sensitivity that is stored with the associations, and then we devise a "grouping" method. About grouping, consider the example in Fig. 1. We not only have (John, Trace) as a sensitive association, but also (Mary, Trace), (x7678, Trace), and so on. Clearly, we can use a cross product of two sets to represent these sensitive associations: The first set consists of all the values in the two tuples shown in the Employees table, and the second set consists of all the values in the P02 tuple of Projects. Then, each pair in the cross product of the two sets will be a sensitive association. We call such pair of sets a *sensitive-pair group*. Obviously, there is more than one way to organize a set of sensitive associations into sensitive-pair groups, and to find the minimum number of sensitive-pair groups to represent a given set of sensitive associations it is likely to be intractable. We use a greedy algorithm to find a suboptimal solution.

The sensitive association concept is closely related to the inference problem studied in the information security and privacy literature (e.g., [4, 9, 2, 5]). Inference problem has long been recognized as a problem not addressed by authorization-based access control. Farkas and Jajodia surveyed the subject in a short paper recently [5]. In the survey, the inference problem in databases is defined as "when sensitive information can be disclosed from non-sensitive data and metadata". With this paper, we initiate a study of inference problem in the scope of information release control. For the general inference problem, the question is how to know sensitive information is actually disclosed, and how efficiently a practical system can discover such a disclosure. Sophisticated mechanisms have been introduced, through logics, conceptual graphs, and mathematical programming (see [5] for references to these techniques). Different from earlier works, this paper stresses simplicity and efficiency. We define sensitive associations through joinpaths, which we believe is a simple and yet effective model. We then turn our attention to developing techniques to efficiently obtain, represent, and check outgoing documents for the sensitive associations. In practice, for any release control mechanism to be useful, it must be efficient. The concept of joinpath has been used in the literature that deals with search and navigation among tables in relational databases [10, 6]. In this paper, we use joinpath in a similar conceptual way but for the purpose of data security.

The remainder of the paper is organized as follows. In Section 2, we introduce the notions required to formally characterize sensitive associations, and a basic procedure for identifying sensitive associations in a database. In Section 3, we propose a representation scheme for sensitive associations and describe algorithms to derive the representations. We conclude the paper in Section 4.

2   Identifying Sensitive Associations

In this section, we formally define the notion of sensitive associations and related concepts. We then discuss methods to efficiently identify sensitive associations. We assume we work exclusively with relational databases.

Symbol	Meaning
DB	database, i.e., a set of tables
$Eq(DB)$	all equality join conditions on DB
Eq-$Join$	a set of tables that are "connected" through equality join conditions
JP	Joinpath
$Tables(JP)$	all tables appearing in JP

Fig. 2. Symbols used in the paper.

2.1   Sensitive Associations: The Concept

As mentioned in the introduction, system managers can assign access privileges to users on different parts of a relational database, including tables, columns, and views. To simplify our discussion, we assume there are only two users, namely, the *public user* and the *insider user*. The insider user can access all tables, while the public user can access only a subset of the tables. The tables that the public user *cannot* access are called the *secret tables*, and other tables are called the *public tables*. The only access modality we consider is *read* (or SELECT in SQL), since we are not concerned with updates.

Given a database DB, we assume there is a given set $Eq(DB)$ of equality join conditions. Each equality join condition takes the form of $T_1.A_1 = T_2.A_2$, where T_1 and T_2 are two (not necessarily different) table names, and A_1 and A_2 are attributes of T_1 and T_2, respectively. An equality join condition denotes some semantic connection between the tuples of the involved tables.

Usually, equality join conditions are implied by the database conceptual model in the form of referential integrity and other constraints, representing metadata information, or data semantics, for the database.

Example 1. In the tables of Fig. 1, we have two referential integrity constraints. The first says that EID of Assignments refers to EID of Employees. This means that each EID value in Assignments must already appear as an EID of Employees, or, intuitively, projects must be assigned to existing employees. The second referential integrity constraint says PID of Assignments refers to PID of Projects. From these two constraints, we have the corresponding equality join conditions: Assignments.EID = Employees.EID and Assignments.PID = Projects.PID.

Since the equality join conditions are decided at database design time, in the sequel, we will always assume the set $Eq(DB)$ fixed for a specific database DB.

Equality join conditions lead to equal joins of tables.

Definition 1. *Given a database DB, an Eq-Join in DB is a set of DB table names, i.e., Eq-Join = $\{T_1, \ldots, T_n\}$, such that, for each pair (T_i, T_j), there exists a sequence of table names $T_{i1}, \ldots, T_{ik}$ in Eq-Join, with $T_{i1} = T_i$ and $T_{ik} = T_j$, having the condition that for each $p = 1, \ldots, k - 1$, at least one condition of the form $T_{ip}.A = T_{i(p+1)}.B$ is in Eq(DB).*

In the above definition of *Eq-Join*, it is required that the involved DB tables are connected through equality join conditions. For example, if we take the join conditions derived from the referential constraints as discussed above for the tables in Fig. 1, then {Employees, Assignments, Projects} is an *Eq-Join*, while {Employees, Projects} is not.

Intuitively, we take *Eq-Join* as the primary way of "naturally" deriving data from a relational database. We believe this being very general. Even if this is not true in special cases, we are not losing much of generality. Indeed, as an example, consider a table with a time period attribute and another table with a time point attribute. A way to derive information (by design) may be to join the two tables in the way that requires the time point to fall within the time period. The framework above does deal with such a case if we assume that a corresponding view (e.g., the result of the special join) is added into the database. Another approach is to have a simple extension that allows inclusion of user-defined join conditions, but we favor not to go into that direction in this paper to keep our framework simple.

There are cases when the same table needs to appear multiple times in order to allow, e.g., self-joins. The above definition of *Eq-Join* can be modified easily to accommodate such a case. Again, for simplicity, we may simply assume that unlimited copies of every table are available, along with the copies of equal join conditions as well as self-join conditions. Hence, we can simply say each table in the *Eq-Join* is a different table without loss of any generality.

In order to further simplify the technical treatment we will focus our attention to a class of joins that we call *joinpaths*.

Definition 2. *Given a database DB, a* joinpath *in DB is a sequence of DB table names* $\langle T_1, \ldots, T_n \rangle$ *with the set of all equality join conditions in* $Eq(DB)$ *of the form* $T_i.A_i = T_{i+1}.A_{i+1}$ *with* $i = 1, \ldots, n-1$, *such that there exists at least one such condition for each* i.

The difference between an *Eq-Join* and a *joinpath* is that a joinpath only takes join conditions (in $Eq(DB)$) connecting consecutive tables in its sequence, while *Eq-Join* takes all join conditions involving the tables in *Eq-Join*. However, both require that all the involved tables are connected through join conditions.

Consider Fig. 1. The sequence ⟨Employees, Assignments, Projects⟩ is a joinpath, while ⟨Employees, Projects, Assignments⟩ is not (since there are no join conditions between Employees and Projects).

Clearly, given a joinpath JP there exists a corresponding set of tuples obtainable by joining the tables in the joinpath accordingly to the equality conditions. Given a joinpath JP, let $Tables(JP)$ denote the set of table names appearing in JP, and $\pi_S(JP)$ denote the set of tuples obtained by the projection on the attributes in S of the set of tuples corresponding to JP. Analogous notation will be used for *Eq-Join*.

Another notational convention we will use is that the values in a *tuple* are prefixed with table and attribute names in the form $\langle T_1.A_1.a_1, \ldots, T_m.A_m.a_m \rangle$. For example, ⟨Employees.EName.John, Projects.PName.Trace⟩ is a binary tuple. Given a tuple $t = \langle T_1.A_1.a_1, \ldots, T_m.A_m.a_m \rangle$, the notation $t \in \pi(JP)$ denotes the fact that t is in $\pi_S(JP)$ where $S = \{T_1.A_1, \ldots, T_m.A_m\}$. Hence, in the same example, $\langle$Employees.EName.John, Projects.PName.Trace$\rangle$ is in $\pi(JP)$, where $JP = \langle$Employees, Assignments, Projects$\rangle$.

Definition 3. *Given a tuple t, a joinpath JP is said to be a joinpath for t if (i) $t \in \pi(JP)$ and (ii) there is no joinpath JP' such that $Tables(JP') \subset Tables(JP)$ and $t \in \pi(JP')$.*

Definition 3 says that a joinpath for a particular tuple is a minimal joinpath such that the tuple can be derived through projection from the set of tuples corresponding to the joinpath.

Given a binary tuple $t = \langle T_1.A_1.a_1, T2.A_2.a_2 \rangle$, assume JP is a joinpath for t. Clearly, T_1 and T_2 are the first and the last table names in JP, respectively. Indeed, otherwise, we could drop some tables from JP and find that the remaining joinpath is for t (a contradiction).

Definition 4. *A joinpath JP is sensitive for a tuple t if JP is a joinpath for t and $Tables(JP)$ contains at least one secret table.*

A sensitive joinpath for a particular tuple t is one that uses some secret to derive tuple t. In contrast, we will use the term *public joinpath for tuple t* to denote a joinpath for t that is not sensitive.

Generalizing the notions, we use the term *sensitive joinpath* and *public joinpath* (i.e., they are not for any particular tuples). A joinpath JP is sensitive if there exists at least one tuple t such that JP is a sensitive joinpath for t. Joinpaths that are not sensitive are called public joinpaths.

The notion of *association* and of *sensitive association* are now formalized.

Definition 5. *Given a binary tuple t and a (sensitive) joinpath JP for t, the pair $\langle t, JP \rangle$, or t alone when JP is understood, is said to be a (sensitive) association.*

Intuitively, associations are pairs of values (along with their table names and attribute names found in the database) with joinpaths that specify how the associations can be identified from the database.

Example 2. Consider the tables in Fig. 1; let tuple t be $\langle$Employees.EName.John, Projects.PName.Trace$\rangle$, and the sensitive joinpath JP for t be $\langle$Employees, Assignments, Projects$\rangle$, assuming Assignments is secret. Then, $\langle t, JP \rangle$ forms a sensitive association.

A natural question arises about the expressiveness of joinpaths. Namely, is it possible that a tuple that can be derived as projection of an *Eq-Join* cannot be derived by any joinpath on the same database? Equivalently, are joinpaths really less powerful than *Eq-Joins*? The following result says the answer is no as long as we limit ourselves to binary tuples.

Theorem 1. *Given a database DB, an Eq-Join in DB, and a binary tuple t such that $t \in \pi(Eq\text{-}Join)$, there always exists a joinpath JP for t in DB such that $Tables(JP) \subseteq Tables(Eq\text{-}Join)$.*

Different sensitive joinpaths, as defined in this section, may give rise to associations of different sensitivity. In other words, not all sensitive joinpaths are equally sensitive. For example, an association involving values that are "closer" to a secret table is likely to be more sensitive than other sensitive associations. The closeness may be measured by the length of the joinpath, by the semantics of the tables, or by system manager's insights.

In general, we allow the system manager to give a set of joinpaths for the release control system to deal with. Only the sensitive associations derived by any of these joinpaths will be considered sensitive and their release will be controlled.

In many situations, the length of sensitive joinpaths may be a sufficiently precise indicator for the sensitivity of the related associations. Hence, we introduce a sensitivity parameter which bounds the number of tables participating in a joinpath. This can be useful for system managers since they can have a "wholesale" way of giving a set of sensitive joinpaths.

Definition 6. *An association* $\langle t, JP \rangle$ *is* k-sensitive *if* JP *is a sensitive joinpath for* t *and* $|Tables(JP)| = k$.

In particular, an association is 1-sensitive means the pair actually appears in the same (secret) table. In our example, the association of John and Trace is 3-sensitive. We believe one should be mostly concerned with up to 3 or 4-sensitive associations. Certainly, this is highly dependent on the particular database schema and associated semantics.

2.2   Computing Sensitive Associations

In this section we illustrate how, given a maximum sensitivity value K, we can compute all k-sensitive associations for $k \leq K$ in an optimized fashion.

An observation is that for each joinpath there exists one having the inverse sequence of tables. It is not necessary to compute both, since they would just derive *inverse* tuples. For each pair of inverse joinpaths we consider a lexicographical order on the names of tables in order to identify the one that should be computed. For example, referring to the tables in Fig. 1, both $\langle$Employees, Assignments, Projects$\rangle$ and $\langle$Projects, Assignments, Employees$\rangle$ are sensitive joinpaths of length three, but only the first will be considered for the computation. This technique will also facilitate the management of the tuples resulting from the joinpaths. That is, as both $\langle$Employees.EName.John, Projects.PName.Trace$\rangle$ and $\langle$Projects.PName.Trace, Employees.EName.John$\rangle$ are sensitive associations (with respect to two sensitive joinpaths that are inverse of each other), we are going to use only the first one (with the lexicographical order).

We can also observe that in some cases, the join result along a joinpath JP_1 is simply a projection of the join result of another joinpath JP_2. If this is the case, we do not need to compute the join along the joinpath JP_1, if the join along JP_2 has already been computed.

Example 3. Consider a database with 3 tables (Fig 3): T_1, T_2, and S, with S being the only secret table, and with referential integrity constraints (i) T_1

refers to T_2 and S, and (ii) S refers to T_2. (We omit the attribute names in the figure.) Assume that the join along the joinpath $\langle T_1, S, T_2 \rangle$ is already computed, perhaps with join operations $(T_1 \bowtie S) \bowtie T_2$ or a direct three-way join algorithm. Consider a tuple t in $T_1 \bowtie S$. Since S references to T_2 and the join condition between S and T_2 reflects this referential integrity, we know there exists t_2 in T_2 such that $t \bowtie t_2$ is in $T_1 \bowtie S \bowtie T_2$. Therefore, t is simply a projection of the tuple $t \bowtie t_2$ in $T_1 \bowtie S \bowtie T_2$. Hence, if the join $T_1 \bowtie S \bowtie T_2$ is already computed, we do not need to compute the join $T_1 \bowtie S$, and we call the joinpath $\langle S, T_1 \rangle$ unnecessary in this case.

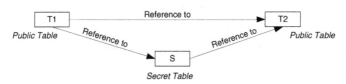

Fig. 3. Three tables with referential constraints.

In addition to the above observation, since we are interested only in sensitive associations, any non-sensitive joinpath is not really necessary for our purpose.

Definition 7. *Given a positive integer K, we say that a joinpath of length up to K is* necessary in terms of computation *if (i) it contains at least one secret table, and (ii) its join result is not a projection of the join result of any other joinpath of length up to K.*

Example 4. Consider the joinpaths of lengths up to 3 involving the tables in Fig. 3. The only joinpaths of length 3 are (after dropping inverse joinpaths): $\langle S, T_2, T_1 \rangle$, $\langle S, T_1, T_2 \rangle$, and $\langle T_1, S, T_2 \rangle$. These joinpaths are all necessary since each contains a secret table, and each cannot be the projection from the result of any other joinpath of length 3 or less.

Consider joinpaths of length 2. As discussed earlier, we know the joinpath $\langle S, T_1 \rangle$ is not necessary. Joinpath $\langle T_1, T_2 \rangle$ is not necessary, either, since it does not contain a secret table. The only necessary joinpath of length 2 is $\langle S, T_2 \rangle$. For joinpaths of length 1, it is clear that the only necessary one is $\langle S \rangle$ since all other joinpaths only involve public tables.

The notion of necessary joinpaths is very useful; indeed, when we compute joins, we only need to make sure that the join results are available for the necessary joinpaths. All other join computations can be avoided, leading to a significant optimization of the whole computation process.

The definition of necessary joinpaths is rather general. As seen above, in practice, one way to identify necessary joinpaths is considering referential integrity constraints. We illustrate this process by the procedure in Fig. 4.

The two conditions of Step 2 in the procedure formalize the reason why, in the tables of Fig. 3, the joinpath $\langle S, T_1 \rangle$ is not necessary.

Input:	Tables, referential constraints, and integer K
Output:	Necessary joinpaths of up to length K
Method:	**Step 1**, mark as necessary all joinpaths of length K containing at least one secret table.

	Step 2, for $m = k - 1$ to 1 mark as *necessary* each joinpath $\langle T_1, \ldots, T_m \rangle$ of length m containing a secret table if one of the following conditions holds:
	  – there is no joinpath $\langle T, T_1, \ldots, T_m \rangle$ such that if $\{T.A_1 = T_1.B_1, \ldots T.A_s = T_1.B_s\}$ are all the equality conditions on T and T_1, there exists a single referential constraint from $(B_1, \ldots B_s)$ of T_1 to $(A_1, \ldots, A_s)$ of T, or
	  – there is no joinpath $\langle T_1, \ldots, T_m, T \rangle$ such that if $\{T.A_1 = T_m.B_1, \ldots T.A_s = T_m.B_s\}$ are all the equality conditions on T and T_m, there exists a referential constraint from $(B_1, \ldots B_s)$ of T_m to $(A_1, \ldots, A_s)$ of T.

Fig. 4. Necessary joinpath procedure.

Theorem 2. *If the join results are computed for all the necessary joinpaths identified by the procedure in Fig. 4, then each of the join results of sensitive joinpaths (up to length K) is either computed already or it can be computed as a projection of one of the computed join results.*

It is also easily seen that, if we only have referential integrity constraints, we can find a database instance such that none of the necessary joinpaths (i.e., the joinpaths marked "necessary") are projections of any other joinpaths (of length up to K). This means that the necessary joinpaths are indeed "necessary".

Once a set of necessary joinpaths is given, an evaluation strategy must be applied to compute the join results for all the necessary joinpaths, and their projections (to find the sensitive associations).

Optimization of multijoins as the one given by a single joinpath is a well-studied problem. In our scenario, a joinpath corresponds to an acyclic multijoin, and hence yields to a quadratic-time optimization algorithm (e.g., [7]). Further optimizations are possible by exploiting the common subexpressions of necessary joinpaths. Since this is straightforward, we omit the details from the paper.

3   Representing Sensitive Associations

In the previous section, we defined the concept of sensitive associations and the procedure to obtain them. In this section, we turn to the data structure used to store sensitive associations with the goal of using this data for realease control.

3.1   Tagged Associations

By definition, a sensitive association is a pair of binary tuple and a joinpath. There are three kinds of information in this pair, namely, the values, the table names and attribute names associated with the values, and the joinpath itself.

The table and attribute names give the information of where the values are from, while the joinpath tells how the two values are related. For different release control applications, different aspects of the association may be used. In order to facilitate our discussion, we introduce the concept of a tagged association.

A tagged association is simply another representation of the an association $\langle t, JP \rangle$ as follows. If $t = \langle T_1.A.a, T_m.B.b \rangle$ and $JP = \langle T_1, \ldots, T_m \rangle$, then we first distinguish the following two parts of the association:

– $T_1.A.a$ and $T_m.B.b$ are the *keywords*
– $\langle T_1, \ldots T_m \rangle$, together with the set $\{T_1.A_1 = T_2.A_2, \ldots, T_{m-1}.A_{m-1} = T_m.A_m\}$, is the *semantic tag*.

The set of join conditions in the semantic tag consists of all the join conditions in $Eq(DB)$ that relate consecutive tables, T_i and T_{i+1}, $i = 1, \ldots, m - 1$, in the sequence $\langle T_1, \ldots T_m \rangle$, exactly as in the definition of joinpath.

Conceptually, the semantic tag stores most of the information about how the association has been identified in the database.

Definition 8. *For each sensitive association $\langle t, JP \rangle$, a tagged representation is $\langle f, s, \tau \rangle$, where f and s are the two keywords, and τ is the semantic tag.*

Since the number of sensitive associations can be huge for some databases, we introduce a form of approximation based on progressively reducing the information in the semantic tag. We distinguish 3 levels of approximation:

– Level 0: the complete semantic tag is preserved;
– Level 1: the semantic tag is reduced to the set of *secret* tables appearing in the joinpath;
– Level 2: no semantic tag, and no table and attribute names in the keywords of the association, i.e., only a pair of values.

We will still call the values in Level-2 representation as keywords, although they don't have the table and attribute name prefixes.

Intuitively, the lower the level, the more precise[3] will a release control system be able to exploit the semantic tags in checking the outgoing documents.

Example 5. Given the sensitive association

$$\langle \text{Employees.EName.John}, \text{Projects.PName.Trace} \rangle$$

along the joinpath $\langle \text{Employees}, \text{Assignments}, \text{Projects} \rangle$, we have the following three levels of tagged representations:

– Level 0: we have $f = \text{Employees.EName.John}$, and $s = \text{Projects.PName.Trace}$ and τ consists of the sequence $\langle \text{Employees}, \text{Assignments}, \text{Projects} \rangle$ and the set of two conditions $\text{Assignments.EID} = \text{Employees.EID}$ and $\text{Assignments.PID} = \text{Projects.PID}$.
– Level 1: the same f and s, but $\tau = \{ \text{Assignments} \}$.
– Level 2: $f = \text{John}$, $s = \text{Trace}$ and τ is empty.

---

[3] By precision of the release control system we mean the overall minimization of false positive and false negatives.

Input:	A set of tagged associations $\langle f, s, \tau \rangle$ having the same semantic tag,
Output:	Cross-product representation
Method:	1. Sort the set of pairs of the form (f, s) according to the f values. Then Group contiguous pairs with the same f value, into a single pair having f as the first element and the set of all corresponding s values as the second element.
	2. Sort the set of pairs of the form (f value, set of s values) by the second element (i.e., the set) so that all pairs having the same set of s values become contiguous. Then group contiguous pairs having the same second element (i.e., the set) into a single pair of the form (set of f values, set of s values).
	3. For each resulting pair P_i, we add a triple $\langle \mathcal{F}_i, \mathcal{S}_i, \tau \rangle$ to the representation $\mathcal{R}$, with $\mathcal{F}_i$ containing each element in the group of first values in P_i, and $\mathcal{S}_i$ containing each element in the set of second values in P_i.

Fig. 5. Deriving cross-product representation.

3.2 Cross-Product Representation

As mentioned in the introduction, for each semantic tag τ, there exists a possibly large number of f and s values such that (f, s, τ) is a tagged sensitive association. The number can be especially large for the representations at Levels 1 and 2. This motivates our effort for devising a compact representation.

Definition 9. *Given a set $\mathcal{A}$ of tagged associations, a cross-product represen-*
tation of $\mathcal{A}$ is a set $\mathcal{R}$ of triples, each called a sensitive-pair group, *of the form*
$\langle \mathcal{F}, \mathcal{S}, \tau \rangle$, *where $\mathcal{F}$ and $\mathcal{S}$ are sets of values, and τ is a semantic tag such that*
$\langle f, s, \tau \rangle \in \mathcal{A}$ *if and only if there exists $\langle \mathcal{F}, \mathcal{S}, \tau \rangle \in \mathcal{R}$ such that $f \in \mathcal{F}$ and $s \in \mathcal{S}$.*

Clearly, since our goal is finding a compact representation, we should try to minimize the size of $\mathcal{R}$.

For this purpose, we propose a simple and intuitive method shown in Fig. 5. The algorithm starts with the sensitive associations derived via the method in Subsection 2.2, and converts them into tagged representations (either Level 0, 1, or 2). We use a two-column table to store the tagged associations (with the same semantic tag) and perform a number of sort and grouping operations to derive the cross product representations. The algorithm is straightforward. It basically corresponds to (1) recognize all the s values corresponding to the same f value, and (2) recognize all the f values corresponding to the same group of s values.

Proposition 1. *Given a set of tagged associations, the algorithm in Fig. 5 cor-*
rectly produces a cross-product representation of the associations.

Example 6. Suppose we have the following set of associations (with the same semantic tag τ): $(1, 2)$, $(1, 3)$, $(2, 2)$, $(2, 3)$. Then the first step will yield the following pairs $(1, \{2, 3\})$, $(2, \{2, 3\})$. The second step will yield $(\{1, 2\}, \{2, 3\})$, i.e., one pair of sets.

In Example 6, we reduced four pairs into one pair. The procedure is not necessarily optimal, since it uses a fixed order in producing the grouping. Nevertheless, our experiments show that this simple method is effective.

An observation is that if Level 1 tagged associations are used (i.e., consider τ being the set of secret tables only), the storage using the cross-product representation has an interesting upper bound, as shown by the following result.

Theorem 3. *Assume all considered sensitive joinpaths have at most m secret tables. Then, for Level-1 representation, we can compute a cross-product representation that has at most c^m sensitive-pair groups, where c is the maximum size of a secret table in the joinpaths.*

4   Conclusion

In this paper, we presented preliminary results on identifying and representing sensitive associations in databases to be checked by release control procedures. Together with the contributions in [1] these results are first essential steps towards a solution for the challenging general task of release control. We are currently conducting experiments on real size databases to study the feasibility of using the proposed representation of associations. Initial results are promising. In addition, we are working on two new fronts. The first is to extend and properly classify the type of sensitive associations. In particular, it may be helpful to consider information gathered at the conceptual design stage. The second is on release control techniques that take into account the many forms in which associations can appear in outgoing documents.

Acknowledgments

This work was partially supported by the National SF under grants IIS-0242237 and CCR-0113515. The work of Bettini was also partially supported by Italian MIUR (FIRB "Web-Minds" project N. RBNE01WEJT_005). The authors wish to thank the anonymous reviewers for their comments.

References

1. Claudio Bettini, X. Sean Wang, and Sushil Jajodia. A learning-based approach to information release control. In *Proceedings of the Sixth IFIP TC-11 WG 11.5 Working Conference on Integrity and Internal Control in Information Systems (IICIS)*. Kluwer, 2003.
2. Keith Brewster. Inference and aggregation issues in secure database management systems. Technical Report 005, NCSC, 1996.
3. C. J. Date. *An introduction to Database Systems*. Addison Wesley Logman, Inc., 7th edition, 2000.
4. Dorothy E. Denning. A preliminary note on the inference problem in multilevel database system. In *Proc. NCSC Invitational Workshop on Database Security*, Baltimore, MD, June 1986.

5. Csilla Farkas and Sushil Jajodia. The inference problem: A survey. *ACM SIGKDD Explorations*, 4(2):6–11, 2003.

6. Vagelis Hristidis and Yannis Papakonstantinou. DISCOVER: Keyword search in relational databases. In *VLDB*, pages 670–681, 2002.

7. Ravi Krishnamurthy, Haran Boral, and Carlo Zaniolo. Optimization of nonrecursive queries. In *VLDB*, pages 128–137, 1986.

8. Arnon Rosenthal and Gio Wiederhold. Document release versus data access controls: Two sides of a coin? *Proceedings of the Tenth CIKM*, pages 544–546, New York, November 5–10 2001. ACM Press.

9. Bhavani Thuraisingham and William Ford. Security constraints in a multilevel secure distributed database management system. *IEEE Trans. Knowl. Data Eng.*, 7(2):274–293, 1995.

10. Richard Wheeldon, Mark Levene, and Kevin Keenoy. Search and navigation in relational databases. July 2003. arXiv.org Computer Science e-print.

11. Gio Wiederhold. Protecting information when access is granted for collaboration. In *Proc. of Data and Application Security, Development and Directions, IFIP TC11/ WG11.3 Fourteenth Annual Working Conference on Database Security*, pages 1–14, 2000.

Appendix: Proofs of Three Theorems

Proof of Theorem 1

Let $t = \langle T.A.a, T'.B.b \rangle$ be a binary tuple such that $t \in \pi(Eq\text{-}Join)$. Hence, t is derived as the projection on the attributes A and B of $T_1 \bowtie \ldots \bowtie T_m$ with $T_i = T$ and $T_j = T'$ for some $i, j \in \{1, \ldots, m\}$ with these tables in $Tables(Eq\text{-}Join)$. By Definition 1, there exist $T_{i1}, \ldots, T_{ik}$ in $Tables(Eq\text{-}Join)$ with $T_{i1} = T_i$ and $T_{ik} = T_j$ such that the conditions $T_{ip}.A_{ip} = T_{i(p+1)}.A_{i(p+1)}$ are in $Eq(DB)$ for each $p = 1, \ldots, k-1$. Hence, there exists a joinpath JP with sequence of tables $T_{i1}, \ldots, T_{ik}$. Moreover, JP is a joinpath for t, since from $\pi(JP) \supseteq \pi(Eq\text{-}Join)$ and $t \in \pi(Eq\text{-}Join)$ we derive $t \in \pi(JP)$.

Proof of Theorem 2

We prove by induction. The procedure states that all sensitive joinpath of length K are necessary. Assume that the join result of each joinpath of length no less than $k \leq K$ is either marked necessary (which is directly computed) or is a projection of a join result of a joinpath of length greater than k. That is, we can assume join results of all sensitive joinpaths of length k are available (from some computed join results). Now, consider a sensitive joinpath JP of length $k - 1$. Two cases. In the first case, JP is marked necessary by the procedure. Then the join result for JP should be computed directly. In the second case, JP is not marked necessary. Then by the conditions in the procedure (and the reasoning given earlier stating that the joinpath $\langle S, T_1 \rangle$ is not necessary for the tables in Fig 3 if $K = 3$), there exists a joinpath JP' of length k such that the join result for JP is a projection of the join result of JP'. Since JP is sensitive and contains a secret table, JP' must contain a secret table and, hence, must be sensitive. Since the length of JP' is k and, as assumed, the join result for JP' is either computed or it is a projection of another necessary joinpath, we can conclude that the join result for JP is a projection of the join result of a computed joinpath (due to definition of projection operation).

Proof of Theorem 3

We consider the simplest case where we have only one joinpath which contains exactly 1 secret table. In this case, the joinpath must be of the form $\langle T_1, \ldots, S, \ldots, T_m \rangle$ where S is the secret table and all others are public tables. Then if (a, b, τ) is a tagged association, where $\tau = \{S\}$ by definition of Level 1 representation, it must mean that (a, b) is a projection from a tuple t in the join result of joinpath and t must contain a tuple t_s from table S (otherwise, contradicting with the definition of sensitive associations). We say that this pair (a, b) is *derived* from t_s. Now consider all pairs (a, b) that are derived from the same t_s. We can see that if (a_1, b_1) and (a_2, b_2) are both derived from t_s, then (a_1, b_2) is also derived from the same t_s. This is due to the fact that are no join conditions between a table appearing before S and another table appearing after S. Indeed, if (a_1, b_1) is derived from t_s, it must mean that a_1 "joins" with t_s (from the left side of S in the joinpath). Likewise, b_2 "joins" with t_s as well, and hence (a_1, b_2) should be derived from t_s. Hence, the number of triples in the cross-product representation must be at most the number of tuples in S. This reasoning can be easily extended to the case of multiple joinpaths and multiple secrete tables in each joinpath. Details omitted here.

Using Delay
to Defend Against Database Extraction*

Magesh Jayapandian, Brian Noble, James Mickens, and H.V. Jagadish

Department of Electrical Engineering and Computer Science
University of Michigan
Ann Arbor, MI 48109-2122
{jmagesh,bnoble,jmickens,jag}@umich.edu

Abstract. For many data providers, the "crown jewels" of their business are the data that they have organized. If someone could copy their entire database, it would be a competitive catastrophe. Yet, a data provider is in the business of providing data, so access to the database cannot be restricted entirely. How is the data provider to permit legitimate access to users who request access to small portions of the database while protecting the database from wholesale copying?

We suggest that delay can be used for this purpose. We show, under reasonable assumptions, that it is possible to slow down the copying of the entire dataset by an arbitrary amount ensuring that queries that return a significant portion of the database introduce a delay that is orders of magnitude higher than that for legitimate user queries. We then consider issues of change, and show, under reasonable assumptions of rates of change, how to limit access so that the voyeur is guaranteed never to have a complete up-to-date dataset. We also present several extensions of these two major results.

We have implemented our technique on a commercial relational database, and we present numbers showing that the analytically expected delays are indeed observed experimentally, and also that the overheads of implementing our scheme are small.

1 Introduction

There are many information providers on the web, providing travel-related information, weather forecasts, directory look-up services, coverage of health-related topics, discographies, and so on – for almost any subject you desire, there is likely to be some provider who has invested time and effort to compile a database on the topic. Most of these providers have invested this time and effort with a business reason: even if they do not charge users for each look-up, they may rely upon user traffic for advertising revenues, for referral commissions, or as goodwill to attract customers to related fee-based services.

---

* Supported in part by NSF under grants IIS-0219513 and CCR-0208740

W. Jonker and M. Petković (Eds.): SDM 2004, LNCS 3178, pp. 202–218, 2004.

1.1   The Problem

Consider an attacker who wishes to steal information from such a provider, for instance to set up a business in competition. This attacker could attempt to hack into the provider's system – such attacks are beyond the scope of the current paper. Here we assume that the provider's computer systems, database, web server, etc. are appropriately protected from system invasion. (There are also many security threats other than data theft – such attacks also are outside the scope of this paper). The attacker still has the "front door" available – the information provider is in the business of providing information from the database to legitimate users, so the attacker only has to masquerade as a legitimate user to gain all the information in the database. To prevent such attacks, most information providers restrict the amount of information that can be queried in one request – users must ask very selective queries. However, such restrictions are easy to overcome – the attacker could trivially construct a robot that repeatedly asks slightly different selective queries whose union is the entire database. Robots can either adopt a *brute force* approach or use available knowledge to generate valid attribute values to pose queries. Such robots are hard to detect especially since each individual query is no different than one a genuine user might make.

1.2   Our Solution

Our scheme involves the inclusion of a strategically computed delay with every data item present in the provider's database. The delays are variable and are based on the popularity of the individual items in the database. They are computed in such a way that, without burdening legitimate users with too high[4] a wait time, they can force an attacker to wait an extremely long time to retrieve sufficient data to recreate the database.

1.3   Contributions

We begin by presenting the basic scheme, assigning delays to tuples according to their popularity; popular items have short delays, while unpopular items have long ones. A simple analysis shows that, for popularity distributions that follow a power law, typical users should expect modest delays, while an adversary attempting to extract the entire database faces delays many orders of magnitude larger. This is true even after capping the maximum possible delay at some value that legitimate users would find tolerable. Such distributions need not be known in advance, and can change over time. Likewise, the cost of computing delays can be kept reasonable.

The success of this scheme depends on access patterns with sufficient skew. If all items have similar popularity, our scheme would assign each of them approximately the same delay. If these delays are small, an adversary bent on extraction would not be penalized sufficiently. On the other hand, if these delays are large, legitimate users would suffer delays beyond their tolerance.

Instead, one can leverage the fact that most databases are updated frequently. We can impose small delays on frequently-updated items, but larger delays on items that are not updated as often. If these update rates exhibit skew, legitimate access to this database will tend to have low delays and fresh data, while an attacker will find that extracted copies of most of the data will always be stale, since the delay incurred in retrieving all of them is collectively greater than the update periods of several of them individually.

We evaluate the success of our approach with a variety of experiments. The first uses real datasets to show that skewed access patterns do indeed produce the desired results. Users can expect to suffer delays on the order of a few milliseconds, while adversaries are faced with nearly 90% of the costs one would achieve by penalizing each query with the maximum individual delay. We also show synthetic benchmarks that explore the range of costs and benefits one might expect if delay is assigned based on access rate as well as based on update rate. Finally, we show that even an untuned implementation of this scheme imposes overheads of 20% in the worst case.

2   The Core Proposal

In nearly any dataset, some items are more popular than others. Legitimate users tend to access popular items more frequently than unpopular ones, but an adversary bent on extraction must eventually request every element in the set. We can use these skewed preferences to assign small (or zero) delays to popular items, but large delays to unpopular ones. Such an assignment does not often penalize legitimate users, but it imposes substantial, frequent penalties to an attacker bent on extraction. Any dataset with a known, skewed popularity distribution is amenable to this technique. What we are leveraging is that the query distribution of an attacker is different from the query distribution of legitimate users. If the legitimate query workload has a uniform distribution over the data elements, then the core proposal described here will not work: however, we may still be able to exploit skews in data updates as we shall describe in Section 3.

For concreteness, in this paper, we will assume a relational model, with each tuple being a unit data element for retrieval. We will assume a query load comprised purely of selection queries against this relation, and assign to each tuple a popularity score reflecting how frequently it is present in the query result. To each tuple retrieval, we assign a delay that is inversely proportional to the popularity of the tuple. With appropriate, often trivial, modifications, our scheme can also be applied to other data models, query models, and delay models.

2.1   A Simple Zipfian Analysis

A Zipf distribution is frequently used to model skew, and occurs in a wide variety of settings. It was originally observed in English word choice [22], and it holds for Web [8] and streaming media [11] workloads. In a Zipf distribution – sometimes also called a *power law* – the ith most popular object is requested at a frequency proportional to $i^{-\alpha}$, where α is called the *Zipf parameter*. This distribution has been widely reported in the database literature as well, and is probably applicable to many data sources on the web. Though our technique is not dependent on the specific form of the query distribution, it is convenient for purposes of analysis to focus on one distribution, and the Zipf distribution is a natural choice.

For purposes of this analysis, we also simplify the query model slightly – we assume that each query to the database eventually results in exactly one tuple. (This is not a major restriction, since a query that returns multiple tuples can simply be considered the aggregate of multiple simple queries that return one tuple each.) The delay, d, for which the database engine pauses before yielding the ith most popular tuple is

$$d = \frac{1}{N}\left(\frac{i^{\alpha+\beta}}{f_{max}}\right) . \qquad (1)$$

Here N is the number of tuples in the relation, f_{max} is the frequency with which the most popular item is requested, and α is the Zipf parameter of the underlying popularity distribution. The constant β is chosen to balance the desired penalty imposed on an extraction attack with the undesirable delays to legitimate users. If an adversary were then to pose a sequence of queries to extract the complete relation, the total delay incurred would be

$$d_{total} = \sum_{i=1}^{N} d(i) = \frac{1}{Nf_{max}} \sum_{i=1}^{N} i^{\alpha+\beta} . \qquad (2)$$

It is easy to see that an adversary must face longer delays with higher β values. Legitimate users, on the other hand, would expect to see median delays, d_{med} for the typical request. For skewed distributions, we believe that a quantile metric such as the median is more representative and fair than other statistical measures such as mean, variance and standard deviation, which often fall victim to outliers in the data, that are commonly found in Zipfian distributions. We can compute the asymptotic rank of the median frequency using the integral test; it is a function of of skew, α, and dataset size, N:

$$i_{med} \in \begin{cases} \Theta\left(2^{\frac{1}{\alpha-1}}N\right) & \text{if } \alpha < 1; \\ \Theta\left(\sqrt{N}\right) & \text{if } \alpha = 1; \\ \Theta\left(\log N\right) & \text{if } \alpha > 1 . \end{cases} \qquad (3)$$

For our technique to be successful, it is imperative that d_{total}, the total delay imposed during an extraction attack, be significantly higher than d_{med}.

$$\frac{d_{total}}{d_{med}} = \frac{\left(\frac{1}{Nf_{max}}\right)\sum_{i=1}^{N} i^{\alpha+\beta}}{\left(\frac{1}{Nf_{max}}\right) i_{med}^{\alpha+\beta}} \in \begin{cases} \Theta\left(2^{\frac{\alpha+\beta}{1-\alpha}}N\right) & \text{if } \alpha < 1; \\ \Theta\left(N^{\frac{\beta+3}{2}}\right) & \text{if } \alpha = 1; \\ \Theta\left(N\left(\frac{N}{\log N}\right)^{\alpha+\beta}\right) & \text{if } \alpha > 1 . \end{cases} \qquad (4)$$

Thus, for skews equal to or greater than 1, setting β to a high yet acceptable value ensures that the delay for an adversary's query will indeed be orders of magnitude higher than that for a genuine user's query. For skew less than 1, the benefit over the naïve approach is only linear in N. However, as these fractional skews approach 1 – as they are expected to – the exponential coefficient dominates, thereby maintaining the ratio of adversary to legitimate user delay at a desirably high value.

2.2   Capped Maximum Delay

This simple scheme provides low *median* delay, but can produce unacceptably long delays for legitimate users from time to time. After all, even the the least popular tuples will eventually be required by some legitimate queries, and the scheme as described above will delay these for a long time. Such delays may displease these legitimate users – something that the information provider certainly does not wish to do.

To prevent excessive delays – and the resulting unhappy customers – we cap the maximum delay that will be added to the retrieval of a single data item, no matter how infrequently accessed. This approach retains the benefits of the simple scheme; the asymptotic relationships between adversary and median query remain the same.

There is some tuple, at rank M, that is assigned the maximum acceptable delay, d_{max}. Since delay increases with decreasing popularity, all tuples that are accessed less frequently will have their delays capped at d_{max}, rather than as computed by the basic scheme. We can express d_{max} as

$$d_{max} = \frac{1}{N}\left(\frac{M^{\alpha+\beta}}{f_{max}}\right).$$
(5)

This alters our expression for the delay for an adversary:

$$d_{total} = \sum_{i=1}^{M} d(i) + (N-M)d_{max} = \frac{1}{Nf_{max}}\left(\sum_{i=1}^{M} i^{\alpha+\beta} + (N-M)M^{\alpha+\beta}\right).$$
(6)

The maximum delay allowed is obviously greater than the median delay. Therefore, the median rank of the distribution does not change in this scenario, and the median delay, d_{med} remains the same as before. The modified relationship between adversary and genuine user delays is now

$$\frac{d_{total}}{d_{med}} = \frac{\left(\frac{1}{Nf_{max}}\right)\left(\sum_{i=1}^{M} i^{\alpha+\beta} + (N-M)M^{\alpha+\beta}\right)}{\left(\frac{1}{Nf_{max}}\right)i_{med}^{\alpha+\beta}}.$$
(7)

Since $M \in \Theta(N)$ (i.e., M increases linearly with N), our initial results remain true.

2.3   Learning the Distribution

While the analysis in the preceding sections was worked out for the Zipf distribution, there is nothing in the definition of the scheme itself that requires that
the workload follow such a distribution. Moreover, even if the query workload
did follow such a distribution, we would still have the task of determining the
popularity rank, and the frequency of access, for each tuple to determine the
correct amount of delay to add.

We associate a *count* with each tuple that tracks the number of times that
tuple has been requested. The value of this count, normalized by a global count
of all requests, directly indicates the popularity of the tuple.

The simplest way to implement this is to add a *count* attribute to each
tuple in the relation. However, this has the undesirable effect of turning every
read access into a read-modify-write access, and therefore causing a substantial
performance hit. We propose several mechanisms to keep reasonable the cost of
maintaining these counts (Section 4.4).

Start-Up Transients. While counts are fine for indicating popularity of a tuple
in steady state, we still have to deal with a (potentially long) start-up period
during which representative statistics have not yet been gathered. Placing caps
on maximum delays gives us a convenient mechanism to manage these start-up
transients. We assume all items are equally unpopular with frequencies of zero.
With these initial conditions, early queries will generate high delays, even if they
are for popular items. However, the capped delay allows us to serve these queries
in reasonable time while we are learning the distribution. The delay associated
with popular items falls rapidly thereafter.

Changing Distributions. Many datasets will have popularity distributions
that change over time. Unfortunately, this presents a problem for our basic
scheme. Because there are often many more newly-popular requests, they have
a significant impact on median delay.

We solve this by introducing a weight for each request which decays expo-
nentially with age. The decay is applied at each request, uniformly to all counts.
We use a static decay term, δ; the choice of appropriate δ depends upon the
underlying dynamics of the popularity distribution. In situations where it is not
known, one can simultaneously track counts with more than one decay term,
switching to the appropriate set as the request pattern warrants – a technique
used previously in both wireless networking [16] and energy management [10].
This adaptive strategy has the added benefit of tracking distributions with non-
stationary second-order terms.

It is expensive to discount the value of every count at each access. Instead,
we inflate the value by which each count increases at each access, and normalize
counts by this value, with the same effect. To prevent overflow, we must reset
counters from time to time, at some loss of precision.

2.4 Attacks

Our scheme applies delays to individual queries, but does not inhibit queries posed in parallel. An adversary able to manufacture identities can use these identities to pose queries in parallel. Because our database engine cannot label these queries as coming from the same user, the adversary pays only the maximum among individual penalties, not the sum over all of them.

It is important to note that true *Sybil* attacks [13] are difficult to engineer. For example, suppose that routable IP addresses are used as identities; clearly, IP addresses are trivial to forge, but it is more difficult to also control the route to that forged address to receive the result. An adversary may be able to control many addresses within a single subnet, but any given subnet can be treated as an aggregate, with responses rate-limited across all users in that subnet.

However, even if an adversary is able to manufacture identities, one can prevent unbounded parallelism through rate-limiting the granting of access to the database itself. If only one new user every t seconds is given an account to access the database, we can place a lower bound on the time it would take an adversary to accumulate enough identities for the parallel attack to become feasible. If this time is comparable to the delay imposed on an adversary with a single identity, then the parallel attack is rendered moot. Equivalently, one can charge a small fee for registration, computed so that a parallel adversary would have to spend as much in registration fees as to collect the data separately.

Storefront and *cached storefront* attacks are more difficult to defend against. Since the attack only forwards queries from legitimate users, the adversary need not register an undue number of identities. If the adversary is of significant size, we will notice the increased traffic, and a simple imposition of a limit on queries from a single user will suffice as a defense. (If the adversary attempts to counter this defense by manufacturing multiple identities, then our protection against a Sybil attack will protect us in this case as well). The success of a storefront attack ultimately depends on the business model of the source data provider – clearly, it costs the attacker at least as much to provide this service as the source provider charges, making it more difficult for the attacker to compete.

3 Exploiting Data Change

The main limitation of our scheme is that it depends on skew in access patterns. If access patterns are uniform, all items in the database have approximately the same rank, and hence the same delay. However, even without skew in access patterns, delay can be used in many cases by exploiting differences among the rates at which elements in a dataset change. Most databases are not static, one-time collections of information: rather, they are updated frequently. Where data changes, it is no longer necessary to thwart an attacker for an arbitrarily long time – it suffices to introduce a large delay relative to the data change rate. In the resulting system, an attacker can never have a consistent, current snapshot of the dataset, since some extracted tuples will always be stale. This scheme is entirely independent of access pattern, and so applies to datasets with uniform access patterns; exactly the scenario our access rate-based scheme cannot handle.

The basic idea is to charge small delays to frequently-updated items, but large delays to infrequently-updated ones. Tuples that stay fresh longer take longer to retrieve than tuples whose values change more often. This ensures that the delay incurred in retrieving the entire dataset is sufficient to cause a large fraction of the retrieved data to be obsolete. While this technique does not depend on skew in access rates, it does depend on skew in update rates. Such skew has been observed in practice [9], and has been used to identify which pages a crawler [15] needs to re-fetch frequently [12].

3.1   Assigning Delays

Consider a dataset with uniform access frequency, but with a skewed update frequency. Let the update frequency have a Zipf distribution with Zipf parameter α. As in the case of skewed access frequency, let the delay of an item, i, be inversely proportional to its update rate, r_i.

$$d(i) \propto \frac{1}{r_i} \tag{8}$$

More precisely,

$$d(i) = \frac{c}{N} \left(\frac{i^\alpha}{r_{max}} \right). \tag{9}$$

An item in the dataset is considered stale if its value changes at least once during the execution of the adversary's query, i.e., its value is no longer the same as that obtained via the query. For the ith ranked item to be stale,

$$d_{total} \geq \frac{1}{r_i}. \tag{10}$$

If the ith item is the least frequently updated item that becomes stale during this time, then all items ranked higher than i, i.e, those that are more frequently updated, will also have become stale. In other words, the number of stale items in the dataset is i. Thus, a fraction S of the dataset (of size N) will be stale if the (SN)th ranked item is stale. From the equation above, the maximum value of S, S_{max}, can be computed as follows:

$$(S_{max}N)^\alpha = \frac{c_{max}}{N} \sum_{i=1}^{N} i^\alpha \tag{11}$$

$$S_{max} \approx \left(\frac{c_{max}}{1+\alpha} \right)^{\frac{1}{\alpha}}. \tag{12}$$

This value of S_{max} tells us what fraction of the dataset is guaranteed to be obsolete and of little use when stolen by an adversary. This fraction is limited only by c_{max}, the maximum allowable value for c, a constant which, given a particular data size and update rate distribution, places a reasonable upper bound on the delay for a legitimate user query.

4   Evaluation

It is easy to demonstrate experimentally that our scheme works with accesses that are Zipf-distributed, since that is precisely the assumption used in our analysis. Running such experiments with synthetic data and synthetic query loads produces observed results that match analytical predictions perfectly. We show results of such experiments in this section.

However, apart from these intuitive results, we also ask how the scheme performs with real data. To this end, we applied our scheme to two sets of real access traces. The first is a trace-history of web-page requests, while the second is based on sales of tickets to movies screened during a single calendar year. Since both datasets exhibit some skew, we can apply delays based on popularity of items, on both of them.

For each of these traces, we ask two questions. First, what is the median delay a legitimate user might expect to see in our scheme? Second, what is the delay that an adversary would expect to see for this dataset? The answers to these questions depend on how well the database has succeeded in learning the popularity of an item, and in tracking changes to this popularity over time. For this purpose, recall that our frequency-of-access observations are weighted with time, with a specified decay rate. We explore a range of decay rates in each dataset. In all cases, an adversary suffers delays many orders of magnitude beyond that of legitimate users.

In addition to these real traces with biased access patterns, we also give results for a synthetic workload with uniform access patterns, but changing underlying data. We consider a variety of rates of bias in update rates. For each case, we quantify the median delay imposed on legitimate users, the total delay expected of adversaries, and the fraction of the extracted database that will be stale.

4.1   Delays for Static Popularity

The first dataset is a year-long trace of web-client usage [2], to analyze user queries posed to a web-server. This trace exhibits a relatively static popularity distribution over its lifetime. While this is a log of accesses to web pages rather than database tuples, it is reasonable to expect that similar access patterns may apply in both cases.

The trace itself loosely follows an exponential popularity distribution with $\alpha \approx 1.5$, as shown in Figure 1. In this graph, the x axis lists the 10 most popular items by rank, while the y axis gives the number of requests to that object over the lifetime of the trace.

We replayed all 725,091 requests in this trace, subjecting each request to the delay as computed by our scheme to assign delays based on popularity, with a maximum delay of 10 seconds. The dataset however, has 12,179 records, which pales in comparison with real-world databases which are often terabytes and quickly approaching petabytes in size. For this reason, we first built synthetic datasets of larger sizes, and created a new scenario identical to the Calgary trace

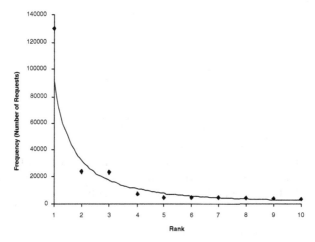

Fig. 1. Request Distribution: Calgary Trace

(in terms of access pattern, delay computation, etc.) except for the number of tuples. This helps to determine how our technique would perform on a real database. Our results appear in Table 1.

Table 1. Delays in Synthetic Traces

Database Size (tuples)	Median User Delay (ms)	Adversary Delay (weeks)
100,000	0.0	2
500,000	0.0	8
1,000,000	0.0	17

The typical user delay is observed to be negligibly small, while delays faced by an adversary are substantial, just as we expect. However, on implementing our scheme on the actual database, the small data size limits the largest penalty an adversary could possibly be subject to, to 34 hours, which is not large in absolute terms. This is due in large part to the very small size of the underlying database combined with a relatively modest ten-second maximum cap. This can be improved in two ways. Real datasets are likely to be much larger, so that total adversary delay should scale appropriately (as we have also shown). Secondly, raising the cap has no impact on the median delay, but directly affects the total delay imposed on an adversary, as shown in Table 2.

At the start of trace replay, we assumed nothing was known about the eventual distribution, but learned it over the course of the trace. After these legitimate requests were consumed, we computed the delay that would be imposed on an adversary if it were to extract the entire dataset, by examining the access counts after the trace was replayed. This was repeated for six different rates of

Table 2. Scaling Maximum Delay Costs

Cap (sec)	Adversary Delay (hours)
0.1	0.33
1	3.16
10	30.17
100	282.70

decay applied to the popularity metric, from 1 (no decay) to 1.0002. Note that because decay rates are exponents, results do not scale linearly; therefore we examine decay rates in logarithmic steps. The results appear in Table 3.

Table 3. Delays in Calgary Trace

Decay Rate	Median User Delay (ms)	Adversary Delay (hours)
1.000000	15.4	30.17
1.000001	24.9	31.06
1.000002	38.3	31.75
1.000005	118.6	32.76
1.000010	421.4	33.27
1.000020	2,241.6	33.61

Because this dataset exhibits a static access pattern, it is best to use the full history of prior accesses in determining delay. Therefore, a decay rate of 1.0 – no decay – provides the lowest possible delay for users without substantially lowering the delay imposed on an adversary. Even with this aggressive scheme, an adversary must wait more than a day to obtain this modest dataset of just over 12,000 objects; this is nearly 90% of the maximum possible delay.

4.2   Delays for Dynamic Popularity

The second dataset is based on cinema box office sales for 2002. This dataset has a rapidly shifting popularity distribution – new movies are released all the time, become immensely popular for a while, and then rapidly fade away as others take their place in the popular psyche. While we were not able to get access to actual traces of access to movie reviews, we obtained weekly box office sales data for all movies released in the year 2002 [3]. We used box office sales as the metric of popularity, and generated user requests to a database of movie records in proportion to the sales data for each week.

Compared to the Calgary trace, the resulting dataset does not exhibit the same degree of skew when viewed in its entirety. This is illustrated in Figure 2. In this graph, the x axis lists the 10 most popular movies by annual sales, while the y axis gives the sales totals for that film. Each week considered separately

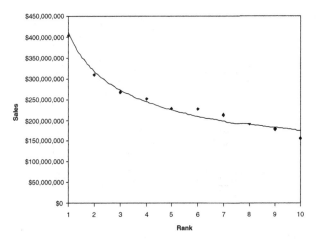

Fig. 2. Sales Distribution of Top 10 Movies of 2002

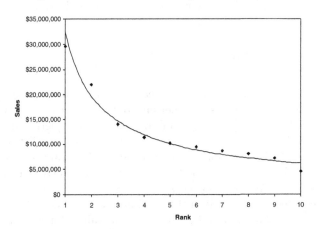

Fig. 3. Top 10 Movies for First Week of 2002

exhibits a more sharply skewed distribution. For example, Figure 3 shows the most popular films from the first week of 2002.

There were 634 films released over the course of 2002. We generated requests by week, one per $100,000 in weekly box office sales. Delays were computed by popularity, applying decay factors at weekly boundaries. The maximum allowable delay was again 10 seconds. With this maximum delay, the largest penalty an adversary could possibly be subject to is 1.76 hours. However, being a tiny dataset, it is important to guage our scheme by the fact that an adversary incurs 100% of the maximum possible total delay in this scenario, which when scaled to a more typical real-world database, is a huge success!

As in the Calgary dataset, the request distribution was learned over time. We computed median and adversary delays for nine different rates of decay applied to the popularity metric, from 1 (no decay) to 5 and the results appear in Table 4.

Table 4. Delays in Box Office Data

Decay Rate	Median User Delay (ms)	Adversary Delay (hours)
1.00	0.03	1.33
1.01	0.04	1.51
1.02	0.05	1.45
1.05	0.08	1.46
1.10	0.14	1.61
1.20	0.26	1.70
1.50	0.53	1.74
2.00	0.79	1.75
5.00	1.26	1.76

The popularity distribution in this set varies quickly. Thus, the different decay factors give fairly similar median and adversary delays.

4.3   Dynamic Data Simulations

Where skew exists in access patterns, it can be exploited to penalize extraction without inconveniencing users. To measure our ability to do so, we created a relation with 100,000 tuples, and simultaneously posed queries and posted updates to this relation. Queries were posed with a uniform distribution, while updates were posted with Zipfian distributions with α values ranging between 0.25 and 2.5. Objects are assigned delays based on their relative rate of updates; the most frequently updated object is given the minimum delay, while the least frequently updated object is given the maximum delay. These delays were set so that an adversary should expect to obtain stale values for at least part of the set once the attempt at extraction is complete. For each skew rate, we measure the median expected user delay, the total expected adversarial delay, and the fraction of the set one would expect to be stale once extracted. The results are in Figures 4–6. Note that the first two have logarithmic y axes.

Delays imposed on adversary queries are effective only when noticeable skew exists in update rate. Thus, when both access pattern and update rate are uniform, the delay technique is not applicable. Such cases either assign high delays to legitimate queries, or penalize an extraction attack insufficiently.

The delay imposed on an adversary can be substantial in this scheme, as much as ten seconds per tuple for realistic skews. However, imposing delay in itself is not the principal goal. Rather, we wish to ensure that some non-trivial fraction of the database is stale once the adversary has extracted it. At modest skew levels, nearly all of the database is likely to be stale, since updates are distributed over most of the tuples during extraction. When updates are more focused, a smaller fraction of the database will be stale. However, at these levels of skew, the adversary will always incur the maximum possible delay.

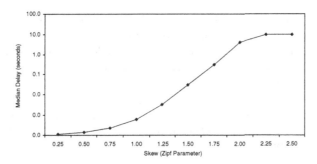

Fig. 4. Median User Delay – Assigned by Update

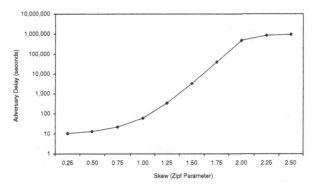

Fig. 5. Total Delay for Adversary – Assigned by Update

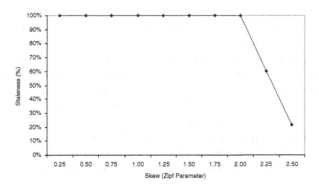

Fig. 6. Fraction of Stale Data – Assigned by Update

4.4   Implementation Overhead

Finally, we must quantify the cost of maintaining counts and computing delay. We do so in the context of the shortest queries possible – a set of simple selection queries. We posed 100 random selection queries to the database, each returning precisely one tuple, averaging across these queries. During the experiment, we maintained a small, write-behind cache of tuple counts. However, not all counts are kept in memory, resulting in some I/O overhead. Using the sampling for synopsis technique described by Gibbons [14] would reduce these modest overheads even further. Nevertheless, overheads are small. On average, each selection query took 55.17 ms, with a standard deviation of 15.61 ms, without any delay computation or maintenance of tuple counts. With the addition of these costs, the average selection query took 66.20 ms, with a standard deviation of 27.84 ms. This yields an average overhead of 11.04 ms, or 20%. These results are summarized in Table 5.

Table 5. Overheads in Simple Selection Queries

Base query cost		Total cost		Overhead
avg (ms)	stdev (ms)	avg (ms)	stdev (ms)	(ms)
55.17	(15.61)	66.20	(27.84)	11.04

5   Related Work

There are several systems which use delay as a security mechanism: password-based authentication [5, 19], self-securing storage [20], and archival repositories [18]. To the best of our knowledge, our work is the first to propose the use of delay to defend against extraction attacks, in a database system or elsewhere.

In addition to raising the expense of an extraction attack, one can consider watermarking – indelibly identifying the source of data in the data itself. A watermark [21] is an undetectable signature embedded in some data object; the watermark serves to identify the source of the document. Originally applied to still images, watermarks have also been applied to video [17], audio [6], and rich-text documents [7]. In general, watermarking relies on embedding patterns in the low-order bits of an object's representation – be it image, sound, or spatial layout. Watermarking has also been applied to relational databases [1], by making minor modifications to the values of non-key attributes. Although robust and high-performance, this technique still requires the challenging task of detecting that theft has occurred and then analyzing the pirated data. Our strategy, which is orthogonal to the use of watermarking, raises the barrier to data theft in the first place.

6   Conclusion

Data providers face a difficult challenge. They spend significant effort collecting their repository. They must provide public access to their datasets, yet they cannot allow another entity to re-use their work by copying the database wholesale.

Delay can be used to provide legitimate access while preventing extraction attacks. By taking advantage of skew – either in access or update pattern – the provider can impose delays such that legitimate users are not inconvenienced, yet an adversary either suffers intolerable delay or retrieves data with a substantial number of stale components. This technique can be implemented with modest overhead, providing increased protection against such extraction attacks.

References

1. R. Agrawal and J. Kiernan. Watermarking relational databases. In *Proceedings of the 28th International Conference on Very Large Data Bases*, pages 155–166, Hong Kong, China, August 2002.
2. M. F. Arlitt and C. L. Williamson. Web server workload characterization: the search for invariants. In *Proceedings of the ACM SIGMETRICS International Conference on Measurement and Modeling of Computer Systems*, pages 126–137, Philadelphia, PA, May 1996.
3. P. Bart, editor. *Variety*. Reed Business Information, New York, NY, 1905-.
4. N. Bhatti, A. Bouch, and A. Kuchinsky. Integrating user-perceived quality into Web server design. In *Proceedings of the Ninth International World Wide Web Conference*, pages 1–16, Amsterdam, Netherlands, May 2000.
5. D. G. Bobrow, J. D. Burchfiel, D. L. Murphy, and R. S. Tomlinson. TENEX: a paged time-sharing system for the PDP-10. *Communications of the ACM*, 15(3):135–143, March 1972.
6. L. Boney, A. H. Tewfik, and K. N. Hamdy. Digital watermarks for audio signals. In *Proceedings of the International Conference on Multimedia Computing and Systems*, pages 473–480, Hiroshima, Japan, June 1996.
7. J. Brassil and L. O'Gorman. Watermarking document images with bounding box expansion. In *Information Hiding First International Workshop*, pages 227–235, Cambridge, UK, May 1996.
8. L. Breslau, P. Cao, L. Fan, G. Phillips, and S. Shenker. Web caching and Zipf-like distributions: evidence and implications. In *IEEE INFOCOM '99: Conference on Computer Communications*, volume 1, pages 126–134, New York, NY, March 1999.
9. B. E. Brewington and G. Cybenko. Keeping up with the changing Web. *Computer*, 33(5):52–58, May 2000.
10. J. S. Chase, D. C. Anderson, P. N. Thakar, A. M. Vahdat, and R. P. Doyle. Managing energy and server resources in hosting centers. In *Proceedings of the ACM Symposium on Operating System Principles*, pages 103–116, Banff, AB, Canada, October 2001.
11. M. Chesire, A. Wolman, G. M. Voelker, and H. M. Levy. Measurement and analysis of a streaming-media workload. In *Proceedings fo teh 3rd USENIX Symposium on Internet Technologies and Systems*, pages 1–12, San Francisco, CA, March 2001.
12. J. Cho and H. Garcia-Molina. The evolution of the Web and implications for an incremental crawler. In *Proceedings of the 26th International Conference on Very Large Data Bases*, pages 200–209, Cairo, Egypt, September 2000.
13. J. R. Douceur. The Sybil attack. In *Proceedings of the First International Workshop on Peer-to-Peer Systems*, pages 251–260, Cambridge, MA, March 2002.
14. P. B. Gibbons and Y. Matias. New sampling-based summary statistics for improving approximate query answers. In *Proceedings of the ACM SIGMOD International Conference on Management of Data*, pages 331–342, Seattle, WA, June 1998.
15. A. Heydon and M. Najork. Mercator: a scalable, extensible Web crawler. *World Wide Web*, 2(4):219–229, 1999.

16. M. Kim and B. D. Noble. Mobile network estimation. In *7th ACM Conference on Mobile Computing and Networking*, pages 298–309, Rome, Italy, July 2001.

17. B. M. Macq and J.-J. Quisquater. Cryptology for digital TV broadcasting. *Proceedings of the IEEE*, 83(6):944–957, June 1995.

18. P. Maniatis, D. S. H. Rosenthal, M. Roussopoulos, M. Baker, T. J. Giuli, and Y. Muliadi. Preserving peer replicas by rate-limited sampled voting. In *Proceedings of the 19th ACM Symposium on Operating Systems Principles*, pages 44–59, Bolton Landing, NY, October 2003.

19. R. Morris and K. Thompson. Password security: A case history. *Communications of the ACM*, 22(11):594–597, November 1979.

20. J. D. Strunk, G. R. Goodson, M. L. Scheinholtz, C. A. N. Soules, and G. R. Ganger. Self-securing storage: Protecting data in compromised systems. In *Proceedings of the 4th Symposium on Operating Systems Design and Implementation*, pages 165–179, San Diego, CA, October 2000.

21. A. Z. Tirkel, G. A. Rankin, R. M. van Schyndel, W. J. Ho, N. R. A. Mee, and C. F. Osborne. Electronic water mark. In *Proceedings, Digital Image Computing: Techniques and Applications*, volume 2, pages 666–673, Sydney, Australia, December 1993.

22. G. Zipf. *Selective Studies and the Principle of Relative Frequency in Language*. Harvard University Press, Cambridge, MA, 1932.

Author Index

Lecture Notes in Computer Science

For information about Vols. 1–3067

please contact your bookseller or Springer